ISBN 978-1-331-70055-5
PIBN 10223267

# 1 MONTH OF
# FREE
# READING

## at
## www.ForgottenBooks.com

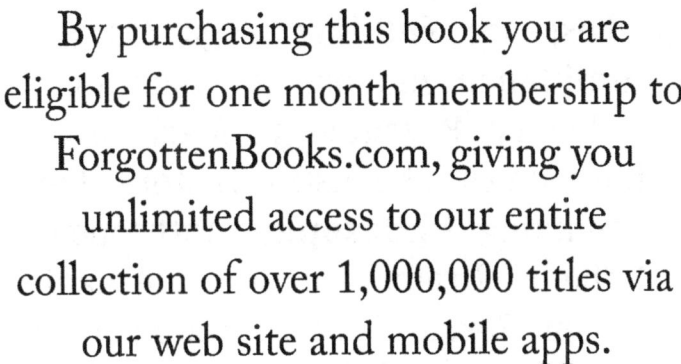

By purchasing this book you are eligible for one month membership to ForgottenBooks.com, giving you unlimited access to our entire collection of over 1,000,000 titles via our web site and mobile apps.

To claim your free month visit:
www.forgottenbooks.com/free223267

English
Français
Deutsche
Italiano
Español
Português

# www.forgottenbooks.com

**Mythology** Photography **Fiction**
Fishing Christianity **Art** Cooking
Essays Buddhism Freemasonry
Medicine **Biology** Music **Ancient
Egypt** Evolution Carpentry Physics
Dance Geology **Mathematics** Fitness
Shakespeare **Folklore** Yoga Marketing
**Confidence** Immortality Biographies
Poetry **Psychology** Witchcraft
Electronics Chemistry History **Law**
Accounting **Philosophy** Anthropology
Alchemy Drama Quantum Mechanics
Atheism Sexual Health **Ancient History**
**Entrepreneurship** Languages Sport
Paleontology Needlework Islam
**Metaphysics** Investment Archaeology
Parenting Statistics Criminology
**Motivational**

# THE

# FULFILLING

## OF

# THE SCRIPTURE,

### FOR

## CONFIRMING BELIEVERS

### AND

## CONVINCING UNBELIEVERS.

### BY ROBERT FLEMING.

#### ABRIDGED FROM THE THIRD EDITION, A. D. 1681.

"My counsel shall stand, and I will do all my pleasure," Isa. xlvi. 10.
"And the Scripture cannot be broken," John x. 35.
"This Scripture must needs have been fulfilled," Acts l. 16.

## PHILADELPHIA:
## PRESBYTERIAN BOARD OF PUBLICATION.

# CONTENTS.

## ARGUMENT I.

## ARGUMENT II.

# ARGUMENT III.

## ARGUMENT V.

## CONCLUSION.

### FIVE INFERENCES.

## CONTENTS.

THE

# FULFILLING OF THE SCRIPTURE.

THERE are two means by which the blessed God
has chosen to reveal himself to the sons of men,
his word and his works. These may be called
the two great luminaries of the church, though the
one be greater and more resplendent, and commu-
nicates light to the other. By viewing the marvellous correspondence of these two lights, it may
be easy to see God's faithfulness in the accomplishment of the Scripture ; and, indeed, this is a
truth of great concern, and one that calls for serious study, the solid persuasion of which will
afford a sweet ground of repose and rest to the soul, .
though the earth were all in a combustion round
about, and give a satisfying answer to our most solicitous thoughts and fears. This being the intended subject of the following discourse, I shall
first offer the propositions generally, and then hold
forth some more particular grounds, whence it may
be clearly demonstrated.

I. That the Scripture of God has a certain accomplishment here in the world.

1. This is the very unfolding of the Lord's decree and secret purpose, bringing forth in time,.
to the view of angels and men, that work which
was before. him. in the depth of his thoughts and .

counsel from eternity. It is an opening up of the sealed book, not of that secret roll of election and the book of life, wherein the names of the elect are written, but the sealed book of God's dispen- sations in the world, showing the counsels and de- signs which should be brought forth in the after ages of time; for as the Lord fully comprehended what he would do, and all that was to befall his church and people from the beginning to the end, long, long before there was a beginning, and be- fore the mountains were formed, so he has copied and written out his heart in the word. Thus the thoughts of his heart, his word, and his works sweetly agree, and each one wonderfully answers to another, for his work brings forth and accom- plishes his word, that his decree and counsel from all eternity may take place.

2. The accomplishment of Scripture is trans- cribed in God's providence, where we may see how the word shines upon all the paths and foot- steps of the Lord toward his church in every age, and what a reflection his work has again upon the word; so that through the whole series and course of providence in the earth, we have a most exact portraiture and image of the Scripture, they an- swering one to another as face answereth to face in the glass; where it may be easy to discern the copy by the principal, and the resemblance which is between the building and the excellent pattern and model thereof which is held forth in the word.

3. The accomplishment of the Scripture is the very turning of that which was the object of our faith and contemplation, into the object of our sense and feeling. It is the real birth and bringing forth of those truths into the world in their appointed time and season concerning the church, and parti-

cular Christians, which were hid in the womb of the promise, and in the dark predictions of the word. It gives the promises and prophecies a visible being; yea, brings truth so near within the reach of our senses, that we may even touch, as it were, and handle the words of life. O what an excellent interpreter is experience! Taste and see, for thus the serious Christian gets a view of the Scripture and spiritual things, which the most subtle and piercing eye of unsanctified school-men cannot reach; yea, by the practice of truth, by nearness to God, and by the retiring of the soul to Him, he has often got more light in an hour, than others have in many days by putting their judgment and invention upon the rack.

4. This is God's own seal, which he puts to the word to confirm and ratify it. I do not only mean that secret seal of the Spirit within, but something more external: a solemn testimony of his works, whereby he every day appeals to men's consciences concerning his truth. By this visible correspondence of the seal and impression, men may easily see whose superscription and image that is which appears on the various passages of Providence.

5. This is something we are not to seek only in the extraordinary acts of Providence, or in any singular and eminent path of a Christian experience. It shines forth in the smallest and most casual things that happen, yea, in every page of the great volume of Providence this may be clearly read.

6. The accomplishment of Scripture concerns every Christian in his personal case, and to it his ordinary experience relates. They whose practice lies much in improvement of the word, and in observation how it is fulfilled, can witness how,

under a spiritual decay, " to be carnally minded is death," and when it is well with their soul, that " great peace have they who love God's law ;" and have often found that God is " a very present help in trouble," and that it is surely good to draw near to him ; and in the close of their life, can, from many remarkable and convincing providences, de- clare the truth and faithfulness of God. It would be well if Christians, in departing from this world, would more generally leave a testimony behind them to the faithfulness of God in his word. This would prove a singular help to strengthen others, and to spread abroad the fame and good report of religion ; yea, thus one generation would declare the works of the Lord to another, and transmit the memory of his goodness to succeeding ages.

7. Besides the general agreement of the word and providence of God in all ages, there is an especial agreement of some portions of the Scrip- ture with particular times. For it is clear, that a part of the word was to have its peculiar accom- plishment under the law ; that part of it also should be fulfilled in the days of the gospel ; and we find a very important part thereof belongs to these lat- ter times. It is true, we do not yet well under- stand how to sort the event exactly to the word, but it is sure that every age hath something of the Scripture peculiar thereto, and that carries forward the Lord's work and design a further step. Every several period and revolution of time still adds something to that excellent history of the word and Providence, which we have since the begin- ning, and brings into the world some additional accomplishment of the Lord's counsel and design respecting his church.

8. The accomplishing of the Scripture particu-

larly relates to the militant and travailing condition of the church; for if the Scriptures were once fully accomplished, and the great mystery of God therein finished, there were then nothing more to do, his work of providence were at an end, and time should be no more. This is something that is not perfected at once, but is still gradually carrying on, and shall be complete at the resurrection of the just, and at the second coming of the Lord, which is the last part of canonical Scripture to be fulfilled, when both his work and his word, and time, shall all be finished together. While the saints are yet by the way, they have the written word, and all the precious promises therein, for present use and encouragement; but when it has brought them to land, it has no more to do; there will then be no more need for a Christian to go to a promise, and adventure upon it; we shall then no more watch with the watchmen in a dark and stormy night, and hope for the breaking of the day; faith then shall not be at a stand to think how such a word shall be made out, because of invincible difficulties in its way. No, faith will then have done its work, and that which is written shall be swallowed up in that which is seen and enjoyed: all the streams of our encouragement will then lose themselves in a greater depth. There will be then no more need of a pledge and earnest to them who have the full possession of the inheritance, and under whose feet the God of peace has trod Satan and all their enemies.

9. Lastly, the accomplishment of the Scripture is something which is not only demonstrated to a Christian by sensible influences, and God's secret working with his Spirit, but is made evident to the observation of men, in the way of providence,

2 *

which is the strongest of all outward evidences; since the world must shut their eyes if they do not see it, and a Christian must deny what he both sees and feels, if he refuse to acknowledge it.

II. The accomplishment of the Scripture is the Lord's peculiar work and design in the world, and the great business which is upon the wheels of Providence, amidst the various changes and revolutions of the world; and for bringing about whereof the blessed thoughts of his heart are fixed and unalterable. It is indeed a grave and serious truth, worthy to be more noticed and laid to heart by men, that the glorious providence of God— which goes throughout the earth, and influences every thing which comes to pass, the smallest as well as the greatest interest of men—in all these operations moves certainly and infallibly for the accomplishing of the Scripture, which is the great object of God's regard : for it is no personal in- terests of men, how great soever they be, that can answer this end. It is something beyond the set- ting up of kings, or overturning kingdoms and nations, that he intends amidst the various changes which are in the world. These things come within the reach of his care and providence, only so far as the fulfilling of the Scripture is therein concerned. He more values the accomplishment of its promises and threatenings, than all the crowns and kingdoms of the earth; yea, He will not let it fall to the ground, though it should be at the rate of laying cities and countries desolate.

Now to clear this further, I shall remark,

1. That the fulfilling of the Scripture is so great a thing, and of such concern, that the blessed God thought it worthy of a place in his heart from all eternity. This marvellous work was such a plot

and contrivance, that as no less than infinite love,
wisdom and power were required to bring it about,
so it was well becoming the majesty of God, and
worthy to be the work of all the three blessed
Persons of the Trinity. Oh, if we could go down
a little to this deep, and see the wonders that are
there, we should find that knowledge, which
usually lessens our admiration of other things,
would heighten it here; it would be new to us
every day, to think how great and marvellous a
thing that is which the Lord is continually accomplishing!

2. Upon the performance of the word the present encouragement and after blessedness of the
saints lie; for the great interest of the church is
adventured upon the word, and embarked with it.
The stock and treasure which is laid up in heaven,
and all that a Christian is worth, which is laid up
in the promise, would perish if the Scripture should
want an accomplishment; the godly man has then
run and laboured in vain, and those who are fallen
asleep in Christ have died in a sad delusion. Providence would be like the work of the foolish
builder, who began and knew not how to finish.
O how highly, then, is the Lord concerned in the
fulfilling his word, that he may perfect what concerns his people, and having surely paid the price,
put them also in possession!

3. There is yet more than the interests of angels
and men, yea, than heaven and earth are worth,
depending upon the fulfilling of the Scripture; even
the glory of God, and especially the praise of that
great attribute, his faithfulness, which he will no
less have to shine forth in the performance of his
word, than his power and wisdom in this great

fabric of the universe, and the marvellous produc-
tions of nature.

4. We should consider this as that great trust
which is put in His hand, who alone in heaven
and earth was found worthy to open the book of
God's decrees and counsels, and loose the seals
thereof; a trust which the Lord did not adventure
upon the angels, the smallest promise being such
as requires no less than an omnipotent power, and
the arm of Jehovah to bring it about; for which
end, He whom the Father has anointed, is gone
forth as a mighty man, who rejoices to run his
race, that he may perform his word respecting his
church and people — a work which he will not
cease from, until the mystery of God in the Scripture, and all that was spoken by the prophets, are
put to a close; when heaven and earth, at the
pouring out of the last vial, shall give that solemn
shout and exclamation, It is finished! It is finished!
Oh, if this were once fully perfect, then the winter
were past, and the summer come, the song of
Moses and the Lamb would be heard, because the
bride has made herself ready; then should all the
trees of the wood rejoice, the hills break forth into
singing, and all that is therein be glad, because
the Scripture, and great design thereof, are fully
finished, and the day of the perfect liberty of the
sons of God is come.

5. The accomplishment of the Scripture is of
such concern, that nothing can be done until it be
once finished. For this, time must wait, the sun
must keep its course, and the ordinances of the
heaven continue as they are. The world is but a
scaffold until this building is perfected; for this
the grave still retains her prisoners, and the dust

of the saints must yet rest in hope; the creation still groans, and the marriage supper of the Lamb is deferred, nor will the cry of the souls under the altar get a full return, until all that is written in the word be fulfilled.

6. The accomplishment of his word is the great thing which the Lord this day is carrying on; the world challenges it, and the hearts of the godly often call it in question; the atheist scoffs at it, and says, "Where is the promise of his coming?" There are often, to appearance, insuperable difficulties in the way of its performance, therefore God so much concerns himself in this, for the accomplishment of which he is, in a holy way, restless, and providence in an incessant motion. In order that the Scripture might be accomplished, the Word was made flesh; and He who counted it no robbery to be equal with God, took upon himself the form of a servant. He will put forth omnipotence for the working of miracles, and change the very course of nature. For this he will make the deep dry, make a way through the Red Sea, and cause Jordan to stand as in heaps, that he may keep his promise to his people. If there is no way for bringing about his word, but through a sea of blood, and over the bones and carcasses of his enemies, he will do it, and bring it to pass, though walled cities, and the sons of Anak, mighty and strong, should stand in the way thereof. Abraham's old age, and Sarah's dead womb, must not frustrate this. If the promise of the church's restoration cannot be made out without a wonder showed upon dry bones scattered at the grave's mouth, this shall not be wanting. When God says he will bring down the enemies of his church, if the dust of the ground should arise, down it must

come: work and counsel of enemies have been
as the spider's web, when it stood opposed to this
end. He will keep his word herein, though the
earth should be overturned, and the mountains cast
into the midst of the sea.

III. The accomplishment of the Scripture is a
truth very clear and manifest, whereof none can
pretend ignorance, if they do not shut their eyes,
and oppose their own light from the fear of such a
discovery. We are, indeed, to look after a more
clear and full discovery of this truth the nearer the
church is to the end of time. There is a labyrinth,
as it were, of turnings and windings, through
which we may see the word often brought, so that
we lose sight thereof, and are ready to stagger concerning its performance; but all ages have so visibly sealed the word by its performance, that we
may say, no Christian can be a stranger to this in
his experience, who is a serious observer of Providence, and the dispensations of the time wherein
he lives.

But to speak a little more particularly.

1. Is that not very clear, which we see every
day brings to light? For these mercies which
bring the word and promise to pass, are new
every morning, and cry aloud, if we could hear,
" Great is his faithfulness." Needs there more,
to convince a blind man that his sight is restored
to him, but that he certainly sees? Surely, they
never wanted confirmation here, who do but seriously seek to be confirmed.

2. Is not that a clear truth, which not only is
found upon the exactest trial, but is witnessed by
such as have tried it in their most pressing
straits and extremity? For it is in the darkest night
that this truth had most brightly shined; and the

more remarkable heroic acts of faith, have still brought forth most convincing results. We may say, there is none can give a better account of the performance of the word, than they who, against hope, have believed in hope.

3. Is not that also clear, whereof there are such solemn, extraordinary confirmations in all ages? I am sure no time could ever deny its witness, that by great convincing providences, both of judgment and mercy, it has been so sealed, as has forced atheists to keep silence. There has never been a time wherein the church had not cause to erect a pillar, and engrave thereon, We have seen with our eyes the great and wondrous works of the Lord.

4. Is not that a manifest truth, which, even in the most strange and dark footsteps of Providence, so clearly shines forth? Though the Lord's way is often out of our sight, yea, contrary to the ordinary road of his walking, through a labyrinth of turnings and cross dispensations, yet at length it evidently clears and disentangles itself, and like the sun breaking out of a dark cloud, shines the more brightly, the more it was obscured.

5. Is not that very clear, which can be demonstrated by such visible effects in the great changes of the world? Men may see the fulfilling of the Scriptures legibly written upon kingdoms and nations, upon the desolate ruins and devastation of cities and houses, great and fair, so that they who go by may clearly read the cause, and bear that witness, Lo! there is sin visibly punished according to the word.

6. How clear is that which we have so evidently drawn out, and acted over in a Christian walk! For what else is the spiritual conversation and

evidences of the grace of God in the Christian's life, but a visible, convincing witness to the performance of the word? Had not this a very audible echo to the great drift and scope of the Scripture? Here men may see the Bible turned into a practical history, written forth, and acted on the heart and conversation of the saints, as on a stage or theatre : the word living, speaking, moving, and clearly diffusing itself through all the veins, as it were, of a Christian's life ; so that if the truth and reality of the grace of God be a thing manifest and unquestionable, we must also see therein the real performance of the Scripture.

7. I shall add, that we may clearly see how one part of the Scripture is nothing else but the punctual fulfilling and accomplishment of the other ; how that which was shadowed out by dark types under the law, and held in a prophecy through the Old Testament, is written before our eyes in a plain and real history in the New Testament, and that the gospel is only a fulfilling of the law and the prophets.

IV. Though it is so manifest that the Scripture has a real accomplishment, in the constant course of Providence here in the world, that I am sure, if men do not blind themselves they can be no strangers to such a thing ; yet we must say, this truth, which most nearly concerns us, is to the most of, men, even such who seem to give a general assent to the word, a mystery and dark riddle. There are a few who even inquire if there is such a thing ; if the promises and threatenings have indeed a certain fulfilling. Few do seriously ponder the providences of God, in which the truth and faithfulness of the word shine forth, that they may thereby be further confirmed. To many, alas too many, the great concern of the law, and everlasting happiness, are a trivial and an impertinent business.

1. For consider, that there are many who not only disclaim the practice of that religion they profess, but do place themselves in the most direct opposition to the rules and principles thereof; to whom the Scripture is but as a romance; yea, who do only converse therewith to prove their wit and parts in impugning it, and who avowedly mock at the judgments and providences of God. I confess these may be reckoned monsters, a very prodigy in the time wherein they live; and which is strange, we see the most horrid atheists usually abound where the light of the gospel had most shined. The savage places of the earth bring forth no such monstrous births as are hatched within the visible church.

2. That indifference which we see among men about religion and the most important truths of Scripture, shows how little this is known or laid to heart; whence there is a generation who do not professedly deny the Scripture, yet can turn it into a school problem, and wonder that men should engage so far upon it. It is not that it is hid from them, but they truly choose to hide themselves from it, as more suitable to the interest they derive. They wish that the truth of God should be rather a matter of opinion, than of faith; a thing which they may dispute about, but not believe.

3. That there is so much barren theory of divine truths in the world, with so little serious Christian diligence, does it not sadly witness how small an acquaintance men have with this truth? Whence we see so great a part of those who professedly acknowledge the word, and are daily conversing

3

with it, yet can give no other account thereof but
report; so many that can discourse clearly of the
Scripture, but could never put their seal to it, that
God is true therein. Hence there are many great
school divines, and able ministers, as to their talents, which are visible atheists in their way and
practice. They judge divinity and religion to be
rather a science and matter of speculation, than a
matter of sense and feeling. But truly this cannot be found in books, men will not meet with it in
a throng of choicest notions; it confounds the wise,
and disputer of this world, whilst the meanest and
most simple Christian often knows more than
those of greatest parts.

4. The great hypocrisy which is in the world, I
mean within the visible church, clearly shows that
this truth is little thought on or laid to heart; for
what is that false show and appearance, which we
may say is not only a sin, but the very sinfulness
of sin, is it not the height of atheism? Could any
be so monstrously irrational as to drive this poor
plot, how to appear that which they are not; to be
at such pains to act the part handsomely of a serious Christian, to personate his tears and grief,
his spiritual frame, his zeal for God, if he thought
gravely on this truth, and believed the threatenings
of the word?

5. Those unwarrantable ways, which in a time
of trial men take for their escape, may witness
that they do not judge the word a sure ground to
adventure on. Whence is their hesitation in suffering times? Is it not that they judge the testimony of the God of truth not sufficient security
to carry them through such a strait, and are not
fully persuaded that what he has promised must
come to pass; for if this were believed, they

would reckon it their greatest safety to embark their interest on so sure a ground, and with much quietness repose their soul, and disburden their care, by putting it over on the word.

6. Do not the frequent sorrows and mournful walk of the people of God, witness how little they are in earnest with this great truth of the Scripture's accomplishment? What mean these distrustful fears, and perplexed complaints? If their eyes are but open to know that they have such a well as the promise of God at their hand, how is it that the smallest straits are so puzzling, and ready to outwit them, that they so usually stumble at the cross? They stagger at the promise, whilst probabilities in some visible way do not vouch for its performance.

Now, from these things may it not appear, that this grave truth of the Scripture's accomplishment is but little known or studied? I confess we may think on it with astonishment, that a matter so nearly concerning us, is not more our work. There are, indeed, many things worthy to be known, but our short life can scarce allow time or give leisure for the study thereof; but though we had only two days to live, this I think might require the one—to be sure and persuaded concerning the truth of that whereon our heaven and eternal blessedness lies, and on which we must lay hold firmly when we are in the passage between time and eternity. O what a wonder that rational souls, who walk on the border of the greatest hope and fear imaginable, can yet be so unconcerned respecting these things. And truly these facts, gravely considered, may seem strange and hard to reconcile.

(1.) That there is such a thing as the very word and testimony of God this day upon record, wherewith we have so much to do, which offers itself to men's trial and exactest search, and yet we know it upon no other account than report or hearsay.

(2.) How, in a matter of such high importance as salvation through all eternity, men can take the truth on an implicit faith, and satisfy themselves with a common assent thereto, as though it were enough to prove our believing the same, that we never doubted or called it in question. I am sure men would not be so lax, and so easy to be satisfied in the most common interest they have here in the world.

(3.) How can men render to others a reason of their hope when it is required, who never asked it of themselves; or will they seal the truth with their blood, who never had it sealed upon their heart by experience?

(4.) Whence is it that men can have comfort in the Scripture, who are not well grounded in the faith thereof?

(5.) How can any think to adventure their immortal souls upon that, whereon they fear to venture an outward interest? or how can they put over their dearest interests into the hand and keeping of God, who could never say they know in whom they believed?

(6.) May it not seem strange, that men can believe the certain performance of the word and promises, and not be more deeply affected therewith? Ought we not· to think ourselves at a loss that day wherein we take not a turn in the meditation of Divine truth, if we are sure that these things must take place?

(7.) I would add, if the Scripture of God surely has an accomplishment, O how are we so little

Christians? Why do men walk so sadly with so great a hope? What manner of persons should they be, that are persuaded that within a little time the heavens must pass away as a scroll, the elements melt with fervent heat, and the earth be burned up? I think if these things will not press home on men the duty of being serious and diligent, they must be in a very sad lethargy.

V. The accomplishment of Scripture is a most clear and undeniable witness of its divinity; that it is His word, who is not a man that he should lie, nor the son of man, to repent. It has this as its distinguishing character, that not one syllable thereof falls to the ground. It is the undoubted and peculiar privilege of God to foresee things contingent, and which have no dependence upon necessary and natural causes; and truly this is a convincing argument, yea, we may say, that of all external testimonies it is the greatest. But it is strange to think what a generation there is, who can sport with the Scripture, and question the truth thereof, who yet never once seriously inquired if such a thing be true. It is also sad to think, at how poor a rate many of the saints here live, because there is so little of that excellent and more noble spirit to search the Scripture for their further comfort and establishment.

It is true, this blessed record bears witness to itself, and is known by its own light, whereon there is such a visible impress of the glorious God, such convincing marks of its true descent, as may thoroughly show whose it is, and how far it exceeds all human invention; and thus by a clear manifestation of the truth, it commends itself to men's consciences as a safe ground whereon they may repose their souls. It is also clear, how

3 *

wonderfully the Scripture has been preserved, and the original copies thereof kept through all ages, that whatever small variation there may appear as to some small points, which in some places have caused divers readings, yet in any necessary or saving truth, the greatest critics will confess, they do not in the least vary! And it is known, (wherein we are to adore the special providence of God,) that the Jewish church, to whom this sacred deposit was delivered, did with much exact and singular care look to it, even in the least tittle and letter thereof, it being the great work and study of the Masorites from one age to another, to see to the preserving of that great record from being in the least vitiated, or corrupt. And do not men see how marvellous the whole frame of the Scripture is; what a correspondence betwixt all the parts thereof, that nothing in it vitiates in the least the proportion and beauty of the work; but all along there is an evident tendency to advance holiness and conform the soul to God? With a wonderful consent and harmony to this great end, we see the simplicity and plainness of its style, backed with a convincing majesty and authority upon the conscience; yea, besides it has been attested by miracles that were great in themselves, famous in their time, transmitted to the church in after ages, with unanswerable evidences of their truth.

Though these are great testimonies to the truth, yet I may say, on very sure ground that, next to the great witness of the Spirit, there is no argument more convincing to reach atheism a stroke, and thoroughly satisfy an exercised spirit which may be in doubt respecting the authority of the Scripture, than a clear discovery of its perfor- mance whilst under the assault of such a temptation. They need but retire within, and then turn their eyes abroad on the world, to see what a visible impress of the word is stamped on every piece of the work and providence of God. Now for further clearing this assertion, I would offer these few things.

1. First, the accomplishment of the Scripture is a very public testimony from heaven to its divinity, whilst the Lord by his works in the earth solemnly avows that this is his word; for his work within the hearts of his people, and that which regards the church, is such, that men, yea, all the wise men of the earth may stand amazed, and confess that nothing less than a divine almighty power can accomplish it.

2. This is the witness of all the generation of the righteous, who from the beginning have proved the truth thereof; yea, it is sealed by the blood of many excellent Christians, some of whom, though they could not well dispute for it, yet had so strong a demonstration of the truth within, as made it an easy work to die for it.

3. This clearly shows the Scripture is an abiding rule of righteousness that alters not, but takes place in all ages; whence they who are wise to bring providence to the word, and compare the experience and remarks of one time with another, may be thus led in a sure path in the foreseing of events.

4. This also demonstrates that it is His word who rules and guides the world, and has a sovereign dominion over the same; whilst we may here see such remarkable events, which both in the present and in former times have fallen out, as show a power that can reach the greatest with a stroke, shake the most established kingdoms, and even, in spite of insuperable difficulties, accomplish the

word. Yea, that surely the spirit of the wheels
which moves them is from Him whose word this
is ; for it is not more clear that the curtains of the
heavens are stretched forth over the earth, than
that the Scripture is stretched out over the whole
work and frame of providence ; so that all the motions and steps thereof, even the most casual things
that fall out, have a visible tendency to accomplish those ends which the Scripture has set forth.

5. This clearly shows it must be His word who
has foreseen all things that were to befall the
church, and the various changes and adventures of
every Christian's life ; it being so wonderfully
shaped and suited to every new trial of the church,
as if intended only for that time, and so adapted to
every case of a godly man, as though it had been
written for him alone.

6. This also shows that He who is the Author
of the Scripture, must have some immediate correspondence with the spirit of man ; for experience
can tell how the word is directed to the heart,
reaches the most inward contrivances thereof, so
clearly reveals and opens up a Christian to himself,
that we may say of a truth, its Author is the God
of the spirits of all flesh.

7. I shall further add, that the fulfilling of the
Scripture in the experience of the saints, shows it
is not a dead letter, but has power and life ; and
that there must be an enlightening, quickening
Spirit, something above words, yea, above nature,
in the written word, that can make such a change
upon the soul, give life to the dead, open the eyes
of the blind, yea, turn a lump of earth, that formerly tended downwards, now without any violence to move from a principle of life towards God,
as the sparks fly upward.

VI. The accomplishment of the Scripture is a most pleasant and truly delectable subject, worthy of our serious thoughts and study; for here is held out the highest truth for the judgment to contemplate, even the truth and faithfulness of God in the word. And here, also, is the greatest good for the affections to embrace and delight in, as that wherein our whole happiness is certainly wrapt up. It is undeniable that it is the godly man who knows best what true and solid pleasure is. Oh, how far do the joy and delights of the soul exceed those of the senses! how far does the delight of a Christian surpass that of a natural man, even in his best estate! The study of the daily performance of the word, is one of those paths of pleasure which would bring in more solid joy to the spirit in a few hours, than some years' wallowing in the carnal delights of the flesh, which is but a pleasure in sport, but quickly turns to grief in earnest. It is one of the great mistakes of the world, to suppose that religion tends to sadden and disquiet the soul, nay, it is certainly because we are so little truly religious. I truly think, though there were not a command for the study of the word, yet the joy and refreshment which the soul would find in such a diligent search, should invite us thereto.

But when I declare what a sweet and delightful subject the performance of the Scripture is, it must be understood that it is so only to the saints; and it is no wonder the world keeps at such a distance from it, for this is a truth it cannot bear. Natural men hate it; for, as* Micah, it prophesies always hard things, and carries a message of death to them, because it foretells their approaching ruin.

To demonstrate how delightful a subject the accomplishment of the Scripture is for a Christian to study,

Consider, 1. Serious converse with this great truth leads forward to practice, and. thus helps to bring down theory to experience; which is the most sweet and desirable of all other demonstrations that we can have of the truth of the Scripture, it turning the exercise of our judgment and reason into sense and feeling; we are then made to see what a difference there is betwixt that discovery which a spiritual man, whose religion is his practice, has of this, and the cold winter-light of natural understanding, that has no heat or warmth therewith.

2. This blessed study of the Scripture's certain accomplishment, is like the act of one going in to look over his charters, and the great things therein contained, which he does not in the least doubt or question, since they are past the seals, and fully ratified.  He now considers those things as his own, which in former times, when he had made no trial of their certainty and of his interest in them, he had regarded only in the general, and as commonly given to all.

3. Here we might see how all the paths of the Lord towards his people are mercy and truth. This would give us a refreshing diary of Providence, to think how in such a plunging strait, we found the word sensibly sealed; what observable confirmations we have had therewith, at such a time, and in such a condition; the after recounting of which in an hour of trial, or in the evening of our life, would exceed the greatest pleasures the men of this world can have in looking over the gold and greatest treasures, which for many years they have been laying up.

4. In the serious study of the daily accomplishing of the Scripture, we should have a most satis-

fying view and prospect of what God is doing in the earth, and how things here beneath do work together for carrying on his designs. We should see what an excellent and curious piece of work this frame of Providence is; how perfect in all its various colours; what an observable harmony appears there; how several discords here, do yet eventually agree together with one consent for the completing of God's design; and whilst we think there must be some disorder among the wheels, we are made afterwards to see that this confusion was an excellent step of Providence, confounding the wisdom of men; every part of his way being so knit to another, as that it discovers to such who make this blessed truth their serious study, a most rare contexture, beyond the reach and skill of the greatest philosopher that ever was. Here also we might go up to the watch-tower of Christian observation, and from thence take a serious look at God's way, and lay his work in the world to the Scripture as the measuring line, by which we should see how the word every day takes place, flows through all the veins and arteries of providence, each line whereof is exactly drawn, as by the pencil of some skilful hand, to that great exemplar of the Scripture. Here we might discern those eminent examples of judgment and mercy that in every age are set before us: how wicked men prosper for a time, yet have a dreadful issue, and are suddenly cast into destruction; they spread as a green bay-tree, and within a little their place cannot be found. How the godly are often sore afflicted, yet flourishing as the palm tree; and the more they are depressed, the more they grow. How the enemies of the church are often lifted up for a sorer fall, and the church brought low in order to her greater enlargement. How judgment finds out sinners, and is often exactly proportioned in measure and kind to the sin. And, on the other hand, how integrity is often sore tossed, yet still falls upon its feet; and is over-clouded, that it may shine more brightly after. How the threatenings of the word visibly overtake kingdoms and nations, bring down great houses, and cause those who are brought up in scarlet to embrace the dunghill, and let not the hoary head of cruel and wicked men go into the grave in peace. O how sweet an exercise were this for a Christian even to lose himself in!

5. From thence we might, in a great measure, discern what of the night it is with the church; if there be any evidences that it is near day. We should be skilful to feel the church's pulse, and thereby find what symptoms there are of life or death, and perceive a dark cloud of judgment rising, when it is but like an hand-breadth. Surely this study should make us wise to know the times, and what we ought to do therein; for amongst these various events which fall out in every age, the Lord's way is consistent with itself and with his truth.

6. Here we should have a most pleasant and clear view how the Scripture of God comprehends the whole state of the church from the beginning to the end of time: that it is a most full and per-fect register of all the vicissitudes and alterations which are to go over her head whilst in a militant condition; and also most exactly points out those occurrences and remarkable events which fall out in the ordinary course of Providence. In follow-ing this study we should clearly see how the Scrip-'ure brings the church to light ont of the fountain

of an eternal decree; and traces it from the first promulgation of the gospel after the fall, through those dark times before the flood, whilst it was but in families, and through that long trial in Egypt, and all its settled and flourishing condition in Canaan; and carries her forward through all the several changes of her case, under her decay, and in the times of the captivity, even to the manifestation of Christ and the dawning of the gospel; and as it thus takes in within its reach the whole estate, and the special events which befell the church under the law, so we may see how the Scripture also follows the church through the whole time of the gospel, and brings her, as a grain of mustard seed, from a day of small things, to her perfection; that it takes her, as it were, by the hand from her infancy, and goes with her through all the turnings of her condition; through that long and dark night of antichrist's reign, it points out her condition clearly, and shows the various assaults that she should endure in that time, and that blessed victory which she should gradually have over her enemies; and that the word and the church do never part, but one walketh step by step with the other, until it bring her safe to land, and, as it were, put her off its hand and guard at the coming of Christ.

7. This would also help us to sweet thoughts, and give us matter of a song in the saddest night of the church's condition; it would serve to silence all our complaints, with wondering at God's way, and triumphing in the works of his hands; we should not then be afraid of evil tidings; a stormy time would not outwit us, being persuaded that though the earth should be overturned, it shall be surely well with the righteous; that the church

must flourish, and all her enemies be found liars, because "He is faithful that hath promised," whose word will as surely come to pass as the sun returns after a dark night.

VII. It more specially concerns the godly in these latter times, to study this great truth of the accomplishment of the Scripture.

1. For herein is the word express, that one part of the Scripture, which from former ages was sealed up, should in the latter days be clear and easy to understand, Dan. xii. 9. The seal is there put on: "Go thy way, Daniel, for these words are closed up, and sealed till the time of the end." But Rev. xxii. 10, we have that bar taken off; "Seal not the sayings of the prophecy of this book; for the time is at hand." Now, by the last days, we are not only to understand the whole time of the gospel, though it is thus termed in the Scripture, but the latter part of these last times, even the close and evening of time, that last epoch and period of prophetic chronology.

2. It is expressly promised, that in the latter days the church shall have a more full discovery how the Scripture is verified; "Many shall run to and fro, and knowledge shall be increased," Dan. xii. 4; which increase, as it clearly points at the last times, and that bright day the church shall have when Israel shall be brought in to Christ, also points at and promises some greater light, and a more full opening up of the mysteries of the word and fulfilling thereof; for the former part of the chapter shows that increase of knowledge relates to these things which were before sealed. We wait and believe that many Scripture truths, now dark and abstruse, shall be made so clear, as shall even cause us to wonder at the gross mistakes

we once had thereof; yea, that after-generations shall have a discovery of some prophecies now obscure, and shall as far exceed us, as this time goes beyond former ages, which, comparatively, we must say, were very dark. O! when that promise of the calling of the Jews shall once take place, what a wonder will it be to them, that their understanding should have been under such a veil, when the truth shall be so clear and evident to them in that day? Will it not be a sweet and easy work for the godly to sort together the predictions of the word, and the events? And truly there is much now wrapped up in Scripture prophecies not yet fulfilled, which in after times, when the events shall unveil their meaning, will exceed, yea, confound all those comments which the wisest and best have written upon them.

3. Is it not also clear, that those prophecies which of all the Scripture were most obscure, and overclouded with dark figures and allegories, concerning which there had been such mistakes and hesitation by the church, have a peculiar respect to the last times? And that they shall then be made plain and easy, when so notable a key as the event opens them; such as those of the witnesses taking life and rising again, Babylon's fall and ruin, Christ's reigning with his saints a thousand years, &c. &c.

4. It is in the latter times that the glory of God in his truth and faithfulness shall most eminently shine forth. The solemn congratulation of the church upon Babylon's fall, not only exclaims, "Great and marvellous are thy works," but, "Just and true are thy ways," Rev. xv. 3; for truly in this stroke of the judgment of God, the fulfilling of the Scripture will be so plain and un-

deniable, that we may say, it will then dazzle the eyes of men, even the greatest atheists, and alarm the world; yea, very effectually contribute to that promised increase of the church and in-coming of the Jews, when in antichrist's fall and ruin they shall see so convincing a seal put to one of the most considerable prophecies of the word, in the accomplishment whereof much of the prophetic part of the New Testament relating to the church's state, and her long trial under antichrist's reign, may be seen clearly verified.

5. The Lord has reserved his greatest works to the latter days; then his judgments shall be manifest, and the word confirmed by such solemn, convincing providences, that men will not pass them without a remark. We are this day witnesses to many such, and are observing what these times shall yet bring forth, that the great and remarkable acts of the Lord may force the world to see a Divine power, and say, Lo, here is an undoubted accomplishment of the Scripture.

6. The church in these latter times has peculiar advantages for understanding this truth of the Scripture's accomplishment. A great part thereof is now fulfilled. The Christian church had in former times but dark glances at these great things, which we see this day visibly transcribed in Providence; the promises were then travailing in birth of that which is now brought forth. We are mounted, as it were, on the shoulders of the experience and observation of former times. The church has now a greater seal and confirmation of the truth than it had in the days of the prophets and the apostles, even when Christ was in the flesh. The temple of God and the ark of his testimony are

now opened in heaven, light more fully abounding and the means of knowledge increased.

7. Is it not clearly foretold in Dan. xii. 4, that in the last times this will be one of the special exercises of the saints, to inquire and make a diligent search concerning the Scripture's accomplishment? For it is there said, " Many shall run to and fro, and knowledge shall be increased." What should be the posture of the godly in these days, but that of the watchman in the last watch of the night, who often looks what appearance there is of the day breaking from the east?

VIII. It is a great duty for Christians to study this truth, that they may have something more than report to show that the Scripture has a sure accomplishment. I must think it strange that there is such a great help as this so near, and yet that we do not inquire and read the faithfulness of God therein; yea, that so great a truth, which can bear the scrutiny of all the critics of the world, a truth wherein our blessedness through time and eternity lieth, should offer itself to our trial, and yet be so little known. O, who can dispense with this duty, to study a practical converse with the word, and to be serious observers of its accomplishment? For let us consider,

1. We are thus helped to declare the works of the Lord, and to give him the glory of his faithfulness. This truth of the Scripture's accomplishment, like a great roll, hath been transmitted from hand to hand, from one age to another, attested and subscribed, as it were, by many witnesses, and it thus comes to our time, and to every man's door, and requires his personal witnessing and testimony.

4*

2. This would make it an easy work to trust the word, and to adventure thereon in the ordinary occurrences of life; for they may well trust God in a strait who have this strong argument to make use of—that often they have tried him, and found him faithful. That was a notable testimony from a serious Christian, in a very sharp trial, " Often have I tried God, and shall I not learn to trust him once !"

3. This lays the Christian in the way of that promise, " Whoso is wise, and will observe these things, even they shall understand the loving-kindness of the Lord," Psa. cvii. 43. Yea, whilst they are serious to observe his works abroad in the world, and his way to others, they shall be no losers thereby at home, but find this promise meet them, and turn their general observation into a personal experience of the loving-kindness of the Lord.

4. Thus the saints, by experiencing the truth of the word, get a convincing seal thereby to their interest in the promise; begun possession is indeed a strong witness to their right.

5. Thus would Christians be helped with much advantage to convince gainsayers; for it is sure that atheism could not make so bold and public an appearance if men did not take their religion so much on trust. The serious experienced man can with confidence own the truth, while he can not only assert, but lead men to the things themselves, that they may see if in such and such particulars the Scripture be not truly fulfilled.

6. Thus the providence of God will have a more sweet refreshing countenance, when from this great height and watch-tower of Christian observation, we take our observation; and truly

without this view men will stumble at the most ordinary dispensations, and think God's work is a mass of confusion; but here we see that the written word, and the way of God, are linked in a most sweet agreement.

7. We may thus trace divine truth, even by our sense and feeling, and join the word and experience in a regular correspondence; yea, thus we should have a clear transcript of the Lord's way with his church, taken out of that great authentic original of the Scripture, and see on what a solid basis and foundation that magnificent structure of Providence is raised up.

8. This is a part of the talent wherewith we are intrusted, and of which all Christians should study a serious improvement, knowing that they must render an account what their observation of this great truth has gained, and what further establishment and confirmation they have thus attained to.

9. The importance and weight of this study should press it much upon us; for if the Scripture's accomplishment be an undoubted truth, then this is sure, that the saints have a great inheritance; they are princes, though now under a disguise, and though yet minors, they are heirs of more than the world can shadow forth. If this be sure, we should look with compassion, rather than envy, on those whom the world accounts happy. We need not question the gain of godliness, for it is sure that those who " sow in tears shall reap in joy;" and the righteous, though now trampled under, at the resurrection shall have dominion; yea, in a word, we may then on sure ground solace ourselves with the thought of that great change which will be within a little time, when the grave must render back her prisoners; and we may lie

down in the dust, with as much assurance of a
blessed resurrection as we are sure there will be
a morning when we lie down at night. O, then,
it is certain that there is a heaven and a hell! eternity is not a night-dream; and one moment will
shortly put an end to all our struggles, yea, the
shutting of our eyelids at death, will but open them
in the paradise of God.

Having touched this truth a little in the general,
I shall now adduce some arguments whence the
accomplishment of the Scripture may be demonstrated.

I. The first argument to prove the accomplishment of Scripture is this—That it is confirmed by
the experience of the saints in all ages: that its
truth is sealed by every individual Christian, from
his frequent and sure experience, and proved by
all believers in their daily walk upon the most
accurate trial.

II. The second argument is—That the accomplishment of Scripture is manifest and legible in
the whole course and tenor of Divine Providence
respecting the church, and made out to the observation of every age by clear convincing instances
both of judgment and of mercy.

III. The third argument for the accomplishment
of Scripture is—That it has not only the Christian's testimony from experience, and that of the
church from constant observation, but is obvious
even to the view of the world; that it forces from
the conscience of the worst of men a testimony
that they can neither shift nor deny; that it is sus-
ceptible of being demonstrated to the conviction of
ordinary observers, and has received a public ac-

knowledgment even from the greatest atheists and mockers of religion in every age.

IV. The fourth argument is—That the greater part of Scripture is already fulfilled, inasmuch as those things which were to take place at certain periods of time have accordingly come to pass, the event exactly answering to the description; and but a little part of it remains at this day to be fulfilled.

V. The fifth argument is—That the Scripture is not only for the most part already accomplished, but we have sure confirmations, yea, a great pledge in our hand from our Lord, that what remains shall be certainly fulfilled.

### THE FIRST ARGUMENT TO PROVE THE FULFIL- MENT OF SCRIPTURE.

ARGUMENT I. That the Scripture of God contained in the Old and New Testaments, wherein our great hope and comfort lie, is certainly true, and has a real accomplishment, may be thus demonstrated—that it is tried and proved in the godly man's experience in all ages.

Experience is a strong demonstration, and such a witness as leaves no room for debate, for here the truth is felt, proved, and acted on the heart. Now the truth of the Scripture the Christian well knows, and is as sure of it as he is persuaded that he lives, or that the sun when it shines has light and warmth. It is true, the world lives at a great distance from this, and only converses with the sound of such a thing; and we know the naked theory of Scripture truth has but a short reach, and that it differs as far from that which a serious prac- tical Christian has, as the sight of a country in a

map is from a real discovery of the same, where
the difference is not in the degree but in the kind:
yet though this grave testimony of experience is a
thing to which many—alas, too many!—are strangers, we must say that so much thereof is obvious
as may force its authority on men's consciences,
and show there can be no fallacy or delusion in
this witness, if they but allow the use and exercise
of reason; seeing it is not the record of a few at
one time, or in one corner of the earth, but a solemn witness from the saints and followers of God,
whose judgment and integrity their adversaries
must often confess; yea, it is the witness of all
the saints in every age through the whole universal
church, in parts of the earth most remote. If this
be not sufficiently convincing, I would add, will
you then come and see? Be but Christians indeed,
and then ye will no more dispute this testimony.
And truly it is a very poor shift for men, who have
the Scripture before them, (which of itself witnesses its authority, and this backed with so solemn
a seal from the Lord by his works and providence,)
to dispute the Christian's witness from their experience, because they do not see this themselves.
For what is the cause thereof? Is it not that they
do not follow on to know the same? The truth of
God seeks credit from no man upon trust; yea, it
asks no more but that by a practical converse they
would put it to a trial, and then it will not decline
their judgment.

Now, to prosecute this argument a little, I shall
point at some special scripture truths with which
Christians have most usual converse in their own
case, and therewith give in their testimony how
these are clearly proved and verified. I do
not intend a particular account how the word is

thus fulfilled with respect to persons, time, or other circumstances. I think it may be sufficiently convincing to instance in the general, such clear uncontroverted experiences which are well known to the godly, and have by them been often proved amidst the various changes of their life, though not by all in the same measure, but in some suitable proportion to their different states, trials, and wrestlings. And concerning these I may with some confidence truly assert, that they are not naked or airy notions, but such as can witness their truth to the serious experienced Christian, to whom on this account I dare appeal.

I shall here instance five special truths of the word, which are much tried and proved in Christians' experience. I. That there is such a contrariety between the flesh and the spirit, as the Scripture holds forth. II. The deceitfulness of man's heart. III. That there is a spiritual and invisible adversary, with whom we have war. IV. That the promises of the word have an undoubted accomplishment. V. The truth also of the threatenings under which the godly may fall.

I. That there is a contrariety between the flesh and the spirit, a law in our members rebelling against the law of our mind, is a truth very clearly proved to the Christian, Gal. v. 17. Rom. vii. 19, 21, 23. This is a part of the word which holds forth man's nature in its true shape and form, yea, so marvellously answers the experience of good men, that to question the same were to put it beyond question that we know nothing of a new nature or principle of grace within. For who ever made earnest of religion, but their first acquaintance with the peace of God was the beginning of this war? It is then that the house is divided, and corruption sets up a standard , yea, no sooner can any begin to be a Christian, but he must be a soldier also ; and we may say, no one ever attained such a measure of mortification, or was so old in the grace of God, as not to feel the stirrings of the old man, and to have no need for that complaint, " Who shall deliver me from the body of this death ?" Rom. vii. 24.

1. They now experience two different parties within themselves, which, at the same time, in the very same action, do act oppositely one to the other ; yea, there is no spiritual duty wherein the flesh, though not always in a prevalent degree, does not show some active resistance.

2. That all the stirrings and motions of the flesh have still a tendency congruous to their own nature, to make the heart carnal, and to alienate it from God.

3. That flesh is a cruel task-master, if once it bear sway, imperious in its commands and violent in its acts ; so that the experience of Christians may herein evidence, that it is a sore and an intolerable thing for a servant to bear rule.

4. That to things most forbidden the flesh moves most impetuously, so as it will even break through the hedge, though sure thereby to be scratched with thorns ; yea, it is often so eager in its pursuit, that it will follow the bait while the hook is most discernible. ·

5. That when once the flesh prevails they may justly cry, " Our leanness, our leanness, woe unto us," Isa. xxiv. 16 ; for, like the scales of the balance, they find a proportionate abatement and depression of their spiritual life as the flesh goes up ; yea, they have cause to know how every step

of their heart going forth to the world, is a step that puts them further off from God.

6. That the more closely the law is pressed in its spiritual extent, yea, the more spiritual a duty is, the more fully opposite they find their carnal hearts; and though the flesh may bear up a little with the form of religion, and has more complacency with that way which lies most in externals, yet it cannot endure the power thereof; it can suffer men to be hypocrites, but not truly Christians.

7. To restrain and bring the flesh under bondage, they find is the way to spiritual liberty; yea, they also know that when the outward man is low and upon a sensible decay, it has not hindered, but rather effectually helped their inward joy and strength.

8. That indulgence to the flesh causes a sensible, thick interposition between heaven and the soul, whence Christians are impeded in their motion toward God, and their choicest duties become a grievous task.

9. That is the true rise of their usual perturbations, and still puts some jar between them and their lot; and hinders a satisfying enjoyment of that which they have, through murmuring at that they want.

10. They also find that the defilement of their spirit helps to darken it; which overgrown with the flesh, can have no clear discovery of spiritual things, but that the more they are separated from the body, the more they find themselves advantaged to converse with divine truths.

II. That the heart of man is deceitful, and desperately wicked, is a Scripture truth, Jer. iv. 14; xvii. 9. Mat. xv. 19, whereto the Christian's ex-

perience answers as the face answers to itself in
the glass. Believers acknowledge that He who
can sound this great deep of the heart, and draw
so lively a portraiture thereof, is surely One before
whom all things are manifest; who searches and
tries the reins, and knows what is our mould and
fashion. This is one of the very first lessons
which experimental religion teaches; and the more
nearness with God and further measure of grace
that is attained, the more clear discovery there
will be of this. O, what sad hours; what bitter
complaints, has it caused! This often mars the
Christian's feast, and mingles his wine with gall
and wormwood. I am sure if that excellent company of the saints, who have been from the beginning of the world, to this day, could be brought
together to give in their suffrage concerning the
deceitfulness of the heart, there would be one joint
testimony to this truth. We should find that Enoch,
who walked with God, Moses, with whom he spake
face to face, the beloved servant who leaned on
Christ's bosom, and Paul, who was caught up to
the third heavens, were no strangers thereto, but
could bear witness to these truths.

1. That which ails Christians most is within, and
their greatest adversaries are men of their own
house; yea, that in the worst of times there is still
more cause to complain of an evil heart, than of an
evil and corrupt world, there being no worse company than that which men are to themselves.

2. That every time of life gives them some further proof that they are fools who trust their own
hearts, which often will escape and over-reach their
quickest reflection, even when their eyes are on
them; yea, that there is no time that allows the
putting off their armour, or to dismiss their guard.

That the best case, the greatest establishment in grace, the evening of the day, which brings us within some minutes of the crown and complete victory, does not privilege us from the experience of a deceitful heart.

3. That under the best frame there will often lurk that which, for the present, though it were told, they could not believe, until frequent experience makes them see that the word knows their heart better than themselves do.

4. That to bring home their heart, when once it goes abroad, is not easy; for it no sooner parleys with a temptation at a distance, or adventures to sport therewith, but it quickly turns to earnest, and is ready to yield.

5. They know the constant need to have a watch upon their senses, and to make a covenant with their eyes, which quickly betray their heart; so easy it is to grow warm, and to take fire upon the smallest touch.

6. They know how quickly also their spirit slackens and loses its balance, even in the greatest advantage of their case; that when, in some measure, they have been raised up in any spiritual enjoyment, they were then in hazard to be lifted up to the wind, and to have the more solid part of their Christianity dissolve.

7. What a sight have they sometimes of themselves; such as would be a terror to them, if the heart and motions thereof could be written out to the view of others, or if there were any witnesses to that which in one room will dwell beside the grace of God as its next door neighbour.

8. In a word, their experience witnesses how soon the strongest resolutions will vanish; that often they are not in the evening what they were

in the morning; but Reuben's character, "unsta-
ble as water," may be considered as theirs.    Their
hearts have often deceived them when they trusted
them most.    Every day may cause them to sit
down and admire the grace of God, which can
mend what they so often mar, and is stronger to
save and preserve, than they are to destroy.

III. That as there is a body of death within,
there is also an adversary without, Ephs. vi. 12.
1 Pet. v. 8. John viii. 44, whose way, and devices, and method of tempting, most exactly answer
the discovery of the word.    This is, indeed, a truth
which Christian experience in all ages witnesses,
that no sooner had they a serious look after God,
but they found themselves pursued by an invisible party, whose approaches, though spiritual,
are yet certain and most sensibly demonstrated;
yea, it is sure none of the saints were ever privi-
leged from such experiences, for herein doth the
Christian's warfare lie.    But O how sweet will
the evening be, when they sit down and sing that
song, "Our souls have escaped as a bird out of
the snare of the fowler!" Psa. cxxiv. 7.    They can
bear witness,

1. That there is surely another party, besides
the world and themselves, with whom they have
to do, even an invisible adversary without; whom
they perceive by that sensible correspondence which
he keeps with their hearts within, by those violent
inroads, importunate solicitations, those impetuous
motions, wherewith they are so strangely hurried
against their light and judgment, yea, contrary to
their strongest resolutions.

2. That since the time when they began to look
after God, and to know any thing of his work
upon their spirits, they have been acquainted with

most affrighting, dreadful temptations, the marks of Satan's rage; feelings which they knew not before, when at peace with their idols and their sinful ways.

3. That the mark he levels at, and to which his usual temptations have a tendency, is their soul and inward man; even to hinder communion with God, and to turn their heart off from him, to break the law, and lay aside commanded duties.

4. That his approaches to the heart are often by a very small avenue; he needs no more than an open door, or a sinful look, for the despatch of a temptation, and knows by a wound in the eye how to carry death to the soul.

5. That he knows his time and opportunity, can change his weapons, and hide the hook with divers baits, and is always at hand when the heart is lifted up, when Christians are out of their duty and in a carnal frame, to throw in some temptation, and fish in such a troubled water.

6. That his way truly answers his name, "Spiritual wickedness in high places;" being discerned, by daily experience, that he has the advantage of the ground, is a most subtle, observing adversary, who lies in the dark to us, while we are in the light to him, and knows how to correspond with our corruptions, and to suit his temptation to our natural temper, and to our calling and our company, to the present strait, to our predominant inclination, and to our retirement and solitude; yea, that he is one who knows how to follow in, and ply with a favourable gale, when we are in hot blood, or in any distemper and discomposure of spirit.

7. That he can "transform himself into an angel of light," 2 Cor. xi. 14, and suit his temp-

**5\***

tations to the spiritual exercises and enjoyments of the saints; that there are temptations on the right hand, as well as the left, which are so refined, and so like a Christian exercise, that they can scarcely discern the weed from the flower, or the most dreadful errors from the choicest truths, to which they often have a great resemblance; though at last it appears that the native tendency even of the most specious error in the judgment is, to looseness in practice, and to make men religiously irreligious.

8. That he is also a "roaring lion;" a fact approved by the dreadful blasphemous injections and darts which are thrown in with violence, without any concurrence of the inclination; but, on the contrary, a discernible force is felt, assaulting them with most horrid atheistical thoughts, even while their hearts rise with abhorrence and enter their dissent against the same.

9. That he is a most restless adversary, who goes about, and gives no cessation, but with purpose to return with greater advantage; is no less terrible in his flight than in his assault; and that he can speak out of a friend as well as out of a foe; yea, and does then most dangerously tempt when the temptation is least seen or discovered.

10. That his temptations do not only drive at engaging the heart to bring sin to the thought, but also to bring it forth to the act, in order to some blot upon the walk and conversation of Christians.

11. That he is one who is overcome by resistance, and flees before those that withstand him.

12. They also find by frequent observations that though he is most subtle, being one who, through long experience and continued practice has attained a great deal of dexterity in tempting; yet

that the serious Christian, by daily experience and
watchfulness, may easily discern and perceive his
temptations in their rise and at a distance, while
they are, as it were, creeping up the wall; yea,
thus, in some measure, he may find out "the depths
of Satan," and know how to avoid the net spread
by that great fowler.

IV. That the promises of the word, which are
held forth to the godly, have a certain accomplishment, is a truth whereto the experience of the
saints in all ages gives a large testimony.

Now, in speaking of this grave subject, it is not
needful to say any thing of the nature of divers
kinds of promises, nor whence it is that we live
at so poor a rate, and so uncomfortably, while
such a well as this is at our hand; for it is easy to
read the cause within ourselves: we sow spa-
ringly, and venture little out, therefore we have so
small an increase; there is a price for wisdom,
but it is in the hands of fools who have no heart
thereto, Prov. xvii. 16. I only design to prove,
that the promises which God has given his people
in the Scripture, are of unquestionable verity, and
have as real and sure performance in the saint's
experience, as those things which come to pass
by the concurrence of natural causes; as that the
fire burns when combustible matter is added, or
the sun rises after its going down; for, indeed, this
truth is so manifest, proved by such innumerable
experiments, amidst the various changes of a
Christian's condition, that we might summon as
many witnesses as have been followers of God in
the world, who in all ages have put the promises
to a trial, and have put their seal thereto that God
is true; yea, to ask such if they know whether
there be a truth in Scripture promises, were to in-

quire of a living man, whether he sees and feels,
or if there be such a thing as motion, since they
have as sure and sensible a demonstration of the
one as he has of the other.

But before I speak any thing particularly to this,
I would first premise some things, to clear what we
understand by the saint's experience of the truth of
the promises.

1. Though the Scripture has here its accomplishment, and is intended for the use of the church,
and every particular Christian while in his militant
condition, yet there are some promises of the word,
yea, and those the greatest, that will not be fulfilled
until Christians have cast off their armour, and are
called to divide the spoil; their experience of which
will be, "the prize of the high calling of God in
Christ," Phil. iii. 14, whereof all which they enjoy
is but an earnest.

2. The great intent of the Scripture promises is
not for contemplation, but that we may know them
by experience, and drive a blessed trade and
commerce therewith; the merchandise of which
is better than that of gold, Prov. iii. 14. Here
lies the Christian's life in the world; yea, a great
part of his talent is in the promises, which are not
to be laid up in his heart and memory as in a nap-
kin, but he is to give an account what experience
he has gained thereby, and thus the diligent hand
should make rich.

3. Whatever be the different degrees of experience among the saints, according to their growth
and age in Christ, yet it is certain that the meanest who have an interest in the promises, and who
did ever lay hold on them in earnest, and put them
to trial, must know something of their performance in their own case; for the Lord does not

suffer his work to want a seal in his people's experience.

4. The experience of the godly is then strengthened when they are much in observation. We know little of the truth and performance of the promises, because we are not more habitually in a frame to observe; thus it goes by, and we perceive not; but they who were seriously seeking to be confirmed in the truth of the word, never wanted confirmation.

5. The special mercies and providences of a Christian's life are a certain return of the promise; they are the sure mercies of the covenant. How refreshing is it, that all the several cases of the saints, their meanest, as well as their greatest necessities, are comprehended in the word, and under some promise, and were all foreseen in His everlasting view, who has so marvellously suited the same to all that his people stand in need of, as if it had been directed to such and such a Christian only!

6. This gives the mercies of the godly man a peculiar and sweet relish; they are, indeed, twice his mercy when he gets them in so immediate a way, reached to him out of the promise, and as an observable return from heaven. When he has had no other escape but to turn in to the promise, and to cast himself upon it, he gained this experience; he trusted in God, and was helped, and can give in this testimony of Him, that he has both spoken it, and himself also has done it according to his word.

7. It is not any extraordinary thing we here understand by the Christian man's experience of the truth of the promises; it is not a rapture or revelation, or such as some of the saints have upon some singular and special account had; for we

have not any promise for these things. But it is something well grounded upon the word, which constantly occurs in the Lord's ordinary way of procedure with his people, according to the tenor of the covenant; for his word does good to them that walk uprightly, and certainly takes place in the experience of every serious and diligent Christian.

8. This is not the testimony of a few, but the record of all the saints since the beginning, whose experience all most harmoniously agrees, and bears this witness,—that "He is faithful that promised," Heb. x. 23. It is not that which a Christian has found once or twice in his life, but is the daily food of such as live by faith.

9. This puts a strong obligation on the godly man to trust the word for the time to come; for those who have tried it often, may with much confidence trust it in the day of their strait.

10. The experience which the godly man has of the real performance of the promises, is a most convincing evidence of his state in Christ; it is the earnest and pledge of the full accomplishment of that which remains; that the Lord, who has been his help hitherto, and will be his exceeding great reward in the end, will perfect what concerns him.

Now, having premised these things, I shall instance some particular promises wherein the Christian's most usual trade and commerce lie. I confess if all the proofs which the saints have had of the fulfilling of the promises could be gathered together, we might make use of that divine hyperbole, "The world could not contain the books that should be written thereof," John xxi. 25. O, what an admirable volume, what an excellent commentary would this be on the Scripture, to see it thus turned over into the experience of every Christian! It would be as easy to number the drops of rain and dew since the creation, as to reckon all those precious drops and emanations of love, those sensible fulfilments of the promise which they have had in their experience. I truly think it would hardly be believed, though it were told, what some of the godly have found in the way of the word; but it is sufficient to answer the design of this work to show, that there is a sensible demonstration and performance of Scripture promises concerning which the experience of the saints in all ages agrees.

There are ten special promises held forth to the godly in the word, which I shall here instance.

The *first instance* is that promise given to such as credit the mere word, when there is no probable appearance of its completion, which we have in 1 Chron. xxviii. 20; Psa. cxii. 7, 8; John i. 50. To clear the accomplishment of this promise, I shall appeal to the testimony of the saints in all ages.

1. That when they have trusted God, and got their spirit quiet in a recumbency on him, he has dealt with them according to his word: yea, from clear, convincing returns of the promise, they have been made to say, it did never repent them that they gave more credit to the testimony of God, than to that of their own hearts.

2. That they have never found a more sweet and observable issue than when their help lay most immediately on the word alone; never a more sensible help than when there was least of sense and most of faith in carrying them through; when little of the creature and much of God ap-

peared in their mercy; and when they were at
the lowest, and there was no way of escape but to
throw themselves on the promise, they have then
had the best retreat; yea, their supply was as
sensibly felt, as their need and burden had formerly
been.

3. That their greatest difficulties and doubts
concerning the promise, have helped to their further
confirmation and establishment; so that which for
the time spoke their case most helpless, made way
for the more eminent appearance and manifestation
of God.

4. That their greatest venture usually had the
richest income; the most eminent experiences of
their life have followed the most adventurous acts
of their faith; yea, upon an after reckoning, they
have often found, that their adventuring of life,
estate, and credit, on the promise of God, has even
in these same things, very observably been their
preservation.

5. That where they have most been a friend to
their faith, there has faith also been most a friend
to them. In their standing to the credit of the
promise even against greatest objections and false
reports, they have found a very evident mark of
God's respect to the same, causing them to see that
he will honour such as thus honour him. And it
is indeed worthy of remark, that because Caleb
took part with the promise of God against that dis-
couraging report which then was raised of the
Anakims and their walled cities, the inheritance of
the children of Anak was given to Caleb and his
sons by the God whom he had honoured.

6. That believing always makes way for sense;
and in their closing with the naked word of promise, they have not wanted the seal of the Spirit

of promise, but have found a sweet calm, and their burden sensibly eased when once they got it laid on the word, which they can say has been their first resting-place. This has been the very fixing of the motion of the needle towards its right point, after restlessness and agitation.

7. That their greatest disappointments have turned afterwards most to their advantage; their returns have not only been according to their faith, but have often exceeded their adventure; yea, that from frequent experience they may say, the issue of trusting the word, how long soever deferred, yet came always in season, and was never too late and out of time.

8. That it never occasioned bitter reflections, nor was their disgrace before the world, that they trusted God in a day of strait and were not helped. But this testimony have all such left who have most credited it in a dismal hour—that faith has often taken them well and comfortably through, where both sense and reason have been ready to sink.

*Second instance;* That God truly hears prayer agreeably to his word. We have this promise in Phil. iv. 6; Psa. xxxii. 6; lxv. 2; xci. 15.

I shall here declare something of that testimony which the saints can give to this promise.

1. That when they have, with Hannah, gone to the Lord in the bitterness of their spirit, they have returned with a sensible and marvellous change in their case; they have enjoyed an observable calm and serenity after much inward perturbation; yea, they have found their hearts thawed, and put into a flush of tenderness, after a most sensible restraint.

2. They have found liberty to pour forth their souls to God, when he has " filled their mouths

6

with arguments," and enabled them both to wrestle and wait, as a pledge of a further answer.

3. That after they have been under a most dark
cloud, they have found their sky clear, and have
got a very sensible taste of God's acceptance in
prayer, and of his taking their suit off their hand,
even while the matter was still in dependence before him; yea, that they have often had such a
satisfying persuasion of his answering their desire,
as has helped them cheerfully to wait, and sometimes to sing the triumph before the victory.

4. That when they had been much in prayer
their spirits have most flourished, the candle of the
Lord has shone upon their paths, and his dew has
been all night upon their branches; and they have
found that there is an evident and proportionate
abatement of their spiritual life and encouragement
in God, according to their declining in the exercise of this duty.

5. They have many times found, when there
was nothing left them but to return to God, a sweet
and seasonable result, so that the most observable
times of prayer have been also the most observable
times of their experience.

6. That it is not in vain to follow out a suit before the throne, but access to heaven is a sure way
to succeed; having found that while many seek
the ruler's favour, the determination of every thing
is from the Lord.

7. That prayer, with quiet waiting in the use of
means, succeeds well, where over-carrying and
carnal policy, in the use of all other shifts, have
miscarried.

8. They know by experience, that as there are
judicial times, wherein a prohibition, as it were, is
laid on them from the Lord in their wrestling, yea,

and a sore restraint on their spirits which has been very sensible; so also they have found times of prayer before some special mercy and deliverance to the church, whereby they could in some measure discern its near approach.

9. That after some solemn address and application to God by prayer and fasting in the day of strait, they have often seen cause even from that day to date a remarkable return, in which even common observers might discern what an evident answer the church's intercession has had with God in times of extremity.

10. I may add, the saints know so well by experience that God hears prayer, even in such and such a particular circumstance, that they can with much confidence adventure, and make an errand of their meanest, as well as their greatest concerns to him, having often tried and found that seriousness and sincerity in addressing God were never in vain.

The *third instance* is the promise of the Spirit, and pouring out of the same, which we have in Isa. lix. 21; Luke xxiv. 49; John xiv. 16; Rom. viii. 15, 16.

The accomplishment of this is so manifest in the experience of the saints, that I am sure this can no more be denied, than the heat of the sun can be denied by those who have felt its influence; yea, the Christian's spiritual walk bears as convincing a witness to the fulfilling of this promise, as any living man shows that he has a soul, and a principle of life within him.

For, 1. That which causes so real a change upon them, which makes them who once were dead, alive to God; that which brings clods of earth so near to heaven, and raises them so far above them-selves to a delightful converse with things not seen, that while their place and abode are here, their company, and fellowship, are above; that which makes all things new to them, and so far changes their nature and inclination as causes them to find more sweetness in a spiritual life, than in the plea-sures of sin; yea, which reconciles them to the law, and to the exercises of a Christian, where once there was such a contrariety—O! is not this a real effect of the Spirit, and no imaginary thing?

2. Since their being born again they find them-selves entered into another world, brought out of darkness into marvellous light, and though once they were blind, they now see; is not this a proof of the truth of this promise?

3. That which makes them see more of God in his word and works at one time than at another; which makes the Scriptures at one time their chief delight, which are at another time but a common record, can be no delusion.

4. That which causes such sensible liberty and confidence in their approach to God, after sore bondage and fear, and which raises them often so far above their ordinary frame, as that they are not only quickened and refreshed themselves, but do observably warm others, must be something real.

5. That which makes such a sudden change in their case under ordinances, that their hearts that died within them as a stone, have suddenly taken life, yea, have been poured out within them, so that they have often wished a perpetual arrest upon their spirits in such a condition; can this be a delusion?

6. That which brings promises seasonably into

their mind in the day of their strait, and makes the word suitable to their present case with a satisfying impression of the same.

7. That which so clearly discovers to men their own hearts, and searches out their most close and retired thoughts: is not this the candle of the Lord?

8. That which demonstrates their state and being in Christ by an argument which is beyond all words; and in an irresistible way, answers all objections, and turns the most froward case into a blessed calm; and has made a simple word more effectual in a moment than most persuasive arguments.

9. That which makes such abundant joy to spring up in the heart when there is no visible reason, must surely be some supernatural and excellent power, that can not only bring consolation out of nothing, but out of contraries.

10. That which gives them so sensible a taste of the powers of the world to come, such a rapturous glance of their inheritance, that they can hardly sometimes forbear to rise at midnight, and sing for joy in the hope thereof; and has given them such a discovery of God at some special times, as has made them judge that all they ever knew of him before was but the hearing of the ear.

11. That which is so sensibly felt in the present time, and has been so sweet when enjoyed, that the remembrance of these times has been very pleasant, can be no delusion.

12. That is no delusion, the withdrawing whereof is so sensible to them, that it makes the duty wherein they have had delight to become their burden; when they are put to row with oars, the wind

being gone, and maketh it like night to the soul, when the sun is gone down.

The *fourth instance* is that promise for direction which God has given his people in the world, that he will guide them with his counsel, and will order and direct their steps, Psa. xxv. 9, 14; xxxvii. 5; lxxiii. 24. I shall attest their experience, to show that they have this testimony to give.

1. That to trust God with their case, and give him the guiding of their way, has taken them much more easily through a plunging case, than over-caring anxiety.

2. That the way of the word has been the best expedient for taking them safely and comfortably through; and that they never repented that they did more consult their duty than inclination.

3. That they were never left without counsel and direction when the eye was single; and it was not so much want of light, as of heart, that made their way often so dark; but when they subjected themselves to God's mind, they have found that such as follow him, shall not walk in darkness, John viii. 12.

4. That light and counsel meet men in following the command, and the practice of known duty has helped them to know more; and that light most abounded when it was their serious study to follow it.

5. They found it was never in vain to inquire after God's mind by prayer, and to seek it in his temple.

6. They also know, that God's gift of light with a powerful impression, his teaching the reins, and instructing with a strong hand, is no delusion, but the sure and well-grounded experience of most solid Christians in all ages; yea, most discernible

from any false impulse: and that some special work and service which God has laid in their way, wants not usually some special call, backed with such light and authority as answers all objections.

7. How God's special directing hand has been often very observable, not only in preventing and crossing their way, to withdraw them by some sharp dispensation from their purpose; but in sensibly overpowering them, so that they have been plucked, as it were, back from unavoidable hazard.

8. They have often observably found, how easy their way was made to them when the Lord countenanced and prospered it, so that they have been forced to see and confess a Divine hand therein.

The *fifth instance* is the promise of pardon, which God has given his people in the word, yea, that he is ready to pardon those who are truly humbled. Isa. xliii. 25; Jer. xxxi. 34; Mic. vii. 18.

Now that there is a real accomplishment of this, I am sure that the experience of the saints in all ages can clearly witness. It is true, pardon of sin does not always infer the sensible feeling thereof; and when it is remitted in heaven, there is not always a declaration of it in the conscience; but it is also sure, that this is often sensibly felt, and that it is found by all the generation of the righteous to have as powerful an operation on a disquieted troubled soul, as ever wine or the choicest cordial could have on the sick or faint. O! if those who question this were in their case, to whom God speaks peace after a storm, they would know how real and certain it is.

1. They feel how this has as sensible a connexion with the serious exercise of contrition and

repentance in their experience, as it certainly has in the word and promise.

2. They know that is no delusion, which is found so certain a cure to a wounded spirit under the sense of sin; a wound which the world and all its diversions could never heal, whose pain and grief no music can allay.

3. That is no delusion which they can no more command than the sun to shine when overclouded, or the wind to blow but when it listeth ; which the most persuading moral arguments, and their former experience, yea, the letter of most refreshing pro-mises, cannot induce.

4. That can be no delusion which causes so marvellous a change, that after the greatest dis-quieting fears, they have found most sensible mani-festations of love; the greatest flood succeeding to the lowest ebb of their spiritual condition: yea, has made them inquire with wonder, whence they are so cheerful to-day, who yesternight were so broken and crushed; whence their spirit should be in so sweet a calm, that lately was so like the raging and troubled sea.

5. That this has often met them as a blessed surprisal, and unexpected welcome, when they have in a backsliding case come to God. That when they knew not at what end of their per-plexed condition to begin, accounts having run long over, yet, on their very first address, they have had their fears suddenly removed, yea, have had the fatted calf killed to make merry with their friends.

6. That which has an audible voice within, so strong an impression upon the soul, which carries with it such a clear satisfying discovery of God's

heart and love, is surely no delusion. The intimation of that one truth, Your sins are forgiven,
or any other word of promise for that. end, is an
argument which they could not resist, but have
been as sure that they saw and felt this as that
they live.

7. That is no delusion which causes them to
approach God with freedom, makes them know
there is a Spirit of adoption, who sets the soul at
liberty from the sore bondage and thraldom under
which their former backsliding had put them ; yea,
this is a thing not only sensibly felt by themselves,
but it may be discerned by others, while they cannot smother the joy of their hearts, or hide in their
countenance such a change of their condition.

8. Have not the saints in all ages witnessed a
joy unspeakable and full of glory, which, though
but of short continuance, yet for the present is so
strong, that it has enraptured their souls with the
hope of the inheritance above ; yea, sometimes
made them sing for joy, in expectation of that
blessed day?

9. Can that be a delusion which has often turned
the poor man's hell into a heaven, which meets
the Christian in the way of his duty, and can make
a sad outward lot to be sweet and pleasant ; cause
them to triumph over the wrath of men, to sing in
a dungeon, to abound and have all things under
greatest wants, and look grim death cheerfully in
the face in its most dread aspect?

The *sixth instance* is that promise of encouragement and support under the cross, which is expressly
held forth, Psa. ix. 9 ; xci. 15 ; Isa. xli. 17 ; xliii.
2 ; xlix. 15 ; li. 12.

Now that this promise is a truth and has a certain accomplishment, the experience of the saints

in all ages will witness. I think it would be a
marvellous record, if the sufferings and prison
experiences of the saints were particularly set
down, what they have found under the cross; but
it is well we know this promise has been, and is
this day evidently sealed.

1. That though they have often experienced
what communion with God is in the secret duties
of a Christian, and in the public ordinances, and
in a special measure at some more solemn times,
they never knew communion with him more sensibly than under the cross; yea, they have found
that the work and service of a suffering time, as it
is not the ordinary service of every day, has also a
peculiar and more than ordinary allowance.

2. That they never experienced Divine strength
more sensibly, than when they have been most
pressed above their own strength; that in the day
when they were cast on God's immediate care,
and their ordinary means of help most withdrawn,
they never had less cause to complain, but might
often say as their experience, that they thirsted
not when he led them through the wilderness;
yea, that they have in no time of their life found
their mercies more observably meet them, than
when by prayer and believing they were put to
dig the well, and wait for the rain coming down
to fill it.

3. That they never found more true liberty than
in the house of bondage, nor more refreshing company than amidst their greatest solitude, while
they found Him near, whom gates and bars cannot
shut out. In the day when all things else seemed
to frown upon them, their midnight songs have
been sweeter than all the prosperity they sometimes enjoyed; they have often proved, that the

deeper any were in affliction for Christ and his truth, the deeper they were in consolation.

4. They find that the most satisfying and clear discoveries of the word are under searching and sharpest trials; that a sanctified affliction is one of the best interpreters of the Bible.

5. That there is a very easy passage between heaven and an oppressed afflicted soul; an observable vent by prayer, and more sensible access to God's face when other things have most frowned; yea, they can witness from experience that "He stayeth his rough wind in the day of the east wind," Isa. xxvii. 8.   While he shuts one door, he has set another open; that when the storm without has been very sharp, they have found a sweet calm and sunshine within; and when he lays on one sore trial, he takes another off.

6. They can tell what a sweet parting they have often had with some sharp trial, which at the first was bitter as death, but in the close, after sanctified exercise under the same, they have found cause to be thankful for, and confess that the time of greatest jealousy and fear has been a time of greatest kindness and love; that the sharpest wound from such a hand and heart as His, has tended to a cure; yea, that very circumstance and ingredient which of all was most bitter and grievous, has often been the most remarkably blessed to them.

7. That the peculiar advantage of a sanctified trial is not so well seen in the present time as afterwards.   When the case has altered, they found a long and rough storm recompensed with a rich load of experience, and a clearer discovery of God, his way, and the certainty of his word, than they formerly had attained to.

8. Their remembrance and after-reckoning upon

this account hath not been sad or bitter; when they sat down, and compared their gain with their loss, they would not then exchange their experi ence, or miss what they have found by the cross, for many more days of trouble and affliction.

The *seventh instance* is the promise that their integrity shall be preserved in an evil time, Psa. xviii. 25; cxii. 4; Rev. iii. 10.

Now to evince the accomplishment of this, I may with confidence appeal to those who have made it their serious study to keep their garments clean in a time of trial, if their experience has not this testimony to give:

1. That though at present honesty in evil times has brought them into danger, and like Joseph to a prison, yet it has brought them out also with ob-servable advantage.

2. That honesty and faithfulness have an au thority even on the conscience of their enemies, and leave usually a conviction upon them; yea, have forced a testimony and approbation from such men; and they have often found better entertain-ment, than those who in a sinful way have sought to please them.

3. They have found this always the choicest expedient and best policy in a dangerous time. A thing whereof they have reaped the fruits in the day of their strait, and times of judgment; yea, though it has occasioned sometime their sufferings, yet it has been also their safety and protection from sadder sufferings.

4. That though integrity is often under a dark cloud of reproach, yet it still comes out well from the same, and has shone usually more bright after-ward. So that they might have had cause to

observe, what unexpected means the Lord has made use of for their clearing.

. 5. That while their enemies might have (were it not for the preventing goodness of God) taken another ground, they have been observably led to pursue them and make them the butt of their malice for their honesty, and that wherein they have peace before God.

6. They find how unspeakably sweet this is in the evening of their life, that then they reap a comfortable harvest of that they have sown with much suffering and tears. O! then it does not repent them that integrity was their choice.

7. They have sometime found a hundred-fold even in this life, and an observable increase in that which they have been willing to hazard most.

8. They must also say, integrity was never their ruin, but a conclusion was often brought about in a way they could not have expected ; yea the Lord's shutting all other doors upon them, has been that he might open one himself, like Hagar's well springing up in the wilderness.

9. That in making their aim, when they had a large heart for God, they have not then wanted an opportunity for evidencing the same ; their encour- agement has abounded with their duty,·and they have got much in, by giving much out for Christ; that there was no such feast in the world, as they have sensibly found in the testimony of a good conscience.

The *eighth instance* is the promise of strength and assistance in duties, Psa. lxviii. 28 ; lxxxiv. 5; Isa. xl. 29—31.

To clear this, I attest the experience of the gene- ration of the righteous :

1. That when they have gone about duty under much deadness and straitness of spirit, they have found a very sensible enlargement, which they could no more command, without the concurrence of Divine help, and something above nature, than those who spread out the sail can command a fair wind when it is contrary.

2. That God's help and concurrence were never more discernible in carrying them through, and making them strong, than in the day that to their own sense they were most weak, when they have gone about duty under the greatest fears and fainting of spirit.

3. That when they had most confidence in themselves, and judged they were at greatest advantage in going about duty, they have usually had the saddest retreat, and found that the "race is not to the swift, nor the battle to the strong." Eccles. ix. 11.

4. They know well what an influence Divine concurrence has not only upon their inward frame, but also upon the exercise of their gifts, yea, upon the common gifts of judgment and memory; and that there is a most remarkable difference between themselves at one time and another, according to the blowing of this wind.

5. They must also witness this as their experience, that they never found duty more easy to them, than when they had most to do; yea, when much work was laid on their hands, they then wanted not an enlarged assistance for the same.

6. That their spirits have been fitted for duty, and carried through difficulties, at which, in some other time and in another frame, they would have fainted; and thereby have seen, that no one need to fear any duty, when God calls him to it; for,

when difficulties have appeared greatest at first, the less they have found them afterward; yea, the hardest piece of service has often been made most easy.

7. They find God raises the spirit of his followers with a suitable elevation for their work, and can fit them for the service and trials thereof even beyond their ordinary reach.

8. That there is an open door and sensible assistance, where there has been work for the gospel in such a place; while, on the other hand, they have found a prohibition sensibly served on them, and the door as it were shut, when the tide was going back, and the word of the gospel stopped.

9. That it is not great abilities which make undertakings successful, it being in vain to rise up early without the Lord.

10. It has often been their experience, that in following the way of God his candle did shine upon their paths; the Spirit of the Lord was with them; whose withdrawing has been no less discernible when they turned aside from him.

11. I may add, that there is no such help and support for going about duties, as a spiritual frame, and nearness with God; for then, light and counsel, inward freedom and sweet composure of spirit, have brought most sensible advantage to them.

The *ninth instance* is that great promise we have, "All things work together for good to them who love God," Rom. viii. 28. "All the paths of the Lord are mercy and truth unto such as keep his covenant," Psa. xxv. 10. I confess, that those who only take an ordinary passing look of Providence, cannot well judge how such things, wherewith often the godly in their life are tried, should contribute to their good and advantage, when nothing seems more directly cross to the same; but the Christian and wise observer know, that there is no real jar between the promise and providence of God in this matter.

1. When God's way and their thoughts have most differed, they have found it was to their advantage, that his choice was always better than theirs; yea, they have been often made to confess, that their saddest disappointments therein have tended to their further profit.

2. That the Lord's denying them some outward thing which they have most desired, was in order to grant them more than their desire; he refused them, as it were, an Ishmael, that he might give them an Isaac.

3. They can often say, they had been undone, if they had not been undone; that it was their mercy the Lord took such a way to cast them in a fever, in order to prevent a lethargy; and by some sharp cross, gave them a wound in the flesh, to cure some gross imposthume in the soul, which would have made their case worse.

4. How the greatest misgivings have wrought their further establishment, so that they were never more confirmed than in that about which they have been most perplexed; yea, they have also found that the Lord's way to cure their frowardness and misbelief was by some further addition to their cross; that when they would not believe, and a small affliction has made them impatient, a more heavy and pressing trouble has been their cure, and helped them to keep silence under God's hand.

5. That the growing of difficulties in their way, and some further pressure in the trial, were in order to its removal, and to the bringing forth of some greater good; and that all visible grounds of

confidence have been often broken, in order that
their blessings should come more immediately out
of God's own hand.

6. How the Lord's deferring their mercy, which
they had often sought, has been indeed their
mercy and advantage; and that waiting on God
without making haste, truly makes the quickest
despatch.

7. Their experience can also witness, how men's
attempts to ruin their reputation, have often been
the very means ordered by the Lord to bring forth
their vindication.

8. How by some sad cross He often prevents a
sadder, as in the man who, riding in haste to the
seaport, to pass over the seas, fell, and broke his
leg by the way, which was the saving of his life;
for the ship and all its passengers perished in that
voyage.

9. How their loss, even by some sad slip, and
failing in their spiritual condition, has really tended
to their further humbling and advantage; yea, that
which brought them under some visible decay as
to the wonted lustre of their Christian profession,
has helped them to grow more under ground in the
substantials of Christianity.

10. They can tell that those steps of the providence of God, which seemed most cross to the
design he was carrying on, yea, which looked
like the very crushing of their hope, have often
been the very means which have wrought most
effectually to bring about their mercy.

11. I shall add, that the sharpest reproofs have
seemed the wounds of a friend, the most pressing
straits made the means for their further enlargement; that the Lord has brought them into some

dark and plunging trial, which then looked like a
fearful pit, that he might bring them out with advantage, set their feet on a rock, and establish their
goings, Psa. xl. 2 ; yea, that in the hottest furnace,
they lost nothing but what they might well spare,
even some of their dross.

The *tenth instance* is that general promise made
to godliness, that to those who make it their serious
study it shall be great gain ; that verily it shall be
well with the righteous, for they shall eat the fruit
of their doings ; and that in keeping of the com-
mandments there is great reward, 1 Tim. vi. 6 ;
Isa. iii. 10 ; 1 Pet. iii. 12, 13 ; Psa. xix. 11.

Now that this promise has a large witness, I shall
here touch some things which, both in the present
and in former times, have been proved, and sealed
by the saints in their experience.

1. That they never more effectually consulted
their good and advantage, than when they did with
greatest singleness consult their duty, and least
with flesh and blood ; they never did more truly
seek themselves than in the practice of self-denial;
yea, when they intended God most, and their
private interest least, they have found a very
sensible advantage.

2. That a serious endeavour to walk before God
acceptably, they have found the best policy, even
in the worst of times ; and have found his way
then very satisfying, when it was most their study
how to please him ; yea, that when the Lord's
way was their choice, they have found it also their
reward.

3. They have found more real joy and peace in
withstanding temptations, than in the temptation
offered ; and more delight in laying their interest

at God's feet, and their wills underneath his, than in all their carnal enjoyments.

4. That inward peace and tranquillity of mind, a sweet calm and composure of spirit, do as really attend a spiritual frame and walk, as the shadow the body; and their best and most comfortable days have been when their hearts were most subject to the Lord.

5. That religion and a spiritual walk is the best friend, even as to a contented and comfortable life here; and that they have then most access to enjoy themselves and their lot with satisfaction, when they enjoy God; yea, that nearness and communion with him tends to the sublimation and refining of their natural spirit, and has been an observable help to their very common abilities and parts.

6. That there is a reality in the blessing, which makes a small thing signify much, and yield more than greater abundance.

7. That when they give God their hearts, it is then sweet to observe his ways; yea, the Lord condescends to their desires when they sum them all up in himself, and make him their delight.

8. That the pleasure of religion is in the practice thereof, and the way to have religion easy is to be thoroughly religious. Duty is then sweet when men act from an inward principle; and holiness would be a more pleasant work, yea, a reward to itself, if there were 'ess mixture of hypocrisy.

9. That real humility and walking low in their own eyes and before God, never prevented their respect and credit with men; but self-abasement observably goes before lifting up, and true honour follows such who least hunt after vain applause from the world.

10. That when they were most faithful to observe and improve a little, more has been added for their encouragement; and they never wanted matter to be thankful, when opportunities were improved and taken hold of for that end ; yea, they have found there is a mercy within a mercy, and in every cross some peculiar mercy, which is only found and brought forth by the exercised serious improver of the same.

11. That much sincerity has also much sense following it. Secret honesty before God has met them openly before men; and faithfulness in Christian freedom has purchased them more favour and respect, even· from the worst, than when they studied most to please them in a sinful way.

12. That they never saw more clearly the gain and real advantage of godliness, and what a difference there is in a time of trouble between those that serve God and those that serve him not. The tenderness which they entertained in the morning, now meets them at night, and pays them home with advantage in an hour of temptation.

13. They have been forced to observe, that there is an invisible guard about godly people in their duty ; that the ministry of the angels towards them is no delusion ; and that hazard within an hairbreadth has been prevented. Relief and help have come as between the bridge and the water ; they have been sensibly preserved amidst greatest dangers, which have only appeared that they might read their preservation from them.

14. That an enlarged heart meets with an enlarged allowance ; and bearing the burden of the people of God, has helped to make their own private burden the lighter.

15. That real godliness and religion has as much

in hand as may be a reward to itself; because it beautifies the soul, and makes the face and conversation shine with an observable lustre, · and guards and preserves the heart from many vexing crosses, prevents sad strokes and sorrows that others who will follow their idols are pierced with.

In a word, it is surely found that God is the best Friend; and when there is peace with ·him, things without do not offend: but it is then understood what it is to be in league with the beasts of the field and the stones of the ground.

V. That the scripture threatenings have also a certain accomplishment.

This is not to be understood of the threatenings of wrath, (from which believers are freed in Christ,) but of a fatherly displeasure; which, because of sin, may bring forth very dreadful effects, to witness that it is an evil and bitter thing to depart from God, and that their own doings shall chastise them. These threatenings of the covenant, "If thy children forsake my law, I will visit their transgression with the rod," Psa. lxxxix. 30, 32, are sure truths, which want not a performance.

To clear this, (before I speak any thing particularly,) I would premise something to be considered.

1. That the word is a perpetual rule which in every period must take place; and though affliction is a part of the common misery of man, yet it does not arise out of the dust, neither fall out at an adventure; but often visibly follows the track of sin, as a blood-hound, pointing at such evils as the cause, and evidencing the truth, and fulfilling of the threatenings.

2. We should adore his sovereignty whose way, both in the measure' and manner of his people's chastisement, is so various, as that none can infal-

libly conclude what God will do in such a case;
yet, this we may assert, and firmly conclude, that
not only the threatenings of the word have a performance, but men may also have, even beforehand,
some more than probable conjecture what such a
case threatens, and what will be the issue of a
sinful course, by considering the Lord's ordinary
procedure, both with themselves and others.

3. Though a gracious state surely privileges
from wrath and condemnation, yet not from affliction and sad strokes of Divine anger, because of
sin; for God takes vengeance on men's inventions,
even when he will spare the inventors.

4. The Lord often contends with his people for
their folly and miscarriages more severely than
with others, and will not let pass in them that
which he passes by in the world; but when light,
and love, and the law will not hedge in their way,
he will set briers and thorns before them, yea, speak
by chastisement upon their bones.

5. It is known that the holy anger of God against
his children, sometimes even pursues them out of
the land of the living, and follows them to the
grave with some remarkable stroke; yea, it has
made them dreadful examples of judgment in this
life, for whom he has accepted an eternal sacrifice
in Christ.

6. I shall add, this is the Lord's blessed end in
accomplishing his threatenings against his people,
that they should not perish with the world. O!
what a blessed exchange is it, that the flaming
sword, which once stood to guard the tree of life,
now stands, as it were, in the way of the saints,
to keep them from running into the paths of death!

Having premised these things, I shall now instance some particular evils, wherewith the godly

are ready to be overtaken, which the word expressly threatens both as to outward and spiritual strokes.

1. Security and carnal confidence, which we find the word threatens is an evil wherewith Christians are ready to be overtaken; but they do also know by sad experience what bitter fruit this brings forth, and that therein the word falls not to the ground, which is held forth, Isa. xxx. 16, 17; Hos. ii. 6, 9; vii. 9.

(1.) That a secure condition is the usual fore-runner of some sad change; that when they are most at ease in a dull and dead temper of spirit, some sharp rousing dispensation is near, as a thorn in the bed of their security to make them arise.

(2.) That seldom reckoning with the conscience, perplexes their case, and makes it a bitter and heartless work to retire alone, within themselves, yea, has a most direct tendency to a further hardening.

(3.) That when security grows within, it quickly makes them dry up and wither in the external performance of duty, and in that vigorous, lively appearance which formerly beautified their walk and carriage before others, so that very by-standers may read the languishing of grace in the dead exercise of their gifts.

(4.) That going about duty with most confidence in themselves, usually gives them the most clear discovery of their weakness; yea, when they have least looked for any cross, they have then been sure to meet with it, with that sad addition, of being a surprisal in a secure condition.

(5.) That sporting with a temptation, may soon turn to sad earnest; and they have found it very hard to dance about the fire, and not be burned and the temptation which at a distance seemed small, upon a nearer approach became another thing than they could have believed.

(6.) That the means whereon they have laid most weight, they have found have given them the saddest disappointment; the putting of them in God's room, and out of their own place, has been the way to make them miscarry, yea, to become their cross; whereas they have often seen something unexpected made the means of their help, that they might know means are ordered of the Lord, and are useful because he makes them so.

(7.) Their experience can also witness that carnal confidence is usually punished with carnal diffidence and despondency of spirit; one extremity being made the punishment of the other, like the hot and cold fits of an ague, which mutually make one another more intense, yea, that their immoderate confidence and expectation have afterwards resolved in as immoderate discouragement.

2. The Christian's neglect of watchfulness, the intermitting of that necessary and commanded duty, is threatened in the word, Matt. xxvi. 41 ; Luke xxi. 34—36.

(1.) They find that it is not easy to guide their walk and conversation when their guard over the heart slackens, but the giving loose reins for a little may make a sad and large breach, that many, many days will not easily make up; yea, a sensible withdrawing of the Spirit, and drying up of their life, is the usual fruit which unwatchfulness brings forth.

(2.) That this causes a low ebb after the greatest enlargement, and that the swelling of the flesh usually follows such a condition.

(3.) That when once the heart lies open, it is

quickly seized on, and made a prey; yea, that sin·
has a swift progress from the thoughts to the ima-
gination, and thence to the affections.

(4.) That unwatchfulness has often turned the
most special times and opportunities for advantage
to the greatest loss, which has put them further
behind than they were, has turned their retirement
and solitude to be their snare, made the desert
worse and more dangerous than the city; and made
them find that vain thoughts, the following whereof
seems pleasant to the mouth, will prove gall and
wormwood to the spirit, there being no sadder company than a man's spirit let loose upon itself.

(5.) That unwatchfulness has an undoubted tendency to cast off prayer, and that it is hard in the
evening to retire to God whilst the heart is abroad
all the day, and to be religious in worship when
men are not so in their walk; yea, that this will
bring their distemper within, to some disorder, im-·
pertinency, or passion in their words or outward·
communication.

3. To restrain prayer, and neglect calling on
God is an evil also which the word threatens, Job·
xv. 4; Matt. xxvi. 41.

(1.) That they have found this giving life and
increase to their prevailing evils, and that corruption is then sensibly growing, when the lively exercise of prayer begins to be intermitted.

(2.) That this wears out their spiritual life, and
brings a consumption upon the vital spirits of
Christianity; so that those who once flourished
and kept green, as by the scent of water, and that
correspondence which they had with the Fountain
of their life while his dew lay all night on their
branches, have through neglect of prayer been

brought to a poor shadow; so that though some-times the greatness of their loss and distemper has been hid from themselves, yet, it might be easily discerned by others.

(3.) That discontinuance of prayer and of de-light therein, will quickly make them disrelish any other part of religion, put them out of frame to meditate, or give thanks, or entertain fellowship with the saints; yea, the more lively and spiritual these are, the more they are a burden, and torment to them.

(4.) That this is a strong temptation to a further forbearance, and will sensibly wear out any sense of their need, and make them stran ers to them-selves and to their own case, so that the less they are in this exercise, the further they shall be indis-posed; and the fewer prayers they offer, the less they feel the necessity of any.

(5.) That the neglect of prayer makes a heavy burden, multiplies difficulties, and causes their care to grow; they must bear their burden alone, and with heaviness take counsel within themselves, while they use not this blessed remedy.

4. We find the word threatens defection from the truth in a time of trial, as an evil into which those that are kept by grace from final apostasy may yet fall, through the violence of a temptation, Psa. lxxxix. 30—32; Jer. ix. 13—16.

(1.) That in one day they may adventure on that which through most of their life they cannot over-come; that their giving the Lord's work a wrong touch is one of those things which scarcely leaves them all their life, but beyond other sins this has still come up with a bitter and heavy reflection; yea, in the evening of their life this has been so

heavy on their spirit, that they were forced to witness their sense of it before the world, ere they
could obtain any ease.

(2.) That the Lord usually meets this with some
sharp and public reproof even before men, to testify
that though he pardon his people, yea, give some
sensible intimation thereof to their souls, yet he has
not omitted. to give some visible mark of his displeasure for such a thing.

(3.) They see that a crooked and unclean way
proves not the means of extricating them out of
trouble, but their difficulties have been made to
grow therewith; yea, they have found that which
they avoided in God's way, has more sadly met
them in another road; and that there is a thick
dreg in the bottom of the cup, which makes it
worse to drink thereof at the close than at the
beginning.

(4.) That it is not easy to make a stand in
turning aside from the way of God; a retrograde
motion is very violent, and yielding in a little will
bring with it some necessity of going further.

(5.) That the rejection of some clear opportunity
to give a testimony to the truth when called thereto,
has turned to be their judgment, and prevented
their being further useful in that manner.

5. The word clearly threatens our want of mortification to outward things, Rom. viii. 6, 7.

(1.) That God has often turned their idol to be
their cross; put a mark of his jealousy on their
dearest things, when once men have put them in
his room; yea, frequent observation of the Lord's
way shows, if they would lose a thing, they may
set their hearts immoderately on it; such eagerness
and exorbitancy of affection being a sure presage it

shall either be their judgment or sorrow, or cease to exist at all.

(2.) That outward things never yielded less than when they pressed them most; that when they are eager in pursuit of the world and satisfaction therein, their spirits are sensibly hurried with many pertur-bations, so that they must say, that which keeps them from enjoying God, also hinders the comfort-able enjoyment of themselves.

(3.) They have found that slow advance in the work of mortification has at last doubled their wound, and been the concurring cause of some very sharp remedy, when the disease came to that height, that an ordinary potion could not suffice.

(4.) That immoderate desire and pressing after an outward thing, has sometimes been answered, but they have also procured therewith a sharp re-proof from the Lord, yea, usually they have found small satisfaction in their enjoying that about which they were so unsober in their pursuit. "Give me children, or else I die," said Rachel: she got chil-dren and she died in bringing one of them forth, Gen. xxx. 1; xxxv. 18.

(5.) Their experience can also witness how over-caring anxiety has often caused things to thrive worse under their hand, whereas they never found a more satisfying issue, than by a quiet, submissive dependence on the Lord.

6. The doing violence to light, and sinning against the conscience, as it is clearly threatened in the word, so likewise the sad effects thereof have been clearly witnessed in all ages, Psa. lxxxi. 11, 12; Prov. xxix. 1.

(1.) That this has a direct tendency to the fur-ther darkening of their light, and to a judicial har-dening; and that reproofs not entertained usually

become less frequent, yea, less pungent and searching; their heart then does not so easily smite them,
so as they can now digest greater things, who would
sometimes have stood at what was comparatively
very small.

(2.) That when they would not read their bosom
sin, which was pointed out both by the word and
conscience, others have read the same written on
their forehead ; and the shifting of discovered guilt
or the serious endeavour to get the quarrel settled
in secret between God and them, has brought the
matter at last to some public hearing, even before
the world.

(3.) That the wilful darkening of their light,
when they would again and again inquire if such a
thing were warrantable, concerning which the Lord
had once cleared their mind, is a most perilous
thing, yea, has procured an answer according to
the idol of their heart, and their choice made to be
their judgment.

I shall but add how dreadful it is to give the conscience a wrench, which is more easily hurt than
healed ; that deliberate adventuring on the occasion
of a temptation, going like Peter to the high priest's
hall without warrant, has cost them dear.

I know it is by serious and experienced Christians, and by them only, that this argument can be
understood. This grave convincing argument of
experience has no weight to others, for strangers
intermeddle not with that joy, and therefore fancy
it a pure fiction, as the only expedient and preservative to their hearts from the horror and inexpressible torment which must seize on them, if the
certainty and necessity of godliness were granted.
But with such I must here crave a serious and free
communion, yea, in so great and important a busi-

ness, must entreat that they would not shut their
eyes, but allow reason that weight which they
would in any other case. On what ground do
you reject this great witness of experience? If
you deny it because you have not found it, do not
others assert this because they surely know it?
And their assertion has these two advantages: 1.
That they once had the same sentiment and opinion with you, which they now reflect on with
much horror. 2. The reality of its effects on
them proves both the reality of the cause, and the
excellency thereof; and now if these men be indeed serious and their testimony true, are you not
in a sad and dreadful case? You cannot think to
lodge together at night, or that your interest and
theirs which have been so very opposite here, will
meet in another world; you must surely land at
some other port, if through all your life you have
walked so contrary to them. O! sit with yourselves alone, and consider this: you hate serious
religion, and therefore you reproach it; will you
take such a revenge on yourselves, and out of prejudice to it, incur so great and eternal a ruin? But
know assuredly it is not what you judged, and if
once you pass in this delusion that great and last
step between time and eternity, you are undone,
undone for ever! And, surely if you admit the
authority of this Scripture, you cannot dispute the
Christian's experience, while there you have so
great a cloud of witnesses, who bear that same testimony.

Now I would here offer some rational grounds,
which may convincingly demonstrate, even to the
world, that this testimony which the saints in all
ages bear to the truth, can be no cunning device or
falsehood; for,

1. That must be a sure testimony if you believe that they who declare the same have the sense of a Deity, and have any truth or moral candour; for it is a clear dilemma, that either they who witness this are impostors of the highest degree, yea, in atheism and gross deceit must exceed all the world besides, or what they witness is true. Now, for the first, I shall crave no more in their behalf, but an appeal to your conscience and sober thoughts.

2. This testimony must be sure, if you but allow them the use of judgment and reason, and do not judge them wholly mad; for it were a strange and unheard of madness, that men should pursue a shadow with such great seriousness, and venture so far, if religion were not a reality. If Christians do not experience what they profess to others, they are either in the highest measure profligate, even beyond the ordinary rate and depravity of human nature, or they must be under a strange madness and delirium; they must either design to cheat the world or themselves. But though their adversaries could wish to have it so, I think their malice will not make them so mad as to own that pretence; and since that cannot be alleged, I profess, were I the greatest atheist, I could not seriously consider the walk of such who are tender Christians without astonishment, or conceive how in such a world, and at so many visible disadvantages, they should be thus engaged on any other consideration, than the truth and reality of Christianity.

3. Do you not see this is their testimony who are willing to be tried therein, and to render a reason of the hope which is in them? Yea, they in this do offer themselves for trial, and with greatest

seriousness entreat the world not to credit impli-
citly their witness and take it on trust, but to put
it to the most exact inquiry and search; and truly .
I know not what pretence unbelievers have to dispute this witness, until from their own experience
they can contradict it.

4. If you grant any such thing as moral certainty, should you not admit this for a sure testimony? for you know by two witnesses a matter
is judicially established; but is it not more confirming when they are of known judgment and integrity? yea, when out of diverse and remote
places of the earth, and strangers among themselves; and yet more, that not only when dying
they own and assert this, but are willing to die
upon a testimony thereto and seal it with their
blood, and this also through all ages? O what can
be more convincing as to moral certainty?

5. You must judge them all to verify the Scripture from experience, on whose practice you see
it so convincingly transcribed. Are not those seen
to be the most tender serious Christians whose
way has the greatest authority over your conscience?

6. Is not this their testimony also, whom on
your exactest and most narrow notice you see to
study religion in the secret and retired duties thereof? Here some other interest than the observation
of men must be an incitement. Yea, may you not
observe there are some who seriously own the
practice of these duties, when the view of those
about them might rather discourage than persuade?
and whilst you are scandalized by the light profession of many within the church, do but also ask
your conscience, if there be not such whose way
you must justify, even in opposition to your hatred

and prejudice against them? Yea, their growth under the ground, and seriousness in what they profess, may be clearly discerned from naked and empty show.

7. Can they intend by such a testimony to deceive others, who have often been in so great fear and disquiet that they be not themselves deceived? O how convincing may it be to the world to consider what perplexing queries and doubts Christians have sometimes about their own inward case. It is strange that this puts not atheists to a more serious inquiry, what such changes can mean which will make men differ so far from themselves, when no outward cause can be discerned? It is true, some matters lie much under ground; the "heart knows its own bitterness, and a stranger doth not intermeddle with its joy;" yea, the deepest plunge and exercise may make little noise without: yet this is sure, there is so much under these vicissitudes as may leave some conviction even to bystanders, that their enjoyments must be true and real, when the want thereof is so sensibly felt; and the world is not so stupidly inadvertent as not to observe this, if they did not shut their eyes for fear of the discovery.

8. Should not their testimony be very convincing whose complaints are oftener against themselves than others; who are often bemoaning over those evils which the eyes of man could not reach? May not the world see how some are pressed with anguish of soul, even to the wasting of their body, when no cause from without is known, though they are otherwise rational and most composed; yea, may it not sometimes be discerned, that there is more smothered within, than appears without? For

grief in earnest wants not some peculiar marks by which it may be evidenced to others.

9. This is their testimony whose confidence and composure of spirit in the greatest exigencies may witness to others the persuasion they have of the truth within their souls. O, doth not this show that the grace of God, and a new nature, is another thing than words; and that they must surely find satisfaction in these duties, which make religion to them a special delight and pleasure, when to you it is an intolerable burden?

10. Do you not see how these men agree every-where, and at all times, that the Scripture is veri-fied by experience; and that the breathings and in-fluences of God on the soul meet them in the way of duty according to the promise, even whilst they most remarkably differ amongst themselves in their natural temper and disposition. And is it not known, that whatever lesser differences are too frequent amongst them through the prevalence of corruption, yet no reflection on the truth of godli-ness will be found amongst them when their reflec-tions are most bitter one upon another? Whilst you have heard the sad regrets of dying Christians concerning their short-coming in the study of godli-ness, have not their complaints tended to commend religion and the excellency thereof, and to reflect only upon themselves?

11. Is not this the testimony of those who act deliberately, and have a rational account to give of the grounds on which they walk? and do you not find they are men as well as Christians, that none are more friendly to reason and the right exercise thereof, than such who are most serious in the study of religion?

12. Is not your readiness to dispute the Christian's testimony, from a rooted prejudice and enmity at the way of the Lord, whereof you can give no reason; yea, have you not often reproached Christians at a distance, whom upon a more particular acquaintance you have from irresistible conviction been forced to justify? For godliness has this singular advantage, that none will reproach it but those who never knew it. O, it is strange with what liberty men can deride religion, who yet dare not go alone to have some serious thoughts about it.

13. I know you will not deny there is such a thing as hypocrisy and a false show of godliness, yet surely you have no ground to question the truth and power of that which is so convincingly attested even by hypocrisy; for there could be no use for that imposture, if there were not also a truth and reality therein. You cannot conceive a counterfeit, but as it stands related to that which is true. If there were not such a thing as serious godliness, the world could never have known how to personate it. Could there be a lie, if there were not a truth? You see, also, that it is the most serious discerning Christians whom hypocrites do usually fear and have an awful regard of; for which there were no ground, if they were not conscious of the truth of that in others, whereof they only study the appearance. Yea, here I must also appeal to the world and ordinary lookers-on, if there be not, even to them, some discernible difference between the power of religion and an empty show; between those who are serious and tender in following the Lord, and others who glory in appearance but not in heart; for the one has a living air and breath, which by no art or cunning can be drawn to the

life, any more than an exquisite painter, with the choicest colours, can paint the vital acts of breathing and moving.

14. Can you not see that holiness must be some excellent thing, which has such credit even with its adversaries and with the worst of men, as to make them grasp at the appearance and shadow of that which others know they hate the power and practice of?

15. Can you deny that there are such Christians in the world, yea, many such, of whom it must be said, even their enemies being judges, that their being serious in that way must be for itself, and has no outward design or interest to which it can be subservient, whilst in this often they run the greatest hazard, and are rendered a prey to others? O, must not that be a marvellous thing, which has such dominion over the soul as to teach men the practice of self-denial, and not only to quit, but to quit cheerfully, their nearest interest, to smile on the spoilers, to rejoice in their sufferings and re- proaches, to forgive wrongs, and take revenge by goodwill? This is indeed above nature, and is peculiar to Christianity.

16. You may see what different sizes are amongst the saints, and how great a difference there is between the experiences of one and another; some made to witness much bitterness in departing from God, and others a singular advantage in drawing near to him; yea, how near sometimes will great extremes in their condition border on each other; and when you see how much these men differ among themselves, and yet that all these differences meet together and concur, do not these very dif- ferences prove the reality of religion?

But O, what can be said here, where weeping

is more fit than words, to see what contempt the great part of men put on serious religion, which truly raises them above the condition of the beasts? Is not the atheism of the time at that height that we must say the assault of the adversary is not so much at one single truth, as at the root and being of all religion? And truly we may fear some sharp and extraordinary cure to recover this generation, of a disease that seems in an ordinary way incurable.

I shall but further offer these few queries, and plead so far with the adversaries that they would, before they pass them, have but some few thoughts thereon. 1. If there be a God, or a truth in any religion, must you not receive this blessed record of the Scripture as the alone rule thereof? Yea, if your judgment and conscience be not both extinct, must you not consent to the law and doctrine therein held forth as good, whatever be your aversion to it? 2. Is not an immortal soul of more value to you than the whole world? 3. You seem to be in doubt whether there be another world, a heaven or a hell; but O, are you sure there is not, and how then can you rest secure? 4. What a horrid and uncomfortable thing is it to be an atheist; and to have no hope beyond this present life? Yea, what a world would this be to dwell in, if there were no true godliness in it, since, without this, no comfortable human society, no kindly and right subjection to the magistrate, can be expected. 5. Is not there a native tendency in atheism to all ungodliness in practice; yea, how far does it debase human nature, and level it with the beasts. 6. Whilst you scoff at serious religion, I dare appeal to yourselves, if in your retirements, when you have any sober reflections, you are not forced

9

to have other thoughts? Why is it you so much fear to be alone, and be in any measure serious with your soul?

I shall only add, is it not rare to find a professed atheist at death, when once the approach of another world awakens the sense of a Deity? It is common to see men who have sported at godliness in their life, weep over that wretched mirth when it comes to death, and call for the ministers whom once they hated; and O, what a dreadful cure will hell be of atheism! for there they know the truth in earnest, though it be their terror: it is sure the devil is no atheist.

I must, before I pass this argument, speak a word to those who know and have experienced the same. O how great should this be in our eyes, and with what astonishment should we consider it! If but one person in an age, or if even every particular Christian were but once, at some solemn time of his life thus confirmed, that he could say, that he did then taste and see the word, and found it surely verified on his soul, at what a rate would he value and preserve so singular a seal and confirmation of the truth, yea, keep up the remembrance of such a special time so long as he lived! But O, must it be said that this grave witness of the Scripture, and of the certainty of the words of truth which we have by experience, loses its weight, and the inestimable value thereof is less regarded, because it is the Christian's daily bread? O what a reach has this argument; what great things are there held forth! I think a serious view of this, if it were brought near to us, might put us to question whether we believe or not. Are we in a dream or awake? Let us bring this argument near, and gravely consider with respect to some of those great truths which are witnessed by this unanswerable demonstration of experience.

I. Does not this argument of experience witness the great truth of a Godhead, whereon the whole superstructure of truth and godliness stands? yea, enforce on men the persuasion of this by a more near and convincing discovery than the greatest works of God, or those glorious appearances of his power and wisdom in the heavens and earth? It is true, those bring him near to our eye and ear, but this brings the blessed and invisible God into the heart and soul, that we may both taste and see that surely he is, and is that which in the Scripture he is declared to be. It is not the contemplation of nature in its highest flight that can answer such an assault of the devil, which may try the most established Christian concerning the being of God. But there is a demonstration within which goes further than the judgment, and passes natural understanding, whence we feel, we taste, we enjoy Him; yea, his voice is heard in the soul. There is, indeed, cause to wonder at the atheism of this world, since men can look nowhere without some witness of a Deity to stare them in the face. But there is a more refined atheism, that lies in the bosom of a professed assent to divine truth, and is not easily discerned; though not the less dreadful because it goes under a cover, not only from the view of others, but even from a man's self. I would here propound some things which witness a special advantage the godly man has to believe, and to be more thoroughly persuaded of the glorious being of God. 1. That he finds the believing of this is a very great thing, and not so easy to reach as the world supposes, for it is no small matter even to attain to this. O what ordinary thoughts have many about it, who think it easy to give an assent to this marvellous truth, because they never considered the greatness thereof! But it is sure that the more serious and grave a Christian is, the more will he be exercised about this. 2. It is a great advantage when we seek after a further establishment in this great truth. What a satisfying persuasion of his blessed being might we have, if our souls were indeed herein exercised! There is a nearer approach to God, which would show us that the faith of a Deity is something beyond the former thoughts we have had thereof. 3. They are at a special advantage to whom believing of this truth is their exceeding joy, and who, amidst their heaviness can say, that the thought and meditation of Him is sweet; that when through a variety of temptations, they are ready to faint, this restores their soul. O what a thing is it in such a world, and in some deep perplexing plunge, to know the Lord is God, a Rock and a Shield now, and in the close of time our exceeding great Reward! Can we have serious thoughts of this, and so easily turn ourselves to other things, without astonishment; yea, is it not strange there should be often so quick a transition between our thoughts of the glorious God and attention to the meanest trifle? 4. It is no small advantage when men can open the Bible, and retire into it under the sense and impression of a Godhead, and that near correspondence he has in this way with his people, to whose soul the words, "Thus saith the Lord," carry awe and authority. 5. They have come a great length, who in their ordinary walk are under some weight and impression that God is near, from whose sight they cannot hide one thought, yea, that on Him they have such an absolute dependence, that without Him they cannot draw their breath.

II. Does not this argument of experience by a sure and unanswerable demonstration witness the truth and reality of grace, that there is such a thing, and that it is no empty sound, seeing it raises man above the natural state of men, as far as reason puts him above the state of the beast! Strange that this should be believed, and that yet we can be at such rest whilst one of these two lies under debate, the reality of grace, or our being really interested therein! O is there not cause of astonishment that such a product of heaven should be found in the earth, whose descent and original is so clearly demonstrated by its breathing upwards after God, by its native tendency and motion towards him, whence it came? Surely, grace is a great subject to think on, and if not so in our eyes, it must be either that we do not believe it, or do not consider what a change it makes in the soul. It lifts the soul up from the clay; yea, by bringing it low in its own eyes, raises it nearer God. This makes a man to have an appearance on which the world is forced to look with some astonishment; one Christian admires this in another, and the more it shows itself, it causes a more near approach between their souls; it will create fear in those who hate it, and has a power even over its persecutors. Now it is the truth and reality of this excellent thing that this argument witnesses; yea, such a witness that can admit no exception. A serious look and persuasion of this may make the Christian's life a continued wonder, that there is such a thing, which by a marvellous surprisal prevented him when he was not aware, led him into a new world, and translated him from a state of darkness to marvellous light; which causes the soul to breathe in another air, brings him near the state of the angels, subdues the will without violence, and subjects it with its own consent! Surely this is one of the most stately pieces of the work of God, and exceeding the whole structure of the universe! O with what astonishment should we look on this marvellous thing, if we could consider the whole frame and structure of the grace of God in a Christian, and make, as it were, a dissection of its several parts and proportions, see its decay and languishing, its different changes and sizes, its vigorous acting and abatements, how it breathes and is nourished, how it is kept green and preserved by a continued intercourse with the Fountain of its being! And lo, whilst we consider this great wonder, both in the whole and in its parts, we may see how it does most exactly answer that model which we have thereof in the Scripture of God!

III. This is a great argument, and should be so in our eyes, which not only witnesses the reality of grace in its acting and exercise, but unanswerably demonstrates a spiritual life and being, which the Christian knows and is as persuaded of, as he is sure that he breathes and has a natural life. O what a marvellous demonstration is this, wherein sense and feeling do in as certain a way concur, as in any discovery we have by our outward senses! 1. It may indeed cause our wonder to think we are men, and that we have a rational being; but a spiritual life is another cause for wondering: a life which comes not by our birth, has no natural causes, yet a life that has its proper operation and vital acts put forth as truly as those natural actions of breathing and moving are put forth by a living man: a life that has in as sensible a way its quickening and refreshing influences, as the earth or bodies of men know the influences of the heavens; which has a pleasure and delight peculiar to its nature, that has no affinity with things we enjoy by the senses, but is a pleasure far exceeding the same. 2. What a demonstration is it which, even to our sense and feeling, witnesses a power on the soul by the word, above the most persuasive words of man, and above all moral influences, by which men are not only touched, but transformed into the same image! 3. If this demonstration of a spiritual life be sure, have we not thus an eternal life and being with God put beyond debate; for, if we be certain of the one, is it not undeniable that this noble being of the new creature, this life that is here begun, must have a more full growth, and be at the furthest stature of the man in Christ; for the one is surely demonstrative of the other, even as a young child, which we see in a growing tendency towards a man, shows that he will be a man in his full growth. 4. If we assuredly know this spiritual life, must we not also admit the undoubted truth of spiritual beings, and of an invisible world with which this life has its correspondence, yea, thus as by a stream be led up to the true Fountain, the invisible God?

IV. How great an argument is this which gives us such a demonstration that heaven is not altogether deferred until we be there, but that there is such a thing as the real presence of the glorious God, and a near familiar approach of him to the soul, which is here as really felt and enjoyed as any thing we can be sure of! O how marvellous should this be to us! I cannot doubt but the report hereof sometimes dazzles the world with amazement, and puts the grossest of men to strange

thoughts. I have sometimes thought it strange
how men are taken even with a kind of transport,
with the discovery of some rare experiment and
demonstration in nature, which could make that
poor man cry out εὕρηκα,* as though therewith he
had gained the whole earth. But O here is another
kind of demonstration, of a more transcendent value
and interest! This indeed rises above the reach of
those who have followed the search of nature with
a most exact and subtile inquiry. O blessed are
the souls who have found it! for they have found
a treasure, the thoughts whereof may make it a
new thing every day ; not only a claim and title to
the inheritance above, but the first fruits and earnest thereof already enjoyed. Have they not cause
both for joy and wondering, who can say, and not
from report, I do surely feel, I enjoy, I am persuaded, this is the Lord ; and thus have come
forth from him with such a change on their souls,
and composure of mind, that even by-standers
might see where they have been ? Now this is the
witness which all who are serious in the way of
the Lord can in some measure bear, that in a way
no less sure and demonstrative than any thing here
beneath can be known, they have had such a discovery ; and now these scripture truths they understand, the meaning whereof they once could not
know, such as, their soul melting within at the
voice of their beloved, to have his name as oint-
ment poured forth, and to be brought near to see
his face with joy, Cant. v. 2, 4; i. 3; 2 Cor. iii. 18.

V. This is an argument which clearly witnesses
a truth and reality in prayer, which may be called

* "I have found it." This is written of Archimedes,
the mathematician.

one of the great wonders of religion. Is not this a very great thing, that poor man, now upon the earth, has such a passage to heaven, and may speak to Him who inhabits eternity, the glorious object of the adoration of angels, without the intervening of any creature; yea, with so sure a warrant may approach the throne of God, and there pour out his soul, and present his requests unto Him who lives and sees? O with what astonishment should we consider this! Suppose at some solemn times in our life only this might be attained, yea, but in one part of the earth, should we not reckon an abode there, were it a barren desert and wilderness, to be preferable to all other advantages, and look on the whole earth besides as accursed? It may truly be a question, whilst we are most in the practice of this duty, if we believe the truth and reality thereof; but it is beyond question what Christians have most sensibly found here. They can say, if they be sure they have souls, they have been as sure that they have had their souls restored in prayer, and that under some desertion they have at last prevailed by wrestling, and been again visited by God's favour.

But does it not seem strange, if seriously considered, 1. That we are not more restless to be surely persuaded concerning this, which we should look on as an inestimable treasure, both for our joy and establishment? 2. It is strange we can find it so easy a matter to pray and appear before God, that we are not afraid to be hasty in uttering a matter before Him, whilst we consider God is in heaven, and we are on the earth! 3. It may seem strange how easily we can step out from the world, and the noise thereof, at once before the Lord, without the least pause or time intervening;

yea, so immediately in our return again step into the world, as if we had wholly forgotten where we have been! 4. How strange is formality in such a business as prayer, which is an address to the living God, one of the most solemn acts of the soul! yea, we may call it the most natural work of a Christian, like the breathing of the child after the breasts; alas! it is sad that this seems many times rather a piece of invention than a matter of earnestness with the Lord. O to what class can such a piece of atheism be reduced, as appears in our nearest approaches to God? 5. Should we look on prayer as a duty, and not consider it as a singular enjoyment also, without which this earth would have an exact appearance of hell? O what thoughts should we have of prayer, if the truth thereof were more believed! I think that man who is sure of the being and faithfulness of God, and of the reality of prayer, need not be solicitous with what face the world looks on him, when thus his great interest and encouragement is secure, and a well is at hand which can supply all his wants.

VI. Have we not demonstration also, by this argument of experience, how near the blessed majesty of God, in the way of providence, approaches to his people, and is surely known by the real correspondence which he has with them in this way? It is true, He is great in the smallest things; but there is a more solemn and near approach to men in some special steps of His providence; yea, He sometimes speaks as with an audible voice, and so opens the ear of men, and seals their instruction, as, "in the hidden part to make them to know wisdom," Psa. li. 6. There is sometimes also so wonderful a series of providences, that men cannot but see something greater than man therein; whilst yea, so immediately in our return again step into the world, as if we had wholly forgotten where we have been! 4. How strange is formality in such a business as prayer, which is an address to the living God, one of the most solemn acts of the soul! yea, we may call it the most natural work of a Christian, like the breathing of the child after the breasts; alas! it is sad that this seems many times rather a piece of invention than a matter of earnestness with the Lord. O to what class can such a piece of atheism be reduced, as appears in our nearest approaches to God? 5. Should we look on prayer as a duty, and not consider it as a singular enjoyment also, without which this earth would have an exact appearance of hell? O what thoughts should we have of prayer, if the truth thereof were more believed! I think that man who is sure of the being and faithfulness of God, and of the reality of prayer, need not be solicitous with what face the world looks on him, when thus his great interest and encouragement is secure, and a well is at hand which can supply all his wants.

VI. Have we not demonstration also, by this argument of experience, how near the blessed majesty of God, in the way of providence, approaches to his people, and is surely known by the real correspondence which he has with them in this way? It is true, He is great in the smallest things; but there is a more solemn and near approach to men in some special steps of His providence; yea, He sometimes speaks as with an audible voice, and so opens the ear of men, and seals their instruction, as, "in the hidden part to make them to know wisdom," Psa. li. 6. There is sometimes also so wonderful a series of providences, that men cannot but see something greater than man therein; whilst

church, amidst the various changes of her condition, yea, in the most strange things which fall out
in the world, convincingly verify his word.

For prosecuting this argument I shall show,

I. How these general promises which belong to
the church universal, and concern her in all ages,
have an accomplishment.

II. How the threatenings of the word, which
relate to her adversaries, are certainly fulfilled.

III. How the Scripture of God clearly shines
upon the darkest footsteps of providence, even on
those which seem most hard to understand, so that
it may be demonstrated that nothing falls out in the
world, or befalls the saints, but what is most consonant to the Scripture.

I. As to the first branch of this argument, I shall
instance in five general promises, which we find in
the word concerning the church, and endeavour to
show their clear and obvious accomplishment.

1. The first promise is the preservation of the
church; that God will be with her to the end of the
world, and though he make an end of other nations,
yet will he not make an utter end of her, but while
the ordinances of the sun and moon do last, and as
the days of heaven, so shall her days be prolonged,
Jer. xxx. 11; Matt. xvi. 18.

(1.) That the church continues and is kept alive
to this day, certainly proves the truth of God's
promise; for she has outlived all her opposers, the
greatest of whom have found their grave in the
quarrel, over whose tomb that last confession of a
great adversary, Julian, may be written, " Vicisti
tandem Galilæe."*     Has not this deadly and irre-

___

* " Thou hast conquered at length, O Galilean!"
The words of Julian the Apostate, addressed in his
dying moments to Christ.

concilable feud been perpetuated from fathers to children? but who has prospered in this enterprise? The archers have often shot and wounded her sore, but her bow abides in strength, Gen. xlix. 23, 24; and even to this day this is her motto, " Persecuted, but not forsaken; cast down, but not destroyed," 2 Cor. iv. 9. She who has brought forth many children, yet ceases not to bear; her age has not marred her beauty, her eyes are not dim, nor has her strength failed; a sight which may cause us no less to stand, and consider this great wonder, than Moses did at that which was but the shadow and emblem thereof—a bush burning, and not consumed: for behold, a church kept alive, yet still in the flames; and when to appearance consumed, it arises more glorious out of its own ashes! This is indeed the only phœnix, of whom it can be said, She has borne deluges, which like an inundation went over her head; even idolatry and paganism in the first times, and antichristianism and Arianism in the after ages, yet she is not swallowed up. Though her enemies have often sung her funeral song, and rejoiced over the dead bodies of her witnesses, yet they have risen again; her dry bones have taken life, and come together, and behold, she is alive at this day!

(2.) Not only the church's preservation, but the continued series and succession thereof unto this time, witness the fulfilling of this promise, that in the darkest times of her condition, she has not altogether disappeared, though long hid in the wilderness. Though the church has often cried out for the want of children, and has been heard weeping, bemoaning herself because they were not, yet she has never wanted an offspring to this day. She did never die without an heir and seed of her own to

raise up her name, even since the covenant was
first made with her in Adam's family; and though
particular churches have their set times, which like
the sun have the usual. periods of height and
flourishing, and afterwards a gradual decay making
way to the departure of light, yet this never made
void the promise of God to the church universal,
whose lamp was never put out, nay, shall never be
extinguished while the days of heaven last.

(3.) The continuance and preservation of the
church is peculiar to her, and can be said of no
other interest and party beneath the sun ; for it is
clear, that there never was a kingdom or empire
so firmly rooted, no society so well governed by
laws, or backed with power, but time at last prevailed over it, and made the same a trophy of her
conquest. Yea, the greatest monarchies and flourishing cities have at last yielded, so as of them it may
be said, " Nunc seges est ubi Troja fuit."* But
time cannot to this day boast of a triumph over the
church of God, though no nation or family in the
earth could ever plead her antiquity.

(4.) It clearly demonstrates the truth of this
promise of the church's preservation, that the
world, yea, that greatest atheists, may see this has
not come to pass at an adventure, nay, not in an
ordinary way of providence, but by a Divine power;
1. Because no interest or party had ever such adversaries as the church, against whom the powers
of the world, and the powers of darkness have always been active. 2. That outward advantages
have usually been on her adversaries' side, they
being not only the great men of the earth, but those
of greatest parts and abilities. 3. That their will

* That which once was Troy, is now a corn-field.

was never wanting to raze her to the foundation.
4. That this enmity has been rooted and irrecon-
cilable. 5. That no interest ever endured such
violent assaults, so many sharp batteries; for it is
observable, that many of the wars and commotions
of various ages have in some way originated on the
church's account; and whatever private quarrels
men have had among themselves, yet it has not
hindered the pursuit of their malice against the
woman and her seed. 6. That even the men of
her own house have often been her greatest enemies. 7. That her real friends have often fainted
in a time of her trial, and stood afar off. 8. That
the depths of Satan, in her enemies, as an angel of
light, have sometimes given her a sore assault, so
that if it had been possible they would have deceived the very elect. 9. No other party was ever
brought so low and near death: the knife was once
at the church's throat in Isaac. She sought to
adopt a bond-woman's son, instead of a lawful heir,
when Abraham agreed to Sarah's overture for the
accomplishment of the promise: and was near ex-
piring in Egypt, when the sentence to destroy her
male issue went forth. Yea, what but a miracle
could have preserved her, when she was between
Pharaoh and the Red sea! How low was the
church in the wilderness; and after, in the days of
the captivity, even broken to pieces with small appearance of life, when her face was all blurred with
weeping, and her enemies made sport over her
ruins at the rivers of Babylon; when the children
of Edom cried out, "Let us raze her even to the
foundation!" Yea, could the church be nearer the
grave, than when her bones were scattered at the
grave's mouth? But above all, in that dark night
when her Head and Shepherd was smitten, and

her hope seemed to be buried in the grave with a
stone put upon it, when she could get no entertain-
ment among the Jews, and the Gentiles in wrath
rose up against her, so that for some hundred years
the great empire which had trodden down all the
nations about, put forth the utmost of its power and
malice for her undoing. O who could have
thought the church should outlive this ! Yea, after
all, we find her tossed and hurried into the wilderness by antichrist, an adversary more cruel than
any that had gone before, where the dragon watched
to destroy her ; but in all these, and through that
long, dark night, she has continued, and marvellously flourished as the palm tree under greatest
weights ; so that her enemies cannot deny that the
promise to the church of her preservation is this
day fulfilled, yea, that it has not in an ordinary
way been brought about. Surely there is no enchantment against Jacob, nor divination against
Israel ; all her enemies have been found liars, for
the eternal God is her refuge, and underneath are
the everlasting arms, Numb. xxiii. 23 ; Deut.
xxxiii. 27.

2. The second promise which I shall here instance is that of the church's increase and enlargement, Psa. ii. 8 ; lxxxix. 25. Isa. xlii. 4 ; liv. 3.

As this promise is express in the Scriptures, so
it is no less clear and evident in its accomplishment: for consider,

(1.) The vast extent which the kingdom of
Christ has had in the world ; for this cannot be denied, that the greatest empire or monarchy could
never so far extend its conquests as the church has
done, since the wall of partition was taken down.
Short are the limits of the Grecian and Roman
empire compared with this, whose bounds have

been the ends and uttermost parts of the earth, where neither Greece or Rome did ever set up their trophies. Has not the gospel as the sun made its circuit from the east to the west? Yes, it has crossed the seas to the dark northern nations, thus fulfilling its course, in order to its return again to the place of its first rising; that it may, as we are sure it shall, visit the Jews again, and the eastern places of the world that now are buried in a night of darkness; which I think will be as sure a presage of the break of day, and second coming of the Lord, as the morning star is of the sun's accomplishing his course, and that it is returning again to the east where it should rise. Has not the gospel been through Asia, where it did not tarry for a night; and the going back of the tide from thence was its flowing to another part of the world? And indeed it is observable of the church, as it is of the sea, that what it has lost in one part it has gained in another. Did the vast distance of Africa, its great barren deserts or scorching heat, hinder the gospel's making a visit thither, so that it was once a fertile soil, and brought forth many famous lights? Yea, something both there, and in the east parts of the world yet remains to show the gospel was truly in those places. And has Europe, though last, been least on this account? What mean the late discoveries of unknown parts of the earth, but to make way for a more full performance of this promise, that the gospel might stretch its conquest over the line, that even America might have her day also, and the voice of the turtle be heard in those lands?

, (2.) Not only the large extent of the church as to its bounds witnesses this, but the great and numerous offspring of sons and daughters which were

**10 \***

brought forth to Christ in those parts where the gospel has been preached ; for what John saw in vision has been very manifest to after ages, namely, an innumerable company of all tongues, nations, and languages, of whom it could be said, These are born in Zion. O how great a harvest of the na- tions is even already gathered! What a marvel- lous increase has there been in some places after special tides of the gospel! This truth is now be- yond debate, that out of one, and him not only as good as dead, but truly dead, there has come forth a multitude as the sand of the sea and stars of heaven in number. The church has inherited Joseph's blessing of a fruitful offspring; the dew of Christ's youth has been as the womb of the morn- ing, Psa. cx. 3. O what a marvellous and goodly company will this be when gathered together!

(3.) This truth may be demonstrated not only from the real conquests of the gospel, and those excellent trophies of her victory over many noted enemies, who have afterwards been vessels of honour, but also from the feigned subjection that so many have been obliged to render. Is it not strange what a multitude in these times profess the truth, and yet hate it, and were never drawn with the cords of love? How very many have courted the name of a Christian, and the shadow of religion, who never knew the truth thereof! which certainly is a convincing evidence of the gospel's conquests.

(4.) It is an unanswerable proof of this truth, that we see the church's increase and enlargement has come to pass most punctually after that manner,, and with those circumstances which were foretold, so that the event does in every thing answer the: word; for,, 1. It is there held out, that from a day:

of small things which men would be ready to despise, it should grow up as a tender plant, and spread forth its branches over the nations; that the children of the desolate should be more than of the married wife, and the glory of the second temple exceed that of the first. 2. This great increase of the church was to fall out in the days of the New Testament, when Christ should be lifted up, that he should draw all men after him; for the promises we have thereof under the Old Testament clearly point at the times of the gospel. 3. The Scripture says that the falling away of the Jews should be the riches of the Gentiles, and that their rejection should make way for the fulfilling of this promise. 4. The isles and uttermost parts of the earth are given to Christ for his inheritance, and foretold as a special part of the church's increase. And do we not clearly see there is no place of the world where Christ's kingdom is more visible, where more children have been begotten to him by the gospel, than in these northern places, even in these isles of Britain and Ireland, which are almost the uttermost parts of the earth, there being comparatively little nearer the pole which is inhabited; yea, we may judge them to have been the Thule, whereof the ancients did so much speak? 5. Was it not also foretold, that the church should possess the gates of her enemies; that at her great increase the world should wonder, the princes thereof see and be troubled, while God should be known in her palaces for a refuge; and does not the event witness this, that over all the counsels and essays which the world has interposed to hinder the church's growth, her rising has always been upon the ruins of her greatest enemies; yea, those who have been a terror in the

land of the living, did often fall and break them
selves in that attempt?

(5.) As the fulfilling of this promise, concerning the church's increase, is undeniable, we must
also say, this is a thing great and marvellous, which
no less than some divine and extraordinary power
could bring about, if we consider, 1. That quick
despatch which the church's growth under the
days of the New Testament has made. O might
not the pagan world wonder how, in the space of
two or three hundred years, it was almost wholly
become Christian! O strange! a Dioclesian and
a Maximin so grievously persecuting Christianity,
and yet near that same age, the empire itself, and
the emperor, submitting to the gospel! 2. How
astonishing was it for the church's rise and increase
to be brought about upon the ruin and downfall of
the idols of the nations; that the world should be
made to renounce its Bible, and that religion which
for so many ages was deeply rooted by tradition
from their fathers; those altars which were had in
such reverence demolished, and their temples made
a ruinous heap; yea, the very name of their gods
obliterated; Dagon has no strength to stand before
the ark of the God of Israel. 3. That it should
be thus advanced by such a mean as the preaching
of the word, even of that which to the Jews was
a stumbling block, and to the Greeks foolishness;
that this voice should put to perpetual silence those
oracles that for so many ages had given a response
to the world; yea, that the church's increase should
be brought about at no less a rate than the overturning of greatest kingdoms; should tame and
civilize the most savage and barbarous, cause the
lion to lie down with the lamb, and even make so
great and universal a change in the face of the

world! 4. Does it not evidence some Divine power that the church's growth has been effected, not only over the violence of men, but over all those dreadful errors and inventions, which both in former and later times have ascended out of the pit to choke her? The church has not only been helped to tread upon the lion and dragon, but on the adder and cockatrice, and carries the trophies of her conquest over all these. 5. Is it not marvellous that the church's increase has been advanced in a way most contrary to all the rules of ordinary policy, by which states and empires have risen: not by dissimulation, but by the greatest plainness and free dealing, for her ministers never flattered the world to embrace the truth; not by open violence, but by a more excellent spirit and power, before which men could not stand, where foolishness was made to confound and outwit human wisdom, and weakness to overcome strength? O how little of man, and how much of God, may be seen herein.

3. The third promise which the Lord has given to his church, is the giving of the Spirit, and pouring out of the same, which is expressly held forth, Isa. lix. 21; Zech. xii. 10; John xiv. 17.

It is true the Christians' inward experience can best witness this, for they have an argument from within; they know, and they are sure they have received the Spirit by the word, whereby they understand those things which are spiritually discerned. But that which here is intended is, to show that the Spirit is truly given to the church according to the promise; that he accompanies the truth and doctrine of Christ, and the purity of the ordinances, as things which from clear undeniable evidences may be demonstrated to the conviction of the greatest atheist: for even they who never knew any saving work of the Spirit, but who live in those parts where the ordinances are dispensed with purity and power, may often see something going forth with the word that is beyond words, a Divine spirit and power, which sends forth its savour in the daily administration of the gospel.

For (1.) Those excellent gifts and endowments given to the church are a visible proof of this. For it is undeniable that where once the gospel comes, instruments are raised, reapers sent forth and shaped for their work, yea, those who were of mean and ordinary parts, when called forth to the service of the church, will have another lustre, and often do not only exceed themselves, but those who were of more eminent natural endowments. Whence is that variety of gifts, so suitable to the various employments the church needs? How are they thus suited to the very genius and temper of their times? Whence is it that every gift and qualification is so fitted and disposed for its proper use, some most peculiarly shaped out to awake and threaten, like Boanerges, while others possess a spirit eminently fitted to comfort; some mighty in persuasion, yet not so fit to expound; others most dexterous to instruct, yet not so powerful to apply; some having great knowledge of languages, and others the tongue of the learned to speak a word in season to the weary; to some the face of a lion is given, when a heroic spirit of courage and resolution is called for; to others the face of a calf, for patient enduring in suffering times? · We may say of this excellent body of the church, as of the natural body of man, how curiously, yea, marvellously is it framed, where every part answers another, and the use of the whole! Each has its peculiar excellency, and something peculiar may be seen in every man's gift, as well as in the variety of the natural face.

(2.) Those more extraordinary outlettings of the Spirit, which at some special times, when the church's necessity requires, have been most discernible, also attest this truth. When he is to plant the church in some place where the gospel will meet with much opposition, is it not then manifest, how some more than ordinary power and irresistible efficacy accompanies the truth, before which there is no standing? The disputer is then confounded in his reasoning by something above reason; the untoward and rude are forced to stoop before the word, and to confess they have to do with power, and not with words: yea, those whom the Lord makes use of, who were feeble and weak as others, in that day are made as a brazen wall, and a defenced city.

(3.) Is it not also undeniable that now under the New Testament there are ministers of the Spirit, and not of a dead letter and empty sound? That with the word, there goes along a ministration of power and life whence a majesty and authority attending the public ordinances is often so discernible, that even those who know not who the Spirit is, are made to see something therein which dazzles them with astonishment? . Whence is it that sometimes such a beauty and power shine forth in ordinances, like a glance of the glory of God, even going before men's eyes, which for the present has made a wonderful change upon some very gross men, and put them in another temper; yea, forced them with fear to acknowledge, that surely God is in the assemblies of his people? Whence is it that the word gives law to men's consciences, and speaks

with such an authority, that even the worst of men
are sometimes made to stand before the ministry
of the word, like men standing at the bar upon life
and death, before a judge whose authority they dare
not decline?

(4.) It is very discernible what a great difference there is, both in ministers and Christians, at
different times in the discharge of duty, as if they
were not the same persons; which appears not
only in the enlargement or straitening of their gift,
but also in its power and life. With what liberty
do they sometimes pray, and are as a ship with a
full gale before the wind! It is then easy to preach;
when at other times even lookers-on may perceive
a sensible languishing, and their very expressions
hampered, yea, they are as men rowing against a
contrary wind, the word wanting that savour and
relish it has had at other times; and this not through
a natural indisposition, or want of preparation, but
that which all who ever served God in the spirit
must confess has most sensibly affected them, when
they have thought themselves at the greatest advantage for going about duty.          .

(5.) It is also clear, that wherever the Lord has
had a church, at some special turns of her condition there have usually been some more solemn
times of the Spirit, and high spring-tides of the
gospel. There was indeed a marvellous flowing
forth of the Spirit of God after Christ's ascension,
which, like a mighty current, carried all before it;
at which time more success followed one sermon
than has followed thousands in another age. This
made the world wonder, as if some universal enchantment had fallen on men, which the more they
sought to bear down, the more it increased; which
made the rich choose poverty, and those who dwelt

in palacés betake themselves with cheerfulness to-
the dens and caves of the earth. But besides this,·
it is very manifest, that in a large measure the
Spirit has been let forth to the church in after·
ages; yea, there is no particular church, where the·
light has shined, but has had its special times,
some solemn day of the pouring out of the Spirit
before the sun went down; which may be observed
either at the first entrance of the gospel, or at some
other remarkable time and change of her condition;
whence a great harvest of souls to Christ has followed, besides the reaching of the conscience and
stirring the affection of many others under a com-·
mon work of the Spirit, which usually goes along,
with such solemn times.

(6.) The going back of the tide, and the visible
withdrawing of the Spirit from particular churches,
where it has sometimes in a large measure been
let forth, is a very convincing witness to the truth
of this promise; for it is clearly seen at what a
stand the gospel is in these places where it most
eminently shined; that the land which blossomed,
and was like a watered garden, has been made as
the heath in the wilderness; and that the ministers
of Christ, whose lot has fallen in such a time, are
put to work as it were with oars, for want of wind,
to cast out the net all night, and catch nothing; a
shut door is opposed to them in the exercise of
their ministry, duty is made burdensome, because
the Lord is against them; there is an evident restraint upon the word, and its intercourse is more
with the ear than with the conscience; yea, all the
liberty they find is to execute a commission of·
judgment, and to denounce the woe of the gospel;
Does not so manifest a withdrawing of the Spirit

11

witness the outletting thereof, and that it is a cer-i tain and real thing?

(7.) Do not the stirrings and strange convictions. which even the worst of men have sometimes under the word, witness a Divine Spirit going along therewith; which forces an assent from their con-. sciences to the truth, which otherwise they hate, yea, makes them for the time wonder they should not have been more serious in the ways of God? Yea, it often puts a thorn in the bed of their security; for indeed the word, and the light thereof, torment those who dwell in the earth: and truly this is a marvellous thing, which enters upon men's secret designs and counsels, reveals to them the most close thoughts of their hearts, which they are sure man's eye could not reach. They are forced to confess what a great difference they find between the word from the mouth of some who are holy and serious, though spoken in greatest simplicity, and from others of greater gifts and eloquence; that surely the one has another sound and relish, and speaks more feelingly home to their hearts, than the most polished discourse of the greatest orators.

(8.) One witness more I shall here·give·to the truth of this promise, even those eminent examples of the grace of· God, which in every age have shined in the firmament of the church; some ·in love and zeal, some in patience and humility; some in the strong acts of faith and self-denial; which certainly demonstrate a more excellent spirit than that which is in the world, whence they appear with another lustre in their walk and carriage, and have a sweet and fragrant savour of the· Spirit to the very discerning of bystanders.

4. We find an express promise in the word of deliverance to the church in a low and oppressed condition, Psa. xviii. 47—50; xxii. 4, 5. Isa. li. 23; liv. 17.

It is true, this promise has its bounds and limits, which should be taken along in the application thereof. We know the covenant of God with particular churches is conditioned only. He promises that he will be with them while they are with him; yea, it is often seen, that a people professing the gospel, confederate with God, following duty, have even turned their back before the enemy, and in the holy providence of God, have for a time been given up to their fierce rage and violence; but it is also sure, that this promise has an accomplishment, and in the day of the church's trouble, the Lord has often appeared by a strong outstretched hand for her help; his own arm has brought salvation to his people when they sought to him; for God is known in her palaces for a refuge, yea, surely the church might often sing that song on such clear grounds as though with Israel she had been standing at the Red sea, "Thy right hand, O Lord, is glorious in power, thy right hand hath dashed in pieces the enemy," Exodus xv. 6. To evince this:

(1.) There are few ages but we have some record of the church's condition, which hold forth such signal, convincing providences of God in behalf of his oppressed church and people, as may be a manifest seal to this truth. It is true, some times have been more remarkable for suffering, times of judgment and of trial wherein this truth hath not so clearly shined forth, yea, that long night which the church had under antichrist might seem to call it in question; but, nevertheless, if men take a seri-

ous look of the Lord's way in ages past, comparing
one time with another, what the straits of the
church have at last resolved in, they will find cause
to cry with astonishment: Great deliverances
giveth he to his people, yea, the Lord hath done
great things for them. I am sure, were there a
full record of those more remarkable deliverances
that particular churches have met with, since the
first planting of the Gospel among them, it would
silence the world respecting the fulfilment of this
promise.

(2.) The confessions even of the church's ene-
'mies have often witnessed, that in pursuing their
malice to trouble and undo her, they have but undone themselves; tormenting disappointments have
caused their very flesh to pine away, and the close
and issue of their rage forced this conviction from
them at last, that the church is a burdensome stone
to be lifted up; a party with whom it is full of
hazard to meddle. They have often discerned
something of a Divine hand so clearly against them,
blasting their counsels and most promising attempts,
as if their eyes, with Balaam, had been opened to
see the angel in their way; yea, in all ages it is
known how the consciences even of the worst have
often betrayed something of a presaging fear, which
they have had of those whom they pursued with
greatest malice, and a dreadful impression they
had of a praying people, and of their prayers.

(3.) This truth has had the clearest witness in
times of the church's greatest extremity, when difficulties have appeared insuperable, and help in the
ordinary way of Providence most hopeless; when
visible means have been withdrawn, all refuge failed, and none to help: in such a day the Lord has
been seen upon the mount, and unexpectedly by

very strange means brought deliverance to a broken and almost ruined church, even as it were between the bridge and the water; so that he who would have a clear view of the accomplishment of this promise, need but turn back on those more remark-able extreme exigences of the church's condition, and there see that a sweet sunshine hath followed the most dark and cloudy times, a raging storm has resolved into a refreshing calm, yea, that with a further growth of the church's trial and doubling of her burden, her enlargement has suddenly ar-rived.

(4.) The greatest advantage which men have got over the churches and people of God, can also bear witness that when the wicked have sprung up like the grass, and the workers of iniquity seemed to flourish, this very way has the Lord taken to bring about a more full deliverance: yea, on the other hand, it has been very obvious that the church's gain has been brought forth out of the greatest loss; that those wounds which seemed most deadly, have turned by the infinitely wise providence of God to her most effectual and thorough cure; and men's unreasonable violence and rage against the church, have often had an evi-dent tendency to bring about even that whereto it seemed most directly contrary, even some further mercy and deliverance, than could have been ex-pected; as the Amorites, in refusing Israel a passage through their land, did by that refusal give them more than they sought, the possession of that land for an inheritance.

(5.) The observation of the church in all ages can attest, that deliverance has often sprung up from a quarter, and by such means, as none would have expected, by such as none but God could

operate; as a sudden report and rumour, 1 Sam.
xxiii. 27: means that have been not only small
and improbable, but that looked directly contrary,
as in bringing the church out of Egypt; yea,
sometimes by the wicked being ensnared in the
work of their own hands. Is it not obvious, that
the Lord has influenced men's private interest to
induce them to befriend his church; and has
caused the earth to help the woman, and raised up
one oppressor to punish another; yea, often has
prepared workmen whence 'they .were least expected, to cut the horns of those who had scattered
his people?

- (6.) There is a convincing witness to the truth
of such a promise, in the sudden, remarkable
change which may be often discerned, both on
men's inward frame and the outward face of the
church, when a time of mercy and enlargement is
come; instruments raised of the Lord, with a discernible elevation of their spirits to act and do exploits; the feeble then made strong, and those who
sometimes would have fainted at an ordinary piece
of service, dare with such a gale of Divine assistance, to run as it were through a troop, and leap
over a wall. For indeed this may in all ages be
obvious, how easy it is to move in the day when
the Lord moves for his people, and strengthens the
girdle of their loins; that it was not their bow or
sword which got them the victory, but the very
finger of God; so that even at some distance, they
who are wise to discern the times did see when
there was a day-break of a church's hope; how a
previous motion and stir among the dry bones has
been then discernible, and given some promising
appearance from the present disposition and temper
of the godly in that time; a promise which, like

the rising of the cloud on the top of mount Carmel, though at first but as a. handbreadth, has showed that deliverance to the church was not far off.

(7.) I would add, those convincing providences which in all ages have been shown against the enemies of the church, such as men could not pass without some remark. How they have become a most abject and contemptible party, like bees which have lost their sting; their countenance has been changed, and they ceased to be any more a terror, when once their work was done, and the date of their commission for the humbling and trying of the church expired; yea, a judicial stroke from the Lord has often been seen upon their very judgment and resolutions, which could not then serve them to trouble and afflict the church, the day being turned, and the time of her deliverance come.

. 5. There is the promise that " all things work together for good to them that love God," Rom. viii. 28.

This is indeed the constant course and tenor of Providence about the church: the turnings and changes of the world, the most strange emergencies of the times, the various motions and interests of men, co-operate together, and have an undoubted tendency to bring forth the church's good, as though they did intentionally act for the same. There will indeed be a more clear and marvellous discovery of this, when the Lord has perfected his work, the mystery of God is finished, and the church brought safe to the harbour; then shall it be fully manifest to what end all these storms and cross winds in the counsels and designs of men were; these things which at the time could not be understood, but seemed perplexed and strange, for

then men will see with their eyes a full perform.
ance of the word. Yet even here in every age,
amidst the various changes of the church's case,
there is no serious observer of Providence but may
bear witness:

 (1.) That not only the church's good, but even
her greatest good, has most clearly had its rise out
of the greatest mischiefs intended against her; that
if we search the Scripture, and other records of
the church's condition, we shall there find the most
remarkable attempts, such as Pharaoh's last essay
to destroy the Israelites, Haman's great design to
root out the seed of the Jews, the great masterplot
of Satan to crush the gospel and the Christian
church, by crucifying her Head; yea, in these last
times, antichrist's killing the witnesses;—have all,
as if really intended by the instruments, as well as
the first mover, brought forth the church's greatest
good, so as the after-mercy has carried some visible proportion to her trial, and to the greatness of
her adversaries' design.

(2.) It may be also clear, if we trace back those
memorable changes which have been in the earth,
how direct a tendency they have had to this end.
We find Nebuchadnezzar raised up as a rod to the
church, and Cyrus for a deliverer; we see the Per-
sian and the Grecian monarchies brought down to
make way for the setting up of the Messiah's kingdom. Antiochus must stand up a little for a sharp
trial, and his downfall gave the church a new breathing. Peaceable Augustus must come in His time
in whose days shall be abundance of peace. We
find a Titus set up to execute the judgment of God
on the Jews, to make way for a further enlargement to the gentile church; a Nero and Domitian
to help forward the church's suffering; and a Con-

stantine to give her some rest after so long and sore an assault; and at last, the Roman empire mouldered down for antichrist's appearance, to accomplish in the church what did remain of the sufferings of Christ by that adversary.

(3.) We may often see a very strange concurrence of instruments bringing about the Lord's end, and advancing His church's interest, even while each one does most vigorously attempt its own proper end; which shows there is surely a living spirit in the wheels that orders these motions, a supreme and first mover that can thus determine them to serve His end and the church's good, when they most directly intend the contrary.

(4.) We have seen how in men's plotting the ruin of the church, there is often an unseen hand determining their judgment and inclination to fall upon that very way, than which we should think nothing could have been more direct for her good and their own ruin; how a Hushai hath been set in, or some have been stirred up amongst themselves, upon their own interest, to break the pernicious counsels and designs of others.

(5.) We have also seen the personal quarrels of the church's enemies among themselves brought to such a height, and to occur so seasonably, that lookers on could clearly perceive that it has been a judgment from the Lord for their rage and violence against his poor oppressed people.

(6.) We have seen the church's enemies raised to a strange height, all advantages favouring them, until their mine has been ripe for springing, and lo! at that very moment something unexpected has turned their former success to their ruin.

(7.) We have seen some temporary evil of the church bring forth her good; yea, when all has been given up for lost, and truth has lost the day upon the field, she has triumphed on the scaffold and at the stake.

(8,) We have seen most despicable things made subservient to some great work of the Lord, a very small thing made the first rise of strange revolutions, and remarkable changes often lying in the bosom of a common providence; yea, truly, we find both Scripture and the observation of after ages witnesses that the church's deliverance did rarely come that way by such a method and means as she had expected, and that God's time of working may be often very contrary to our time of expecting.

Is it not often seen, that men's endeavours to darken the truth by error, have been an effectual means for its further clearing? That a trial upon the church hath wrought towards .her deliverance; her meat hath been often brought even out of the eater? A time of persecution will help to cure the divisions amongst the godly, and bring them together in the furnace, which prosperity could not do; yea, the very undoing of the church has been God's blest way to keep her from being undone.

II. The second branch concerns those scripture-threatenings which are held forth in the word, with a respect to the visible church, and against a people professing the gospel, that no privileges they have above others shall exempt them from judgment.

I here intend to show how judgments from the Lord, which point, as with the finger, to the abounding sins of the time, do reach particular churches, according. to the threatenings of the word. The greatest monuments of wrath have usually been set up, where the largest offers of the gospel had been made; yea, the anger of the Lord may draw so deep against a people professing his name, as to make their land desolate, and the highways thereof mourn.

1. Consider that we find the threatenings of the word point at the time of a people's judgment, 1 Thess. ii. 16; Rev. xiv. 15, 18. That when they fill up the measure of their sin, and their cup is full, the Lord will not then defer the execution. Until the cup of the Amorites was full he did let them alone; and we find answer deferred to the cry of. the souls under the altar, for avenging their blood on antichrist, because that accursed party had yet more to do against the church, and the saints more to suffer under their hand. For, let us consider, (1.) That there is an ordinary growth and height of sin, which a land comes to before destruction; some national and universal spreading thereof, pro- digious outbreakings, the utter rejection of reproof, all which show that a people's case must then be on some turn; yea, it is evident that strange and unusual sinning goes before some strange stroke. (2.) Before judgment cometh, the sin of a people has become so daring that it has had a loud cry; yea, their case has been such as did justify the Lord's procedure against them, even in the con- science of all lookers on. (3.) It is easy for such as are wise to know the times, to see night coming on a land when sin is at some dreadful height, by considering the Lord's usual way with a people in such a case. Yea, there have then been some spe- cial forewarnings, and a more than ordinary impres- sion of judgment upon the spirits of the godly: the hiding of many of them in the grave has showed. the near approach of a penal stroke. (4.) Some Noah or Jonas is sent forth to threaten, who, as

watchmen upon the wall, discern the danger at a distance, and cry out and give the people warning when the time of judgment has been drawing near.

2. There are some special evils and sins of a time, which we find the word does threaten most dreadfully, that though the Lord should pass by many infirmities in a church and people professing his name, yet for such and such sins, he will not turn away the punishment thereof, as we find in Amos iii. 2; but has solemnly declared by his truth and faithfulness, that these shall not pass without some visible mark, even before the world, of his anger. Such as idolatry, perjury, and covenant breaking, Ezek. xvii. 15; also departing from God and his way, Jer. ix. 12, 13; yea, blood-guiltiness, 2 Sam. xii. 10. Now, to evince the accomplishment hereof, I shall show, (1.) That in these sins men may plainly see that judgments are not wholly deferred to another world, but though much is often passed here, and laid over to that last and great judgment, yet upon such sins the Lord has put some mark of his displeasure, even in this life. (2.) That for these he uses to contend before the sun, and in the view of men; his judgments are, indeed, often secret, and do consume as a moth, but, upon such sins, we may frequently see some public visible stroke is made; to follow. 3. That the Lord also uses to be a very swift witness against such evils; those forementioned sins do much hasten judgment, so as seldom that generation passes away without some witness thereto. It is rarely found that some great revolt of a people from God, and breaking covenant with him, do lie long unpunished, nor does the hoary head of the violent and bloody man go

often to the grave in peace. (4.) That these sins are followed with some very dreadful and eminent stroke, which has made the land desolate, its cities waste and a ruinous heap; yea, houses great and fair to be without inhabitants. (5.) That a Divine hand uses to be most discernible in the punishment of such sins, because of a very clear resemblance between them and the stroke, which has forced their own consciences as well as that of spectators to confess the righteousness of God therein. (6.) That the Lord will put some mark of his anger on the choicest of his servants for any acceding to such sins: for this the sword shall not depart from David's house, and idolatry rent the kingdom from the posterity of Solomon; Jonah shall not escape for his rebellion; yea, God was wroth with Moses, and no intreaty could hinder his dying in the wilderness. The Lord's controversy on this ground has even reached their posterity, which shows that these threatenings are exactly fulfilled.

3. A people's lukewarmness and their slighting of the gospel are sadly threatened in the word, 2 Thess. ii. 10, 11; Rev. iii. 15,1 6, and that threat fully accomplished. (1.) A people's entering upon a religious way, and pursuing a form of reformation. on carnal grounds, has put them in a worse condition than before; for truly men's hypocrisy in going about a good work, threatens more than the performance thereof promises. Jehu got a temporal reward, but his posterity must at length reckon for all the blood of Jezreel. (2.) That no people are further from the gospel than such as have been under most clear convictions, and have profited little by them; so that it is found there is often more success amongst the savages,

than amongst those who have made no progress while the tide did flow. Yea, ministers have found most discouragement to labour in those parts where the word has been long preached. (3.) Light not improved will turn a people more gross, and is usually followed with some remarkable growth in sin ; that the more the word puts a restraint on men's corruption, the more it rages ; so as it may be observed what a very black colour the powerful preaching of the gospel has put upon a people, as a visible mark of judgment on such as profit not thereby. (4.) Men's formality in the matters of God has been often punished even with the taking away of the form. Error and delusion do seldom want a harvest amongst a people who receive not the truth in love. (5.) Slighting of the gospel has been at last followed with some visible restraint both upon the ordinances and dispensers thereof ; a judicial withdrawing of the Spirit as to the work of conversion and conviction, whereby the Lord doth plainly cease to be a reprover to them ; yea, even saith, "Bind up the testimony and seal the law."

4. The word also threatens carnal security ; yea, it holds forth a certain connexion between spiritual judgments upon a people and some outward strokes to follow thereon ; they are then near to some judgment upon their persons ; in hearing they shall not understand, until their cities be consumed without inhabitants and there be an utter desolation. Yea, judgment begins as a moth in the fifth chapter of Hosea, but in the 14th verse it turns at last to be a lion. (1.) As the first part of the church's deliverance is usually spiritual, so the first step of judgment against a people has been upon their spirits. Serious discerners of the time might

know that the night was fast coming on, and some
sad outward stroke on a land, by the abounding
of spiritual judgments. (2.) The most dreadful
strokes that ever come on a particular church do
usually find it judicially hardened, and under
many warnings plagued with security; thus did
the flood find the old world; and, before that desolating stroke on Jerusalem by the Romans, the
Jews were in such a case. Salvian can tell how
it was with the African churches before that dreadful inundation of the Goths and Vandals; yea, the
church's records in all ages do witness that before
any sad persecution came upon a people, a deep
sleep and lethargy has preceded; gray hairs might
have been seen upon them. (3.) Spiritual judgments, when they grow upon a people, make great
dispatch, and do quickly ripen for some further
strokes; when men have run down their consciences, and are past reproof, going on from evil
to worse, the case comes then to be clear and ready
for the final process.

5. The word denounces woes against the trou-
hlers of the church, Isa. x. 5; 2 Thess. i. 6. (1.)
Eminent oppressors of the church have seldom
gone out of the world without some mark of Divine anger upon them; surely, if there were a record of such instances that in every age have been
conspicuous, men would be forced to see that the
most noted enemies and persecutors of the saints,
have been also the most convincing and noted examples of judgment. (2.) That the church's sufferings use to go before a day of vengeance on
the instruments thereof. We find Jehu got an
outward reward for executing the judgment of God
on his enemies; but such men who have been the
rod of the church, have not long wanted some

scourge as sore upon themselves as they have been to his people, and at last they have paid dear for their service. (3.) For this God has taken many away in the midst of their day, and made them cease to be, who would not cease to trouble the church while they had a being; yea, he has taken them whom men could not reach into his own hand, and completed their destruction.

6. The Scriptures threaten carnal confidence, Jer. xvii. 5, 6. To clear the accomplishment whereof let us but compare the word and the church's observation together, and we shall find, (1.) That outward means have never more miscarried than when most promising; yea, that very eminent instruments, when much depended on, have been observably blasted, and made to shrink under such a burden. (2.) That they whom the Lord had made much use of, yea, honoured to be great instruments in the service of the church, have often had some discernible blot, to reprove men's over-esteem of them. A Tertullian, an Origen, in ancient times; yea, even a Luther, in latter times, must go with some halt to the grave. (3.) That many who have been useful in the church for a time, the Lord often lays by; and by putting a further weight on some instruments than they could bear, has often rendered them useless. (4.) That none are more ready to shrink in a day of trouble, than such as at a distance seemed most daring; yea, none more ready to fall into that excess of undervaluing instruments, than those who have most exceeded upon the other hand.

7. The word threatens, and in a special way points at, corrupt ministers, Mal. ii. 3, 9. The accomplishment whereof hath in all ages been very discernible. (1.) How such have usually been

most noted as the greatest and most violent enemies which the church has had ; yea, that no course
has been so evil, that has wanted some of these
to help it on ; their hatred and persecution of the
godly have been found to exceed that of the most
openly profane and profligate. (2.) That as they
are particularly threatened above others in the word,
so they also receive some special mark in their
judgment; and having once lost their savour, become vile and loathsome even to the worst of men,
are contemptible in the eyes of such, whom they
seek, in a sinful way, to please ; yea, have a worse
savour than the profanest wretches, that being verified in them, Corruptio optimi pessima.* (3.) That
they seldom make a good retreat from an evil way ;
so that it is an usual observation, that it is rare for
corrupt professors to repent, or a fallen star to shine
again. (4.) They are often smitten even in their
gifts, which wither and dry up when not faithfully
improved. (5.) I must add another remark, though
I desire to deal with fear and much tenderness in
such an application of the judgment of God, that
the Lord often puts some note of his wrath on the
children and offspring of unfaithful ministers ;
whereto, as their evil practice and example have
been a special help, so likewise are they thus
punished of the Lord.

III. I would now proceed to show that the Scripture has a manifold accomplishment, even in those
most strange and dark passages of Providence,
whereat men are ready to stumble ; for if we lay
them to the measure and line of the word which
is stretched over the whole work of Providence,
we shall see how well they agree one to the other ;

* The worst corruption is that of the best.
12 *

yea, that all the paths wherein God walketh towards his church are mercy and truth.

1. It may seem strange how the church's trouble and strait is often seen to increase with the first stirrings of her deliverance. When some remarkable mercy is in the bringing forth, the first step thereof would seem sometimes to put her further aback, and in a worse condition than before. This is, indeed, a part of the Lord's way with his church; but let us take the word along therewith, and we shall find, (1.) How the church is often at the brink of the grave even when her case is upon a turn; and how it is congruous to his way, whose paths are in the deep waters, who clothes himself with darkness, that men should not find anything after him, or lay down absolute conclusions concerning his dealing—that the motions of Providence should be often so perplexed. (2.) Did not the case of the church in Egypt seem much worse, their burdens doubled upon them, even when their deliverance was near at hand? (3.) The selling of Joseph as a slave, and his confinement to a dungeon, would seem extraordinary steps of Providence, and yet we see how kindly these did work. (4.) When the church was even at the next door to a deliverance, her trial was even at the greatest height; "Be in pain and labour to bring forth; for thou shalt go to Babylon, and there shalt thou be delivered," Micah iv. 10. (5.) The step of the providence of God, which of all seemed most dreadful to the church in the days of Esther, was the sealing of the decree, and the sending it forth to root out the whole seed of the Jews; but this was the very step that wrought most thoroughly for her deliverance.

2. The sore interruptions which a people's endea-

vours for reformation and to promote the kingdom
of Christ have met with, would seem strange, but
that it is often seen, as an usual attendant on reformation, how insuperable difficulties.and unexpected
hindrances grow up in the way thereof; thus,
when Luther and other instruments were raised up
in Germany, to pursue the church's reformation,
what cruel edicts were then set forth to retard its
progress! What a pure and thorough reformation
was on foot under Edward the sixth in England,
and what a dreadful storm did quickly break it up!
(1.) There is a lively portraiture of Providence in
the affairs of the church, in that vision which Eze-
kiel had of the wheels, whose mysterious motions
and turnings, so cross one to the other, without
any discord therein, as to the end to which they
were directed, witness the rational and wise conduct of Providence. (2.) Nehemiah, Ezra, and
Zerubbabel, had an express call for building the
temple, yet they found great and frequent interruptions; " Who art thou, O great mountain, before
Zerubbabel?" Zech. iv. 7. Yea, they were obliged
to hold the sword, and build; to watch and work
at once. (3.) What a very painful interruption
did the church experience; " O Lord, revive thy
work, in the midst of the years," Hab. iii. 2. (4.)
We find a special reformation set on foot by Hezekiah, with a solemn covenant by the princes,
priests, and body of the people, with a setting up
of the pure worship and ordinances of God; but
lo! a sharp storm is soon after raised by Senna-
cherib; yea, Hezekiah is scarcely in his grave,
when his son brings in both corruption and persecution. And when the Christian church, in the
times of the apostles, began to flourish, did not a
sad scattering follow immediately? Acts viii. 4.

Zion's walls are ever built in troublesome times; and her being brought to a heap of rubbish is but making way for a further advance, that in the building of her again the Lord may appear in his glory.

3. That a sad overclouding and darkness shall come on a land after most special manifestation of the power and glory of God, would seem a strange act of Providence, and cause a very serious inquiry how such eminent appearances of God for a people, such observable success for a time, with many signal encouragements, should all seem to resolve into a desolating stroke and ruin! This may be instanced in the Protestants of France, instruments remarkably raised and fitted of the Lord for the service of that time, yet who perished in a bloody massacre. Also in the confederate German princes, Saxony and Hesse, men eminent for piety, carried forth with much zeal for God; yea, in the beginning of that war having many promising encouragements, yet remarkably deserted of the Lord, with very sad consequences. Let us also consider the Bohemian war, commenced upon the necessary defence of religion and liberty, and at first attended with some smiling providences, yet it resolved into a great desolation and ruin. Yea, a dreadful massacre of the Protestants in Ireland followed one of the most solemn times of the power of God and outpouring of the Spirit, that we ever heard of since the days of the apostles. (1.) It might seem as strange what Baruch got from the Lord in answer to his complaint, that he would pluck up what he had planted, and cast down that which he had built, Jer. xlv. 4. Yea, after that discourse, and all those large promises which Christ gave his disciples in John xvi., we find all

is concluded with this, "The hour cometh that ye shall be scattered." (2.) What strange providences met the church in the wilderness; sometimes brought back to the Red sea, tried with hunger and nakedness, consumed with various strokes and many years' wandering, until most of that genera- tion who came out of Egypt found their graves in the journey; and yet this was after as clear signs of God's presence as ever a people had. (3.) We find a public reformation most zealously prosecuted by Josiah, which looked like the renewed espousals of that land with God by a solemn covenant; yet, quickly after, night came on that land with a long captivity, and Josiah fell by the sword. (4.) There was a flourishing plantation of the gospel in Judea ·a little before the desolation of that land by the Ro- mans; yea, it is clear from the word, that times of much light and reformation do ripen much sooner for a stroke than any other times. (5.) It is very manifest that particular churches have their day. I truly think that Bohemia's case may have this ob- servable in it, that it had the enjoyment of the light even from the times of John Huss, and Jerome of Prague, which was near an hundred years before there was any day-break on other parts, so that we should consider if their night did come on soon, that their day was also much longer; yea, the stroke might coincide with the ebb of the tide, and arrive when their harvest was gathered in; though I dare not think the Lord's work is utterly extinct there, but that Bohemia's dead and withered root has life yet in it, and shall once again bud forth.

4. Is it not usually seen when judgment comes on a land, that the godly get the first stroke? (1.) Judgment must begin at the house of God and the green tree; and the church's trouble and persecu-

tion is a forerunner of vengeance on her adversaries. There is a cup of the judgment of God, and
it is of a strong composition, for the wine is red
and mixed, and the dregs are reserved for the trou-
blers of the church, and for such as are at ease
in a day of her grief; and truly they have the advantage that drink first, "Blessed is the man whom
thou chastenest, that thou mayest give him rest in
the days of adversity, until the pit be digged for
the wicked," Psa. xciv. 12, 13. Yea, we find
keeping of the "word of patience," which imports
suffering to the church, goes before some more
universal stroke, Rev. iii. 10. (2.) Men may be
raised up of the Lord, and followed with success,
when he has them for a rod to his church.

5. That prosperity and success should follow
sometimes the worst of men in an evil course and
cause, such a concurrence and series of providences
as seemeth to smile on them, even to the bringing
of their sinful devices to pass, while the people of
God have been made to fall in a just quarrel before
their adversary, would seem an astonishing providence; but let us bring it to the word, and there
we shall see, (1.) That there is a prosperity which
tendeth to destruction, Prov. i. 32; Job xii. 6.
The church was shaken with such a providence,
Mal. iii. 15; but in the ver. 18, they were taught
from further observation to discern, and to put a
difference between the righteous and the wicked.
(2.) We find that even the predictions of false prophets in favour of a sinful way may come to pass,
Deut. xiii. 1, 2, for the trial of his people, whether
they will love and fear the Lord, and cleave to his
way, when Providence seems to shine on a crooked
path. (3.) Did not success for a time attend Ab-
salom? Israel as one man, yea, the friends and

counsellors of David, went after him; a fair wind did also favour Haman in his attempt to ruin the church. Jeremiah is almost shaken with this, "Yea, they have taken root, yea, they grow, they bring forth fruit," ch. xii. 2; but is not this usually found an ominous presage of a storm? Israel's falling before Benjamin was an astonishing providence; and Habakkuk was surprised that the Lord looked on while the wicked devoured the righteous, ch. i. 13; yea, Joshua cried out in amazement, "O Lord, what shall I say, when Israel turneth their backs before their enemies?" ch. vii. 8. But we have the Lord witnessing by his word, that thus he beats them off from all carnal grounds of confidence, and wounds them to a cure; that by bringing them low, he may raise and fit them for a further mercy.

6. The church has met with great disappointment when outward grounds of confidence and ordinary means have been most promising; but let us bring it to the word, and the case will be there answered, "How should one chase a thousand, except their rock had sold them?" Deut. xxxii. 30. Their strength is gone with the Lord's departing from them; for when a time of judgment is come, even the mighty then find not their hands, counsel fails to the ancient, ordinary means bring not forth their wonted effects, thus showing the race is not ever to the swift, nor the battle to the strong. We often see that the people of God are much carried out after means, or lifted up therewith; they will ride on horses, Isa. xxx. 6; and this shall be their punishment: but, on the other hand, the Lord's way in his greatest works has not been by might and power, but often by means most improbable and unexpected.

7. The long continuance of a heavy, afflicting rod on the church, without the appearance of its removal, seems a strange step in God's way with his people. But, (1.) The Scripture does not tell how long a sharp storm may afflict either the church, or any particular Christian; for it is a part of the Lord's secret counsel, but not of that which is revealed; it is enough that we know from it, that men cannot make the church's suffering longer than God's time. (2.) Israel's trial in Egypt, and under the captivity, was a long term; three hundred and ninety years must the church suffer, Ezek. iv. 5. O how many sad days and wearisome nights were there in the seventy weeks determined upon Jerusalem! (3.) The saints, under a long trouble, have almost gone the length of blasphemy in their complaints; "My way is hid from the Lord, and my judgment is passed over from my God," Isa. xl. 27. How pressing with the Lord was Daniel, that God would "hearken, and not defer," and yet the return comes not until the first year of Cyrus! Yea, that cry from under the altar, "How long?" doth get a dilatory answer. (4.) There are many prayers before the throne, the return whereof is suspended, until God shall build up Zion; and then the prayer of the destitute shall be remembered, even as to the Christian's private enlargement. (5.) The church's enemies must have time to ripen; and it is not a storm of a few days that will purge away the filth of the daughter of Zion.

8. When there is some remarkable work of God in a land, and some great outpouring of the Spirit, Satan often sets up some counterfeit thereof; thus with the preaching of the freedom of grace, liber- tinism sprung up. Thus we find there were some

parties set up in Germany to run down the church-reformation, under the show of a more pure and spiritual way; and of late, some in England, under pretext of a more spiritual dispensation, have cast off the very letter of the Scripture, turning it to an allegory. (1.) That Satan himself is transformed into an angel of light, and in no way proves more dangerous to the Church. (2.) That the most dreadful errors often imitate the choicest exercises of the saints, and have such a resemblance, that, if it were possible, the very elect should be deceived. (3.) Simon Magus, with false miracles, opposed himself to the apostles: and when the time of the Messiah drew near, a Theudas, and a Judas of Galilee, arose to deceive the people. We find also an altar from Damascus set up near that which was showed to Moses in the mount; yea, when Moses and Aaron were showing forth the marvellous power of God, then did the magicians cast down their rods also, by which the heart of Pharaoh was hardened.

9. That abounding of error and heresy in the times of the gospel seems strange, but, (1.) We find the apostles, yea, Christ himself, has given express warning that this should be one of the special trials of the Christian church. (2.) The event also answers the word as to the particular way in which error should be propagated, even by subtle undermining, and under the pretext of liberty: so that not only the matter, but even the manner, is expressly foretold in the word. (3.) This is a judgment on men who receive not the love of the truth, that when he who rides on the white horse is gone forth, the black horse and his rider quickly follow. And truly it is seen that the church has not been so much troubled in the time of the hottest per-

secutions, as when she was at rest, and in the eri joyment of outward liberty. (4.) That the depths of Satan are engaged in the breaking out of heresy is evident, if we consider, [1.] Its marvellous growth, rapid as the plague, and like the arrow that flieth by day. [2.] With what violence men are thus driven : yea, often a change of their very natural temper is most evidently seen. [3.] The monstrous and horrid things which are often brought forth, show whose hand is at the birth. [4.] The usual tendency that error has to irregularity in practice ; for as it poisons the spring, and corrupts the leading faculty, even the judgment, so it moves towards the vital spirits, and influences the coversation : and the leprosy in the head breaks forth in outward eruptions.

10. The great commotions that usually attend the gospel, when it comes to a land in power, may also seem strange, but herein is the word verified, Joel ii. 28—30, for the gospel gives the world an alarm, makes the kings and great men of the earth run together to hinder the rising of Christ's kingdom, Psal. ii. 3. Truly, in all ages the gospel has made its enemies fear that this would be their fall and ruin. When the apostle has an effectual door opened in his ministry, he has also much opposition thereto. But, on the other hand, all is still and quiet, while the strong man keeps the house ; yea, where the gospel comes there is a red flag hung forth, and if men will not receive it, and be subject to him who rides on the white horse, he shall come again in another character, even to take peace from the earth, to put the world in a flame, and to accomplish the judgment of the despised gospel ; to divide between the husband and wife, the parents and children ; for our blessed Lord

Jesus is express, "I come not to send peace on the earth, but rather a sword." Matt. x. 34. The message of the gospel will either be the best, or the worst sight that ever a land had.

11. It may seem strange that, in all ages, men of the greatest parts and learning have been so generally opposers of the truth; yea, the most sober and calm will even appear violent, the more the gospel is followed with power; for the wisdom of this world is at enmity with God; not many wise according to the flesh are called. Of all the beasts of the field the serpent was Satan's choice; and to an Ahithophel the simplicity of the gospel is foolishness, and Christ is a rock of offence. The light of the gospel torments them that dwell in the earth, and will cause men to blaspheme, and discover that which would not appear so long as they enjoyed their sinful peace without disturbance.

12. The strange judgments which sometimes befall the saints in their outward lot, would at the first look, put men to a stand, but let us weigh it in the balance of the Scripture, and we shall find (1.) That such has been the complaint of the saints, yea, it seemed strange even to Solomon, that there are just men to whom it happeneth, according to the work of the wicked, Eccles. viii. 14. (2.) That was a strange stroke which forced David to this complaint, "My enemies speak evil of me, and say, An evil disease," or as the original readeth it, "a thing of Belial, cleaveth fast unto him," Psa. xli. 5, 8. Josiah fell by the sword; Eli with one stroke has his sons killed, his daughter-in-law dying, and himself falling from his seat, and breaking his neck; yea, Aaron has both his sons killed before his eyes, by an immediate stroke from the Lord. (3.) There is no jar between this, and the

tenor of the covenant which God has made with his people, to punish their transgression with rods, yea, sometimes by a strange rod, while he takes not his love and kindness from them. Great suf- fering may be ordered of the Lord to give some great examples thereby; "Ye have heard of the patience of Job, and have seen the end of the Lord," James v. 11.

13. The gross falling of those who have some- times shined with much lustre in the church, may be astonishing, but it is clear. (1.) There is some particular spot and blemish noted even in Noah, Lot, Moses, and David; yea, under the New Tes- tament, even in that great apostle, whose denial of his Master is set forth, to show how far some may fall, whom grace will again restore. (2.) It is clear, that some do fall for a judgment to others; that those who will stumble, and whose prejudice at the ways of God is their choice, may thus further fall, and be broken. (3.) This should teach us watchful- ness, that those who stand may take heed lest they fall; and an adventuring on the grace of God, that none, after such eminent examples, should fear to repent and ask for mercy.

14. The contingency of events, which appear to happen without the rational conduct of Provi- dence, might, at the first look, put men to a stand, yea, would seem to give atheists some shadow to say, "The Lord shall not see, neither shall the God of Jacob regard it," Psa. xciv. 7. But, upon a more serious inquiry, we are induced to consider, (1.) That though the providence of God in things here, moves suitably to the nature of inferior causes, whether necessary, free, or contingent, not violating them, nor making use of them contrary to their nature, so that though the event be necessary

and infallible with respect to the first cause—the determined counsel of God, it is nevertheless contingent in respect of its nearest cause ; yet it is also clear, that the smallest and most casual motions do certainly fall under the comprehensive reach of Providence, so that even a sparrow falls not to the ground by chance. Rebecca comes not with her pitcher to the well, nor Ruth to glean in Boaz' field, without the providence of God. (2.) That those things which to us seem most casual, we often see by their tendency and product to have been intended by the Lord as a special means for the promotion of his glory. If prejudice do not shut men's eyes, they must confess this can be no blind chance, but some higher counsel. What would look more contingent than that Ahasuerus was indisposed to sleep, and could have no rest in the night; or that a reflection of the sun upon the waters should make them appear as blood to the children of Moab? But we see what great things the Lord accomplished by these means. (3.) Is it not often manifest, that Providence guides the stroke of a man's sword in the battle, and directs the bullet to its appointed mark ; and does even determine those things which in themselves are most free and absolute, the heart and will of man? Did not the crowing of the cock, and the soldiers dividing Christ's garments, accomplish the Scripture? Though it was at a venture that a man drew the bow which sent Ahab to his grave, yet it was not chance that directed the arrow between the very joints of his armour. (4.) Amidst the various emergencies and hazards of men's lives, does not experience show that things contingent are not abandoned to fortune, but there is a Providence which does number our hairs, without which they cannot fall to the ground? What surprising hazards have been often obviated! By what unexpected means have men been delivered from violent assaults; how unlooked-for help has come, even while the foot was slipping; yea, between their falling and fall they have been met with some remarkable mercy! (5.) It is easy to discern that many accidents, which seem most casual, are observably brought about, and guided to fulfil the threatenings of the word on ungodly men. How was Sisera led into the house of Jael, passing by other places; how was Haman's petition for Mordecai's death delayed to that very morning when the king's thoughts were favourable to him, for it would appear that if Haman had been one day sooner, he would have obtained his desire!

This is a grave and serious subject, and should be much studied now, when so many are ready to quarrel with the way of the Lord, when prejudices against the truth are so universally abounding; in order that we may see what a witness there is, even in the most dark and astonishing steps of Providence, to the truth and faithfulness of God; yea, how great a confirmation we may have of our faith, from those very grounds which are so much made use of the strengthen men against it. I know the holy sovereignty of God should teach us to adore and keep silence, when we cannot fathom the depths of his providence; and on this great satisfying truth we should stay and fix ourselves, "The Lord is true, and there is no unrighteousness in him," John vii. 18. It is a necessary duty, when a matter is hard for us to understand, to inquire in the sanctuary; there is a warrantable search after the works of God, that we may know them.

Now, besides the instances already mentioned,

I would yet further touch some few steps of Providence, with a special respect to the present time, and which, though strange, yet when brought to the test of Divine truth, will be found a most satisfying confirmation thereof.

1. It may seem strange to see the church of Christ this day so universally brought low, whilst the whole earth besides is at such rest and quiet. If we look anywhere abroad, affliction and contempt from men are seen in a very great measure to attend the profession of godliness, but more especially the power thereof; yea, almost in every place the church seems to be decaying and declining, rather than in an advancing state. This may cause great thoughts of heart, when we consider the inestimable value which He to whom the church belongs has put thereon, what glorious things are spoken of her in the word, especially with respect to the latter days; and we have expected that this would be a solemn time of fulfilling the promises, which yet point to a more universal raising and enlargement of the church of Christ; yea, we have seen some performance thereof begun, and therefore should conclude the Lord's work herein cannot halt until it come to the full height and to the perfect day. "Shall I bring to the birth, and not cause to bring forth? saith the Lord; shall I cause to bring forth and shut the womb? saith thy God," Isa. lxvi. 9. But let us go to the Scripture, and we shall find, (1.) That the church and the world in their joy and grief, as well as in other interests, are in most direct opposition. "Verily," saith Christ, "ye shall weep and lament, but the world shall rejoice," John xvi. 20. These cannot be at rest together, since the trouble and suffering of the church are a part of

the world's ease and quiet. What a solemn jubilee
does that cause to her adversaries, when they see
before them the dead bodies of the witnesses of
Christ! Rev. xi. 10. But when once the truth
casts off her sackcloth, and the witnesses get on
their feet, O what a terror does this cause! They
are pained by the remembrance that they have done
so much against the church, and yet cannot undo
her. Should this be more strange now than when
the city of Shushan, and the whole seed of the
Jews, were in perplexty, whilst the king and Haman sat down to feast, and rejoice over the threat-·
ened ruin? Was not that a broad and dark cloud,
when Zion was a wilderness, and Jerusalem a desolation; yea, she could find no rest, no comforter
anywhere? Lam. i. 16, 17. But, if such a providence seem strange, let us consider his way,
who by the greatest straits uses to bring about the
most remarkable mercies; and remember that the
devil appears with greatest wrath, and raises the
sorest storms, when he knows that his time is short.
(2.) If we consult the Scripture, we shall find the
adversaries of the church have an hour, which is
their hour and the power of darkness; their sunshine is indeed a black and dark time. And then is
there a strange astonishing concurrence of outward
advantages on their side; they are thus established
for judgment, and the wind must serve, and the
tide flow until their work be fulfilled. They could
never have been such a rod on the church, if they
were not appointed of the Lord. Yea, it is observable, that whilst this their hour continues, there is
then a power of darkness that has an unusual force,
and would seem to carry all before it, until it is
said, " Arise, shine, for thy light is come, and the
glory of the Lord is risen upon thee," Isa. lx. 1.

(3.) Nor should we be amazed at this, when we read Ps. cii. 16. The Scripture is very manifest, that.when the Lord is about some great building, a great deal of rubbish and breaking down uses to go before. There is in every age a filling up of the sufferings of Christ in his people; and a testimony thus required to his truth, which the great Witness himself did once seal and confirm with his blood—even he who before Pontius Pilate gave a good confession; and through all ages, even to the close of time,' there must not be wanting some witnesses to the same. It is known that some times of the church are beyond others, made re-markable for suffering; but it is no less clear, that in these times also the truth has had the greatest victory. Thus we see some ages of the church have a larger part of this testimony assigned; yea, not only particular ages, but particular churches also. (4.) We shall also find some remarkable proportion that the turning again of the church's captivity has to her former bondage, Isa. xlix. 19, 20; lv. 13; Jer. xxxi. 38—40. In the last passage, the restoration, as with a measuring line, is made to answer in breadth and length to the former down-casting. Zion's rejoicing when the time of refreshing comes from the presence of the Lord, must be as universal as once the cause of lamentation was, Isa. lxvi. 10. Such an hour sometimes occurs to the church in which a refreshing report is nowhere to be heard, but the tidings of the next day add more grief to the former day's sorrow; yet a time has quickly followed wherein the church might say, " The Lord hath increased my greatness, and comforted me on every side." She has had a spring and reviving, upon the return of the sun, as universal as her decay and withering once was through the dead winter, Isa. li. 3. And, truly, whilst we consider the time in which we are now fallen, how the church of Christ is every-where low, and in a most languishing condition, antichristianism now upon a formidable growth, as if there were an universal conspiracy to return again to Babylon, we may thence conclude a cer-tain delivery; yea, that even by a day of vengeance the Lord will bring about the year of his redeemed. I humbly think we may judge, with a safe Scrip-ture warrant, that so universal a decay, such a great overspreading of darkness over the reformed churches through the whole world, may give us ground to hope for such a spread of the Gospel as shall be even to the filling of the earth therewith, as the waters cover the sea. It will not be a par-ticular shower and sunshine of refreshing influ-ences on some church; it will not be the reviving of the work of God in these nations which will an-swer so broad a cloud, and so universal a devasta-tion through the whole churches of Christ; but we may, according to the Scripture, look on this as a part of the last and most remarkable assault that the universal church shall have from antichrist before that full stroke on the seat of the beast; yea, that this is a very promising forerunner thereof, for when this party seems now to get up, and begins to war, we have sure ground to believe his further falling thereby, and that every new assault which that grand adversary makes upon the church shall so far put forward her interest, and hasten his own ruin. Blessed are they who are helped in this dark hour to watch and wait until the vision break up, for it will assuredly speak in the appointed time.

2. It may also seem strange, that we see the sun-

shine of the church so quickly darkened with clouds, and followed with showers, that any lucid interval she enjoys is not long without a new storm. She draws but a little breath for some new trial. This would be puzzling, if such a piece of Divine providence be viewed without the Scripture; but there we may see the fate and condition of the church under the gospel, the most remarkable steps in her way, the sharp assaults and short breathings she was to expect, most clearly foretold. Yea, by consulting this blessed record, we shall find, (1.) That a more continued rest than that which the church enjoys, could not well be reconciled with the Scripture. There was indeed a most remarkable cessation under Constantine's reign, after a storm of some ages' continuance; but how short! and it is said, "There was silence in heaven for half an hour," Rev. viii. 1. [1.] The cross has a more peculiar respect to the dispensation of the gospel than to the times of the law; it is in accordance with a greater manifestation of grace under the New Testament, that greater and more frequent trials for its exercise should also be realized. [2.] We find such sore and unusual assaults are not only suited to the most excellent condition of the church, in regard to spiritual privileges, but often happen to the most excellent of the saints, Heb. xi. 32. [3.] Every particular church, beside the ordinary changes in her lot, has also some more solemn trials, and some great assaults beyond others, and accordingly has some more singular breathings and mercies suited thereto. [4.] We cannot find any such calm and breathing, which has not been very short; the clouds have returned quickly after the rain; yea, the most excellent princes and magistrates, under whom the church has had some sweet repose, have been often in a very short time taken away, and have but lived a few years. (2.) Do not the Scriptures show the need the Church has to be emptied from vessel to vessel? a long calm being no less her hazard than a sharp storm; and there is more cause often to watch over her outward rest, than weep over her trouble. O how often has the church lost more by a few years' peace, than by a long continued trouble! Yea, the necessity of a sharp winter for her recovery has been so discernible before it came, that, if it were not for the sake of truth, and the shaking of the faith of the saints, the continuance thereof might be almost wished as her advantage. (3.) Do not the Scriptures also witness that continued lasting quarrel which is between the world and the church, a quarrel which time cannot wear out; so that if she had not so great a party for her, and an immediate support from heaven, we might find more cause to wonder she yet breathes, than to ask why her breathings are so short, when there is so great a power against her? O, if the church had not this to answer, " That the Lord hath founded Zion," sure the design of so many ages would at last have taken place, even to the razing of her foundation. (4.) The most singular fellowship with Jesus Christ on the earth is by the cross, so that if such afflicting times did not often return upon his people there would be a shut door between the church and a large part of the Bible, both as to its meaning and as to its consolation; refreshing truths are there, with which the godly cannot have so feeling a converse in an outward calm as under the sharpest wrestlings. O what an excellent commentary has a suffering time given upon these words,

"Persecuted, but not forsaken; cast down, but not destroyed; as sorrowful, yet always rejoicing!" (5.) Let us also consider what warrant there is, to expect before the end, a more solemn and remarkable time of the church's enlargement, that not only shall be universal in its extent, but more lasting and continued than has formerly been; which I humbly judge, on clear Scripture grounds, we are to expect upon the coming of that full stroke on Babylon, and the solemn espousals of the Jewish church to Christ; and though this will not want some sharp trials, and a mixture of outward trouble, yet we find no ground from the Scripture, after the discomfiture of antichrist and the throwing down of the Turkish empire, to fear any remarkable interruption, or that the church shall have any great assault, until that final gathering of the world and her forces together, to the last battle of the Lamb.

3. It is a usual complaint through the church, that with a greater increase of light and knowledge, there is seen a visible wearing out of life and power; tenderness and the serious exercise of godliness is less evidenced than in the times of greater ignorance. Let us but look through the Reformed Churches, at this day, and then turn home to ourselves, and we shall find this remark too sadly verified. We know there is a sweet agreement between the Christian's light and life, which have a mutual subserviency to each other, and yet we see at this day but little proportion between the one and the other. The Scripture is clear, (1.) That there is a time of a people's espousals to the Lord, Jer. ii. 2; but we find also how rare it is for a people to continue that measure in their life and love, whatever advance there may be as to light; thence

14

we find the church holding up with the name and profession of godliness, when very sore spent in her life, Rev. iii. 2 ; yea, this decay is so insensible, that it is hard for them to remember whence they are fallen. (2.) If we ask the Scripture, it will show the judicial tendency which light not improved hath to a further hardening; how, under the gospel, men may be made deaf with hearing. "For judgment I am come into this world," saith Christ, John ix. 39. Light is surely one of the greatest talents of the church, and brings with it either a remarkable gain or loss; nothing so dreadful as this when it is abused; for thus men are not only more deadened, but become the more deaf and blind. (3.) This is one of the devil's greatest engines to turn men's light against themselves, and to incite them to turn the grace of God into wantonness. Thus, knowledge, whose true and native tendency is to humble and abase, being thus poisoned, works the contrary effect; for often when light hath made a further advance in the church, the devil is there at work to destroy love, by many bitter contentious debates, more for personal repute and credit, than the interest of God and his truth. I am far from any intended reflection on the necessary duty of appearing in defence of the truth, a dispute wherein they should know neither friend nor brother, where with that excellent man Melancthon they can say, "Non quæro gloriam propriam, sed veritatem."* (4.) Though this is a very sad symptom that night is coming on a church, when the light shines, but the heat and warming influence thereof is gone ; yet the Scripture explains how the Lord makes things bring

* I seek not my own glory, but the truth.

forth contrary effects, and causes a remarkable consumption that seems to reach the church in her
inward and vital parts, to resolve into an overflowing with righteousness, Isa. x. 22. He makes his
grace marvellous, in connecting his people's rising
with so low a step of their condition; and in
causing his church, when brought to a small remnant, to "take root downward, and bear fruit
upward," Isa. xxxvii. 31. It would seem a strange
connexion, that the time of his favouring Zion,
even the set time, Psa. cii. 13, should find her in
a heap of stones and rubbish; yea, that a reviving,
and the breaking of her day, begin with the weeping of her friends over her ruins. And with respect to the present time we may believe on very
sure grounds, that godliness and the power thereof
will yet flourish in the world, though it be at
the lowest ebb, yea, at its last breathing; that
little spark now under ashes will revive, and blow
up to a flame, yea, send forth its heat to warm the
nations; for if such a death-like decay had respect
only to some particular church, and if this withering abatement and languishing were confined to a
corner, it might be a sad presage that their sun,
when so far declined and gone down, were near to
the setting; but since this seems to be a consumption over the whole earth, and through the whole
Reformed Church, we may look on it as a very
promising ground of confidence and hope of a recovery. For if the universal church cannot die
under such a disease, it is also sure that this sickness is not unto death; yea, so remarkable an opposition to the power of godliness we may judge to
be a very refreshing presage of some more universal
revival of the same; for there is hope of this tree,
which the Lord hath himself planted, that it shall

grow by the scent of waters, even by the river, the streams whereof make glad the city of God. O what life is there in the church of Christ, even when it seems to be buried! She is in the root, that cannot dry up; her dry bones shall flourish as a green herb. There is now no less appearance of this than at that time when the Lord turned again the captivity of his people; a thing so little expected, that they knew not whether it was a dream or real, Psa. cxxvi. 1. It is indeed a very humbling confession that our ruin is of ourselves; yet must it not ruin our hope, since in the great things which the Lord hath done for the church, the greatness of his power hath not been more clearly witnessed than the freedom and sovereignty of his grace, that men may see this is the Lord's doing, and should be marvellous in their eyes.

4. It may seem a matter of astonishment, that the great men of the earth, and they who sit in the place of judgment, are usually found to be the greatest adversaries of the church. I do not deny that there have been great men in the world who have no less outshone others in fervour and zeal for the truth, than in their place and quality; but that which Salvian says of his time hath been true in most ages of the world, that the contempt of religion by those who were in greatest power had this effect, " Ut mali cogantur esse, ne viles habeantur."* I confess this may cause wonder, if we consider how men should so far counteract his interest from whom they derive their power; and that they should expect homage from others, who

* Men are constrained to be wicked, lest they should be considered contemptible.

themselves deny their subjection to the great Judge. But we learn from the Scripture, (1.) That it is not strange, though iniquity have a throne, under whose shadow mischief may not only find shelter, but be framed into a law, Psa, xciv. 20; yea, it must not be thought strange that the adversaries of the truth are among the chief of the time, Lam. i. 5. The world is not yet cured of that madness of which the prophet speaks with amazement, Psa. ii. 1; but the kings and rulers of the earth attempt to ruin the church, and make his decree void who by his word created the world. It is not only of late that the servants of Christ have been brought before rulers in defence of the truth, and have suffered by the law, where the crime was an adherence to the express command of the great Lawgiver. Luke xxi. 12. The kings of the earth for many ages past have, amidst all their private differences, with one consent agreed to make war with the Lamb, and to give their strength to antichrist; yet this is nothing else but what the Scripture hath foretold, Rev. xvii. 13. (2.) If this be strange to us, does not the Scripture prevent our stumbling, by a most sweet antidote; that when we see the oppression of the poor, and the wrathful aspect which rulers usually have towards the church of God, we should not marvel? Piety is in all ages run down by power; but it is written, " He that is higher than the highest regardeth," Eccles. v. 8. The further they seem raised above human reach, the nearer they lie to some immediate stroke of a Divine hand. When there is no reprover on earth, he sits in heaven who laughs them to scorn, who will speak to them in his wrath, and vex them in his sore displeasure. (3.) The Scripture in this witnesseth the Lord's blessed design to make his church thrive, when she is destitute of the help and countenance of civil authority. It is thus he declares the greatness of his power who can keep her alive, and preserve his interest in a destroying flame, and under a cruel oppressing magistrate; yea, thus cause her to flourish in his days, and have peace in his reign, even under the grievous reign of her adversaries. The church's distress makes her resolve upon a nearer conjunction with God; "And because of this we make a sure covenant," Neh. ix. 38. (4.) As the Scripture prevents men's stumbling at this ordinary suffering of the church, it does also witness that no human greatness can secure men from him who cuts off the spirit of princes, and is terrible to the kings of the earth; consider Psa. ii. 9, and xciii. 4. Here we may read the cause of the changes of kingdoms and states, so frequent in the world. Whatever influence personal interests have, there is a holy revenging God, and his arm is made bare that he may recompense tribulation to those who have troubled his church. None need wonder that flourishing states are broken in such a quarrel; for he who must reign, and have all dominion and power subjected to him, will carry that war back upon themselves, and stand up against them for his own right; he will strike through kings in the day of his wrath, yea, pursue the race and seed of such oppressors from generation to generation.

5. It seems strange to see some of greatest repute in the church, who have been singularly useful to engage others in the way of the Lord, change their principles with the time, and turn at last to opposition thereto; yea, make it their work to cast down what once with great zeal they seemed to

build. I confess there is nothing that infidelity takes more advantage of to question whether there be any thing further in religion than a human interest, when men are found so opposed to them·· selves in matters of religion with the changes of the time. But let us consult the Scripture, and, instead of being shaken, we shall find this a special con- firmation of the truth, for, (1.) Such a shaking trial is clearly foretold, Eph. iv. 14 ; yea, in 2 Cor. iv. 2, a warning is given of those who handle the word deceitfully, by accommodating it to their pri- vate interest and design : for when men do once come to compliance with a sinful course, they then wrest the Scripture by misapplying it, 2 Pet. iii. 16, that they may keep from such a visible oppo- sition between it and themselves in their prac- tice. Now if it seem strange, that amongst the dispensers of the mysteries of God, and those of greatest repute in the church, such should be found, read 2 Cor. ii. 17, and you will there see the cause why many corrupt the word to be, that they are not in sincerity, and walking in religion as in the sight of God. (2.) When we have so sad a discovery in the church, we have likewise this antidote from the Scripture, not to be shaken or moved thereat, Heb. xiii. 9. Let us study to know and be persuaded of the truth. Though we should be left alone in following duty, the testi- mony of God is sure and immovable, and he is true though all men should be liars. We must have the persons of none in admiration, but though an apostle or an angel from heaven should come to oppose the Scripture of God, we ought to say, "Let him be accursed." (3.) Here also is the holy counsel and design of the Lord made known, that they who are approved may be made manifest, and

that they may discover themselves who turn aside:
to crooked paths, to the prejudice of the truth, Psa.
cxxv. 5. They may dig very deep to hide their
opposition to God not only from others, but even
from themselves; but Providence has a deeper
reach, and ensnares them in the work of their own
hands; yea, thus brings them forth with the workers of iniquity, and as his greatest adversaries,
who wound and betray his interest under the mask
and disguise of friends. It is strange to think, how
small the first entry of a further declining will be,
when once there is a tendency and bias that way;
and how hard it is to join in a familiar correspondence with the adversaries of the truth without
joining in some measure with their way. It is a
sad truth which is said of Ephraim, "Strangers
devoured his strength, yet he knew it not," Hos.
vii. 9. When men go the length of holding the
truth in unrighteousness, and withstand the giving
of a testimony to it when called upon, the next
step will be an appearance against it. (4.) They
often become a stumbling-block whose lips should
preserve knowledge, and whom the people are to
consult concerning the law. It is a strange ground
which is given of the departure of those from the
faith who were once in repute of the church, 2
Thes. ii. 12, that it was to punish them who believed not, and would not embrace the truth.

When this seems strange to us, we should learn
to adore and justify him who thus stains the pride
of all flesh, and will silence the confidence or boast-
ing of instruments, that the church may know
where her strength lies. The greatest endowments
and gifts, where men are swelled with pride, have
a more easy and native bias against the truth, than
for it; and threaten the church's hazard more than

any advantage the exercise of these gifts can promise; and the greater repute men enjoy, where humility does not keep them low, the nearer they are to some humbling stroke, 1 Cor. i. 26. The greatest heroes in the church of Christ, who have shone, even to their last, most brightly, have been also the most humble. The falling off of such characters from the truth, is a trial most expressly foretold, and a convincing testimony to the truth of the Scriptures. So it must be granted also, that there are ministers and watchmen in the church of Christ, in all ages, who are found faithful to their Master's interest; who not only confess the truth and deliver the counsel of God to the world, but witness their adherence to it by suffering. Can the world deny that in the worst of times some are found who are in earnest, and have the weight of their work upon them, without respect to outward encouragement?

6. It is an astonishing thing to see how some have walked under a profession of godliness, and for so long a time have had the appearance of being serious and exact, whom an after discovery has proved, not in some particular only, but in the main interest of religion, to be without reality and truth. It may indeed seem strange, that men, having the use of reason, should be at so sore a toil to hold up a form of godliness, and the external exercise only of Christian duties, who might, with facility and unspeakable pleasure, have reached both the shadow and the substance by being serious; and it is certain, if such have not the impression of a Deity erased from the soul, there must be terror in their approach to God, when they have a witness within that it is their deliberate work to deceive at once the great God, their generation, and their own

soul. Many such pretenders are, and will **be,** within the pale of the visible church, and there is often a Divine hand marvellously seen in rending that veil, in such a way as may witness this is from the Lord. But, (1.) It is expressly foretold that men should have a form of godliness and deny the power thereof, 2 Tim. iii. 5; that they will profess to know God, being abominable, disobedient, and unto every good work reprobate, Tit. i. 16; yea, that they will come in sheep's clothing, yet be ravenous wolves, Matt. vii. 15. (2.) This blessed record of the Scripture shows, with what singular art such characters may act that part, and with Jehu inquire if another's heart be right, whilst his own is most false; they will cry unto God and make mention of him, but not in truth, Isa. xlviii. Yea, we should not wonder, though such charac-ters be found, who can mask their private interest with such a profession, whilst they seek a rule for their religion out of Machiavel, but not out of the Bible. (3.) Consult the Scripture, and you will know that they will invite the world to see their zeal for God, who dare not endure the view of their own conscience: therein you will find an Apostle, and one of the twelve, and yet a devil. (4.) The Scripture does not allow or flatter any in such a way; you cannot there find one line for its encouragement: but though human law does not, yet Divine law most severely threatens, Job viii. 13; Matt. vii. 19. And there you may see how horrid a thing it is, which, the more near it ap-preaches religion in the false show thereof, is the more hateful and loathsome. (5.) You cannot ac-cuse the followers of Jesus Christ that by them any such thing is owned or justified, but it is rather an offence, and wound. It is indeed a cause of grief, but no cause of reflection on the truth of God, for "they went out from us, because they were not of us," 1 John ii. 19. (6.) That horrid and black roll mentioned by the Apostle, 2 Tim. iii. 2—4, is connected with a form of godliness, but a denial of the power thereof. It is not strange, when religion is attended with much power in a place, that hypocrisy is found there also; but it is clear, that remarkable discoveries have been made thereof, and that seldom they who have most industriously studied that accursed art, have gone to the grave under this cover. Some special incitement and concurrence of the devil is here oft very manifest, and his power as remarkably put forth as in any lust of the flesh, to put men forward on such a design ; yea, he may be subservient to them in the exercise of common gifts, that may deceive for the time very discerning Christians.

7. The sad jars and divisions so frequent in the church of Christ may seem very strange, and be a cause of offence to many ; that whilst the world is at such an agreement to oppose the truth, professors are often found at war, and most bitterly contending amongst themselves, and smiting one another, when they should be striving together about their Master's work. This is sad, and is a rock whereon many split; yea, it is strange that this destroying plague doth so observably attend a state of peace. But there is no cause for such stumbling, if we will allow it some serious thoughts; it may rather help to fix and establish us in the way of the Lord, and instead of being a poison, may be an effectual antidote against the infidelity of the times, which pretends to so great an advantage from this. For the Scripture is clear, (1.) Though it is a sore stroke on the church, yet it is one which

usually overtakes her in such a torn and divided case; yea, we have no warrant to expect the church militant shall be in that condition in which there shall be no differences; no, in heaven only will perfect peace and concord be found, 1 Cor. i. 10; Rom. xv. 5. (2.) There is no cause of reflecting on the truth, but on those who profess it, since the Scripture shows "we know but in part, and prophesy but in part;" and that there is such a prevailing mixture of corruption here, that some will preach Christ out of strife and contention, not sincerely, Phil. i. 15. Yea, there are always different sizes of saints; and they who eat not are ready to judge them who eat, and they who eat are ready to despise him who eateth not. (3.) If we consult the Scripture we shall find, that peace and concord within the church must be severely qualified with a respect to holiness, Heb. xii. 14; for else such an agreement would not be the true peace of the church, but her plague: that " wisdom which is from above, is first pure, and then peaceable," James iii. 17. They are its best friends who have least latitude to take or give in the interest of truth; but indirect tamperings for peace have often caused a further breach. There is no jar between zeal for God and an ardent desire and endeavour for peace, but what our corruption causes. He is indeed a blessed peace-maker, who can go the furthest length to yield his own credit or private interest, yea, overlook the most sharp personal reflections to promote that excellent design; but hath nothing to yield or quit upon his Master's interests. We have the heroic practice of the Apostle recorded, Gal. ii. 5, " to whom we gave place by subjection, no not for an hour, that the truth of the Gospel might continue with you."

They who caused divisions in the church, and were therefore to be noted, Rom. xvi. 17, were the same who did oppose the doctrine of the church; for it is men's falling off from the truth which is the cause of schism, but not their adherence to it. (4.) Whatever advantage some may take to accuse the way of the Lord from these breaches, I am sure they cannot deny that there is a fellowship and concord in the church of Christ beyond any in the world; that there is a communion of the saints even here, with one heart and mind, yea, in such a measure, as may show the world that this is a bond exceeding the most near and strait ties of natural relations, Ephes. iv. 3—16; and truly every jar and difference amongst the followers of Christ makes not a breach.

8. I know that it will seem strange, that when the church is brought low by her adversaries, the hand of God, in a very immediate way, also is so heavy; yea, seems more sore upon his people than the hand of men, and does even appear more remarkably against them than against any others. This may occasion great thoughts of heart, when we consider the tenderness which the Lord doth witness toward his people, that he stirs not up all his wrath, nor will lay upon them above what they can bear, but stays his rough wind in the day of the east wind, and hath promised to be a sanctuary and hiding-place when they are scattered by men, Ezek. xi. 16. With another party the church might debate, but there can be no standing when the Almighty pursues. Let us consult the Scripture, and we shall see, (1.) That it is no strange case, but we shall find the prophet, Jer. xvii. 17, crying, "Be not a terror unto me, thou art my hope in the day of evil; and the church complain-

15

ing, Jer. xxx. 14—16, that the Lord seemed to wound her "with the wound of an enemy, and the chastisement of a cruel one." It was the appearance of this that was a very sad addition to her trial beyond any other thing, Isa. lxiii. 10, that she found the Lord turned to be her enemy. (2.) The Scripture shows that the rod may have a dreadful appearance, and the way of the Lord may be matter of amazement, when he designs a further increase of their grace, yea, their trial more than their punishment; this we have discovered, Job i. ii. Satan may very effectually concur in a stroke on the church, or some particular Christian, and thus cause a strange concurrence of imbittering things, whilst God only intends his people's trial. And the fiery trial, mentioned by the apostle, 1 Pet. iv. 12, may have such singular circumstances, that the godly will question if such did ever befall others, and yet it is there held forth more as a ground of joy, than of fear. O how deep in afflicting times may the plot and contrivance of the devil be, which, in the holy counsel of the Lord, is oft forced to run against its own bias, and to bring forth a very contrary effect! (3.) From the Scripture we may know, that the trials of the church may surround her on all hands; "Thou hast called as in a solemn day my terrors round about," Lam. ii. 22: yet, when it is so, we find it may be needful for the church and particular Christians to be "in heaviness through manifold temptations," 1 Pet. i. 6; and truly, such an unusual concurrence of trials may have as manifold use and advantage, as the many afflicting ingredients in that trial have been remarkable. (4.) We may also see from the Scripture what a resemblance there is between the public lot of the church and the private case of the saints; how under some sad trial and departure of the Lord from his people, his dispensations are many ways corrective and judicial; read Lam. i. 2, where you find the sword abroad devouring, during a time of public judgment; and it was at home also as death. And in verse 16, under such sore afflicting strokes there is one held forth that was most imbittering of all to the godly—the Comforter, who should relieve their soul, was far off. Nothing does more endear a mercy, and make it sweet, than the Lord's immediate appearance therein; and nothing does more imbitter the rod, which put David to that cry, "Remove thy stroke away from me; I am consumed by the blow of thine hand," Psa. xxxix. 10. (5.) Upon a serious inquiry concerning this strange thing, we may understand that there is some provoking cause whereat these providences point. When the godly are pursuing their ease and satisfaction under the rod, rather than listening to its design; when they are ready to take mortification under trouble for a crouching beneath their burden, it is not strange though that sad woe, Amos vi. 7, reach them: for thus the righteous God suits their stroke to the sin, and keeps such a proportion, that a light sense of the care of the church should make their care abound, and their own affairs shall press them with much trouble, when they interfere with the interest of Christ. There is a saving of things by which we put them in further hazard, and a securing thereof by a surrender to the Lord. An immoderate fear of man, to the prejudice of present duty, may bring with it some sad strokes of the displeasure of the Lord; yea, that he thus bereaves his church of many choicest instruments by his immediate hand, to make it appear that the anger of the most high God is more. to be dreaded than the violence of all our adversaries. But yet, in the close of these judgments, when a church may seem quite con‐ sumed, and her strength worn out, we have some ground of hope that the Lord may prevent his people's thoughts by as marvellous immediate re‐ storing providences, when he sees their power is gone and that there is none to help; yea, it is easy with him, and like his way, to restore what the former years have taken away by the locust and caterpillar, which he had sent amongst them, Joel ii. 25.

9. There is a step of the holy and unspotted judgment of God, which would also seem strange, which is inflicted upon the soul by an immediate stroke of judicial hardness. How undeniably evi‐ dent is it that men under great light, after known convictions and wrestlings of conscience, yea, after solemn engagements, and their declared resolution to follow the Lord in his way, have yet gone a great length in a deliberate resistance to him and his truth, without the least appearance of a check or trouble. I confess this is one of the marvellous things of God, and of his dominion over the soul both in its hardening and softening. It truly calls us to fear, and is a stroke that may force on athe‐ ists the awful conviction of a Deity; for though it is not felt by them who are under it, because the want of feeling is a part of the disease, yet all who look on may know this is the very work of God, and a part of his judgment. But let us ask the Scripture and we shall find, (1.) That the way of the Lord in this is holy and righteous, for he is under no obligation to the sons of men, Rom. ix. 18, but is absolutely free to give grace to, or with‐

hold it from, whom he pleases; his blessed will being alone the rule of righteousness. He comprehends the reason of all his counsel and judgments, which are to us incomprehensible; yet he so far condescends to let men see his unspotted justice, as well as his sovereignty, that they who are unjust by a deliberate choice, shall be unjust still, Rev. xxii. 11, and they who will have none of him should be delivered up to the lusts of their own heart, Psa. lxxxi. 12. We see in what a measure Pharaoh was hardened of the Lord, which was a plague worse than the other ten; but we find, Exod. ix. 34, that Pharaoh hardened his own heart, and thus was a stroke suited to such a resisting of light. (2.) The Scripture shows, Isa. vi. 9, how this sad sentence is immediately passed on the soul, even by the very word and ordinances; men preached deaf and dead by the means which convey life to others. This is a stroke that does not draw a bar between them and external fellowship with the ordinances, but it draws an invisible bar between them and the power and efficacy thereof. It is a judgment that walks in the dark, and binds where none can loose; it kills without a cry; yea, gives men a death-stroke, when the pain of that wound is not felt. (3.) This strange judgment is as plainly held forth by the Scripture as you see it in any example before your eyes; men will be mad in their opposition to God, even when he is most remarkably opposing them; as Ahaz, who trespassed the more, the more he was distressed, 2 Chron. xxviii. 22; yea, like the men of Sodom, they grope after the door, and persist in that wickedness, for which God hath already smitten them with blindness. O what may be the next stroke, when men renew their assault against God after he has once and again smitten them! Is not that a strange degree of judicial hardness, Acts vii. 57, that when they saw the face of Stephen shine, and looked steadfastly thereon, they then ran with fury against him? Yea, to such a length this judgment will come, that the posterity of persecutors will take up the same quarrel, and pursue it, though they have seen their fathers fall under the stroke of an avenging God. (4.) We may also know from the Scripture how deep this judgment may be: the bands of such deluded beings are made strong on them, so that they can neither stir nor move, like malefactors shut up in jail, and under fetters. It is known what Pharaoh's last rebuke was after he had rejected many. Is there not something of hell and of its everlasting fetters, in some measure, made visible in the earth? Surely, where light and conviction resolve into rage and malice against the truth, nothing can be more like hell, or have a more near resemblance to the state of the devil.

10. It is strange that the righteous should fall, and have one event with the wicked in a time of judgment, whilst we see some, notorious for wickedness and opposition to the church, go to the grave in peace. I know men are ready to wonder at this; yea, hence an atheist will infer that things fall out at a venture, but the Scripture shows, (1.) That by no external providences, yea, by no affliction obvious to sense, the way of the Lord and his respects to his people can be judged. We are, in this, obliged to adore God, whose judgments are incomprehensible, when we see "a just man perish in his righteousness, and a wicked man prolong his life in his wickedness," Eccles. vii. 15. (2.) The Scripture teaches us concerning this provi-

dence, that though Saul and Jonathan fall together, yet there the Lord in a special way puts a difference between one and another. Josias died in peace, as was promised, 2 Kings xxii. 20, yet he fell upon the high places of the field in the common judgment; but he was taken from the evil to come. Some may be hidden in the grave from a further storm, by the same judgment wherein the Lord is pursuing the land. It is clear from the Scripture, how small an accession to a sinful course may, in the holy displeasure of God, bring some of his people under the same stroke with his adversaries, and involve them in judgment. We find, Psa. i. 1, there is a standing in the way, and joining in the counsel of the ungodly, held forth as a partaking with them in their sin; and Ezek. ix. tells us, that not mourning for, and dissenting from the national sins of the time, puts men out of that blessed roll of those whom the Lord marks for preservation. Now, as to the prolonging of the days of the wicked, the Scripture will show, [1.] It was no less strange to the prophet Jeremiah, ch. xii. 2; "yea, they prosper, and take root." It amazed that blessed man, Psa. lxxiii. 4, 7, that not only "their eyes stand out with fatness," but "they have no bands in their death." [2.] But God prevents some by a sad temporal stroke, and can serve himself of a scaffold or gibbet to bring about their mercy, as he did to the thief on the cross, whilst he plagues others by a long forbearance; "Because sentence is not executed speedily, therefore the heart of the sons of men is fully set in them to do evil," Eccles. viii. 11. [3.] As in every age we are called upon to adore the sovereignty of God, so also to observe his great judgments. "Lo, this is the man that made not God

his strength," Psa. lii. 7. But we must wait for
the full discrimination which the last sentence of
the Judge shall put between those who fear the
Lord, and those who fear him not.

## THE THIRD ARGUMENT TO PROVE THE FULFIL-
## MENT OF SCRIPTURE.

ARGUMENT III. The third argument for the
Scripture's accomplishment is this—That not only
the Christian's experience, and the observation of
the church, bear witness thereto, but it is suscep-
tible of being demonstrated even to the view and
conviction of the world.

It is true, the world cannot reach those sweet
and sensible enjoyments which the saints have of
this truth; but it is also sure, that in every age the
works of the Lord, and some more convincing providences, both of judgment and mercy, do solemnly
invite men to observe the accomplishment of the
word therein; yea, no time hath wanted something
of a public witness from ungodly men, who, under
the constraining power of conscience at death, or
in some day of trouble, have been forced to seal the
truth by a very open confession of the righteousness of God towards them. I confess we may
wonder why the world looks so little upon this,
and why the conviction of so great a truth, which
they cannot shun, does not more press them; but
the Holy Ghost beautifully resolves this, because
the "brutish man knoweth not, neither doth a fool
understand this," Psa. xcii. 6.

I shall instance some special truths, wherein the
faithfulness of God in fulfilling his word may be
obvious to the most ordinary observers.

1. I shall show that man is fallen from that excellent estate wherein he was formed, Rom. v. 18,

**19.** It is true the Scriptures alone discover the, cause and original of this dreadful contagion; but it is obvious to all that man is thus diseased, and bears the marks of such a fall as we read of in the word.

**1.** There is some remainder of that excellent fabric, which may yet appear among its ruins; some print and appearance, though dark, of that primitive lustre and beauty; some impressions which sin has not wholly worn out, that may clearly show what man once was, and point out his former excellency; that he has been another being, one without blemish from the head to the foot; for we see the deep impressions of a Deity still rooted in men, even the most wild and savage, which no invention can utterly erase; we see some common principles of reason imprinted in the most rude and ignorant; some notions and ideas which the soul has of good and evil, among all, and in every place of the earth; natural truths, which are no ways impressed on the soul from any objects of sense, but such whereto men, by an unavoidable necessity, are forced to assent. Do not these things witness that from some great height poor man has fallen?

**2.** Does not the present appearance of man's nature clearly show it is fallen into some dreadful disease, that it is surely overspread with some horrid, leprosy and contagion, the symptoms whereof now are most discernible? What an exorbitancy appears in his desires, with what contrary tides is he hurried; always at jar with his present lot; his reason and will, once in a sweet league, are now at war, between which he is often rent in pieces as between wild horses! How is he now restless in an unreasonable pursuit; he labours in the fire, and for a shadow! Yea, what do these tumults and commotions of the earth mean, men upon the smallest account sheathing their swords in each other's bowels? Homo homini lupus;* insatiable in revenge, and making the earth by their quarrels· resemble the raging sea. O do not these things too visibly witness, what a dreadful disorder and perturbation there must be within? Here we may see a very manifest rupture, and breach of a build-ing, once well knit and framed.

3. I would ask wherein man's true advantage and excellency above others of the creatures, can be seen, if not with respect to what he once was, and to the blessed restoration by grace? For his knowledge often serves only to increase his sor-row, to show the good he wants, and the evil he is subject to. Is there any of the creatures subject to such outward misery and pain, to so many dis-eases; yea, as to a sensual life, may we not say the beasts have even some preference? Are they so unruly, do they so much go out of their bounds and station? The many laws made for man in the world, with the convincing necessity thereof, sufficiently answers this. We see also that sore travail is appointed to man; to how much toil is he obliged for an outward subsistence, how often does he sow and not reap! The beasts withdraw from the yoke, and those over whom he had dominion are ready to assault him. Women bring forth their children in sorrow; men are attended with fear, their life is often made bitter with care and labour; yea, as men increase in the world their care and discontent increase therewith; but besides all, he is in the greatest slavery of all the creatures through

---

\* Man is like a wolf to man.

the violence of his lusts. He pursues the bait, though he knows it will undo him ; his corruption oft, like a strong man, binds him in fetters, and his flesh imperiously drags him at its heels. Was poor man thus framed at the beginning, or raised so far above the rest of the creatures, only to make him the more miserable? Truly, if a lively protraiture could be drawn of sinful depraved nature, there are none so gross but should abhor, yea be affrighted to see that in the third person, with which, alas! they so easily comply in themselves.

II. That so great a change is truly wrought upon men in conversion, as the Scripture holds, John iii. 3—6; Ephes. ii. 1—5; Colos. iii. 10, wherein something above nature, even the marvellous power of the grace of God, may be seen, is a truth, I am sure, known and undeniable to the world.

1. That they, who in their practice have been notoriously profane, have been reached by grace, and thus the leopard has been made to change his spots; and such as were accustomed to do evil, have learned to do well. Many famous instances witness this in every age. 2. That on men most determined in their judgment against the way of God, and who were wont to deride holiness as fancy, even on such so great a change has been wrought, as has made the world to wonder; they have been forced to lay down their prejudice, yea, to wonder how they could oppose the truth so long. Surely atheists must grant there have been professed atheists as themselves, who have been made eminent examples of grace. 3. That in the height of their wickedness (like Paul breathing out cruelty, and Vergerius while he was writing against the truth) grace has sometimes reached them. Some

such trophies of the gospel's conquest have been conspicuous in every age ; yea, it is often seen that some remarkable height in sin has proved an evident crisis and turn in men's condition, either to judgment or mercy. 4. That some, from being eminent adversaries of the truth, have, through grace, been made eminently useful instruments in the church ; yea, there have not been choicer vessels of honour, and more zealous for the Lord in their time, than they who were once most violent in their opposition. 5. That grace has reached such, whom the world reckoned most wise and discerning, yea, that knew the value of outward things as well as others. Can the atheists object, Do any of the rulers or rabbies believe in Christ ? when it is so clear that some who are most serious in the matter of religion, have been amongst the wisest, most learned, and judicious of their time. 6· This change hath been discernible upon the simple, the most stupid, •and dull ; yea, upon some such as in whom a natural incapacity might have obstructed the work, if something above nature had not carried it on ; yea, there has been a change even in their understanding, to show that this can make the simple wise, and that in the way of holiness, the wayfaring man, though a fool, shall not err. 7. That by a very improbable mean, even the word, and that sometimes by weakest instruments, this great change has been wrought; and it is remarkable how little of the work of conversion followed the miracles of the primitive times, whereas by the simplicity of the preached gospel this effect often follows. 8. That they are not a few on whom this change has been wrought; and truly, besides the ordinary proofs, I think there should be some more special record by the

church of those illustrious and eminent instances
of the grace of God which occur, as well as
of remarkable instances of judgment. 9. That
falls not out at an adventure which is wrought
upon one, and not another, while both are
alike discerning; yea, some who seem furthest
from the grace of God, very gross and rude,
have been taken, when the more civil and refined, and of a more promising natural disposition, have been passed by. 10. This change is
often discernible upon men in a time when no advantage from without appears; even times of persecution and hazard, from which many have dated
their first acquaintance with God. 11. It is known
how great a cloud of witnesses have sealed this
truth. O! can that be a universal enchantment,
that in every age, and in most remote places of the
earth, has fallen upon so many, or can all these be
void of understanding? What outward advantage
could they design in that which is so usually attended with outward hazard and loss; or what
credit from men, while it makes them the very butt
of the world's hatred and reproach? Yea, can it
be thought that all these could have combined to
engage in so great a cheat? 12. The marvellous effect of this change witnesses this is no delusion, when even one word has made the stout-
hearted and most daring tremble, and show by their
very countenance that there is another tribunal than
man's before which they are arraigned. That is marvellous power which can make so willing a divorce
between men and their idols, which were once as
their right eye to them; and beat them off that
ground of self-righteousness, which they had been
so long establishing; that causes them also to choose
the reproach of Christ and his cross, before any out-

ward advantage; and to abandon that society, without which aforetimes they could not live. This
evidences something above natural reason.

It is strange the world does not more wonder at
conversion which is so great a miracle, yea, one
of the greatest, since it is no less then to raise out
of the grave such as are truly dead, Psa. xix. 7.
Should we not with astonishment look on a Christian, if we seriously considered what a change the
grace of God makes here from what he once was,
and how great a change glory will, before long,
make from what he now is? I know there are
many things we wonder at from our ignorance;
but it is men's ignorance and estrangement from
this, which makes it so little their wonder, for if
we be assuredly persuaded of the truth of conversion, we have then three great truths unanswerably
demonstrated: 1. That the Scripture of God which
holds this forth is faithful and true.   2. That there
is a Divine Spirit and a power above nature that
certainly accompanies the same.   3. That there
are two contrary states in another world, since they
are here so manifest.

I shall here endeavour to show that the very
immediate power of God is exercised in conversion.
1. That is a strange and marvellous thing that can
change one species of a creature into another, and
turn a wolf or tiger into a lamb; yet such a change
is here.   Conversion makes a vast difference between a man and himself; takes him away from his
former delights and exercises, his old friends and
society; yea, causes the man who was a persecutor of the truth, and took pleasure therein, to rejoice in suffering persecution on that account.   I
think the world will not debate, where so many
known instances are at all times obvious.   2. This

is marvellous which can estrange men from their
worldly interests, and take their heart off that which
was as their right eye, and subdue under them that
which once took them captive at its pleasure. Yea,
they whose predominant passion was love to the
world, and who have been in their natural disposition so narrow, that they could not allow themselves the comfortable use of what they had, have
been brought to a willing surrender of all for Christ.
3. Would you debate the efficacious power of that
which should melt and dissolve in tears those who
through their life were known to be most obdurate
and stupid? Yea, is not this great change sometimes ushered in with such terror, that may convince lookers-on, it is a matter of the greatest earnest,
and not a counterfeit? 4. How great a thing is
that which takes men unawares, without their
thoughts and intention! It is sure many have been
thus surprised, yea, in one hour have gotten a
sight which will never go from their heart; they
now see what report could never have made them
believe; they know now what it is to be taken
out of a dreadful gulf of darkness into a marvellous
light: and truly it is usually discernible, that some
one word will force its passage, and take fire within,
as a word beyond all others fitly spoken and fitted
by Divine appointment to open the heart. 5. It
is a marvellous change which reaches the young,
and those sometimes of an age little above infancy, whose years may show there was no design
to cheat the world. Yea, from a family where
little advantage of education has appeared, select
some who, even at death, have witnessed the power
of the grace of God and his Spirit on their souls;
they have expressed their hope, and the grounds
of it, with such judgment and seriousness, as has

convinced bystanders of an immediate teaching of
the Spirit, and of the mighty power of God, who
can impart to those who can scarcely speak or
exercise reason, the power of religion.  6. What
a change is that which also reaches men in their
old age, who have been long rooted and inured to
the world, who have resisted many a call of the
gospel! They have been made to weep and confess,
after sixty or seventy years living under the gospel,
that then only they began to know what it is to be
Christians.  I confess this is one of the rare trophies of the grace of God ; yet no age wants some
such instances to prove how far grace can prevail
over nature, custom, education, and all these disadvantages which follow old age.  7. What a strange
power is it which has been so evidently witnessed
on some who have outrun others in all manner of
wickedness; yea, even then, when justice was
crying for punishment to cut them off, grace has
stepped in to save, and reached them at a scaffold
or a gibbet!  Should it not be convincing to see
two persons brought to a public death for some
gross crime, who have the same hazard before
them, the same means made use of for their conversion, yet the one melting in contrition, the other
most obdurate?  You cannot say that this is from a
different nature and constitution, since sometimes
those of a more promising nature and better disposition have been seen further off, than those of
whom least was expected.  8. Is it not a strange
change which has been realized, where no company, no example, no usual way for instruction can
be alleged, so that it may be seen they have been
truly taught of the Lord, and by his immediate
teaching; that in a very extraordinary way, and
by means most improbable, he can convey himself

into the soul? This can be no result of natural disposition, for then it would appear in their younger years in some measure, and grow up with them. This change occurs also in those of most different natures, most unlike and opposite in their humour and disposition. Here the foolishness of preaching is found more effectual than any other way; yea, the most sublime and polished strains of oratory, and the greatest gifts, have often come short of that success, which has followed more improbable means.

I shall here mention two remarkable instances of the power of grace in conversion. First, that excellent man' Junius, whose life we have in some measure written by himself. He testifies that being carried away with evil company, yea, tempted to atheism, he was one day moved to go and read the Scripture; and beginning with the first chapter of John, whilst he read, it suddenly astonished him, and left so marvellous a conviction on his soul of the divinity of the subject, and the majesty and authority of the writing, that all day he knew not where and what he was. He then saw that the Scripture exceeded all human eloquence, and this was followed with such power, that his body trembled, and his mind became astonished, with such a surprising and marvellous light; and from that day he began to be serious in the way of the Lord.

A second instance is the remarkable conversion of worthy Mr. Bolton, a choice minister of the church of England, in whose life this is recorded, that being eminently profane, a horrid swearer, and much accustomed to mock at holiness, and those who most shined therein, and particularly that excellent man of God, Mr. Perkins, then preacher in Cambridge, whom he much undervalued for his plainness in preaching the truths of God, yea, was in his views near the length of popery; but on the Lord's gracious appearance to him, he was put to have other thoughts, that, as he said himself, the Lord seemed to run upon him like a giant, throwing him to the ground, and with such a terrifying discovery of sin, as caused him to roar in anguish, and often rise in the night on that account, which continued for some months, but at last a blessed sunshine appeared, and a shining light.

III. That communion and fellowship with God, whereto the saints are in this life admitted, is a most real thing, and no delusion, is a truth which may be very convincingly demonstrated, 1 John, i. 3; Phil. iii. 20. I know this is a truth that must be spiritually discerned, and therefore the world cannot know it, or reach that unspeakable joy which is found by the saints in that sweet path; yet there are some convincing evidences which may rationally demonstrate the same, if men consider,

1. How great and excellent a company bear this testimony, even as many as in every time ever served God in the spirit; a truth not once or twice proved in the Christian life, for the proofs thereof are innumerable and past reckoning; yea, amongst all the saints, from the days of Abel to this present time. There was never one contradictory witness produced. 2. They who thus testify are those whose testimony in any other matter the worst of men could not refuse. 3. They have had as great interest in, and share of the world as others, and been of as discerning spirits to know the true value of things, who declare that there is an undoubted reality in converse with God. They wanted no

outward allurements, had not lost their taste, and were flesh and blood as well as others, and yet they turned their backs on all for Christ, and by their walk testified they had found some more satisfying enjoyment in fellowship with God. 4. Must not this be very convincing, that when men become once serious in the way of God, they have got some new evidence of another world, and some other society and intercourse than that of men? Whence are those frequent retirements from which they come forth with greatest satisfaction? does it not thus appear they are not alone when they are alone? 5. Is not this also testified in times when men could not well dissemble; in times of great outward affliction, when the world also has been most tempting with its offers; yea, at death, when they are stepping over the threshold, a time wherein our words are of greatest weight, the spirit being then more unbiassed, and free from ordinary temptations? How oft have they at such times declared that surely God is familiar with men, and that though they were going to change their place, yet not their company! 6. Can that be a delusion whereof the saints are not more sure that they live, than they are sure of this truth? When God comes near to their souls, what a discernible elevation of their spirits is evident! yea, on the other hand, as the withdrawing hereof is very sensible to themselves, is there not something of this even obvious to bystanders? 7. Does not something of this truth appear on the very countenance and outward carriage of Christians; a lustre and resemblance of Heaven, a holy gravity and composure of spirit, when they have been brought near to God in secret converse with him, and taken up to the mount? Does not the walk of a serious, mortified Christian convincingly witness this; yea, what should make them look so well, and with such satisfaction, when there is no visible cause for it, when shut up in prison from converse with friends and acquaintance? Surely men will not think a rational man so mad as to quit his former pleasures, and choose the cross, in order to deceive the world with a counterfeit joy and satisfaction; and while it is too evident what a dreadful society and commerce many have with the devil, should any man question whether the saints have communion and fellowship with God the Father of spirits?

IV. That "the righteous is more excellent than his neighbour," Prov. xii. 26, is a truth which I am sure men, notwithstanding all their prejudice, must needs confess, and that therein the Scripture is verified. I confess the saints are under a dark cloud here, through the prevalence of corruption, yea, are often accounted as the filth of the world; but when grace, in any greater measure and vigorous exercise, shows itself, then there appears so much as will darken all the grandeur of this earth, and force men to see an excellency in the saints beyond any others.

1. What an evident difference is there between their way who walk with God, and that of the most polished moralist! Something is in the one which witnesses a more excellent spirit, a higher elevation, a sweet harmony and equability, so that they move in a higher sphere, act from other principles, with a respect to some greater interest than anything here, and have more of a large heart to serve their generation, than they whose self-interest is seen to be first and last in all their motions.

2. Do not tender, serious Christians who live near

God, truly resemble Him to whom they move, as their great and last end; yea, evince an excellency of spirit, a sweet calm and serenity, while going through things that are most vexing; a discernible quietness in looking upon most affrighting revolutions in the world, as those whose treasure and great interest is beyond hazard, though the earth were all turned to ashes? 3. Is there not such a majesty and authority attending holiness, as forces respect and fear even from those who most hate them; yea, and forces men to justify those in their conscience, whom they openly reproach and persecute? Whence is it that a serious, tender Christian is oft a terror to the profane, when there is no outward cause for it, but that they are struck with the conviction of a more excellent spirit, one carrying such a resemblance to the image of God, as causes fear? 4. Does not a holy walk cause men to shine as lights in the midst of a crooked and perverse generation, yea, darken all their neighbours; and is it not seen how grace shines with the greatest lustre in the darkest night; what a sweet and odoriferous scent this sends through the country where they live, that may show the difference there is between such, and those who are wallowing in the puddle of this earth? 5. Is it not obvious what a greater lustre and beauty there is in the self-denial of Christians, their bearing injuries, forgiving such as injure them without reviling, than in the proud, vindictive spirit which is in the world? 6. It may be also evident to the world, that there is another spirit in those who do not bow with every time, nor yield to men because of their outward power, from that spirit which is in the world. While the one presses men to save themselves on any terms, the other causes the

Christian to take up his cross, yea, to lay down his life, to save his conscience. Whence is that patience and resolution, by which the godly, in times of suffering, have overcome their persecutors, their bold avowing of the truth before men when hazards are most obvious, and the advantage wherewith they appear above others in such a time? O! does it not clearly witness they are of another metal who thus abide the fire, yea, become more bright by that wherewith others are consumed!

How has this spirit, which is in the saints, prevailed over the greatest enticements of carnal gain and pleasure, which to many may seem a wonder; as the popish party once said of Luther, "Bestia hæc non curat aurum:"* this did in effect show him to be something above man; for that is a thing before which the spirit of the world could never stand.

V. That the promised encouragement which is held forth to the people of God under trouble and suffering for his name, is a truth I am sure not only Christian experience can witness, but may be demonstrated even to the observation of others, Psa. ix. 9; Isa. li. 12.

1. The very countenance and outward appearance of the godly in a suffering time, often declares the peace and tranquillity of their soul, so as surely they must have joy and satisfaction which the world does not know, and have some other correspondence than with things visible; for it may be often said, as of Daniel and his fellows, that under greatest pressures, and a very mean condition, they look as well, yea, with as much cheerfulness, as

* This beast does not care for gold.

those who live on the king's allowance. 2. That can be no counterfeit which thus reconciles the Christian with a suffering lot; for affliction and trouble prove very searching, and often broach the vessel, and bring forth what had formerly lurked most closely. Does not that holy confidence and freedom, which the saints have evinced in confessing the truth before the princes of this world and their most cruel adversaries, yea, their cheerfulness in extreme suffering, even when resisting to the blood, speak something beyond the fortitude of a merely natural spirit? 3. Is it not seen that the cheerfulness of the godly under suffering, when there is no outward ground for it, not only astonishes, but is an exceeding torment to adversaries, when they see that all their endeavours have been in vain, either to turn them aside, or to ruin their encouragement; but that the most sharp sufferings of the godly help to strengthen others to justify God's way, and evince the tender respect he has to his suffering people, even before the world? 4. Is it not also manifest, that those whose natural disposition was known to be very fainting and timorous, when called to suffer for the truth, have, without the least appearance of discouragement, shown an invincible resolution? O! is there not a visible fulfilling of the Scripture, that shaking reeds should be made to stand where strong cedars have bowed; yea, that some of very mean and ordinary parts have been so discernibly raised above themselves, as to confound the wise and learned? 5. Must it not be confessed that the zeal and resolution of the saints did never more appear than in times of greatest opposition? that at no time they have looked more like Christians, with more advantage, and with more peculiar beauty and lustre.

of the grace of God, than under suffering; a thing which, as it eminently commends the Gospel, has also so far convinced their enemies, that in some measure it has taken off their prejudice against the way of God and followers thereof. 6. I may appeal to the greatest atheists, if any moral arguments could ever produce such effects as rejoicing in tribulation, choosing affliction before sin and all its pleasures, triumphing over persecutors, and going with a calm cheerfulness to a scaffold, singing amidst a dark prison; yea, and abounding and having all things under greatest want? O! whence is this? Something above nature must be here; something that is stronger than moral reasons, by which the saints have thus overcome the world. Yea, is it not obvious to all who look on, how great a difference there is between the pretended resolution of a natural spirit in death and suffering, and the joy and confidence of a Christian appearing in the composure and tranquillity of his soul within? The one is but a dark shadow, and the other a picture drawn to the life.

VI. That there is a conscience within men, whose power, both as a judge and witness, answers that clear discovery the Scripture gives thereof, Rom. ii. 15, is a thing obvious even to the world. To prove the reality of conscience, consider,

1. There is something within which makes men afraid to be alone with themselves, yea, causes them to go abroad, and frame diversions to be out of its noise. He would gladly be at peace, but amidst his greatest mirth and prosperity, this mingles his wine with gall and wormwood. 2. Men have often an accuser within their breast, even while they seem to brave it out before others; this judgment they can by no means decline, but after the

committing of sin, yea, on the back of their sinful pleasures, it follows with a bitter sting, and rings this dreadful knell in their ear, that the end of their way will be bitterness. 3. What is it that makes men's guilt so legible often in their countenance, even when they study most to conceal it, and makes them betray to by-standers, whether they will or not, some secret trouble?

4. Whence is it they are so much disquieted for secret sins, which the eyes of others could not reach; yea, that even the most profligate amongst men have a horror for some gross sins which yet can bring no outward danger? 5. How is it that even the greatest men whom the world cannot reach, and in the midst of advantages, have yet often most affrighting thoughts, terrors, and dis- quieting reflections? 6. What must it be which forces men to justify God when his hand pursues them, and makes them so easily find out sin in a time of their strait? Why is the sense of guilt so very affrighting at death? 7. What should make men tremble at the word, and so much hate a searching ministry? 8. How do the worst of men often justify those in secret, whom they openly condemn; yea, what is it that causes a secret fear and awful regard of those whom they hate? 9. Whence is that horror which wicked men, who were wont to sport at sin, often have in their sick- ness, such as Spira, Latomus, Olivarius, and others?

That there is a conscience, a power which every man has within him and over him, that forces the soul to a reflection on itself, even when it trembles at the sight, and with an awful sound tells the atheist there is a God, is an important truth. This is that great tormentor and troubler of the world from which there is no retreat, though one should flee to the uttermost parts of the earth; this keeps a high court of justice under the authority of the great Judge, and there, without respect of persons, summons great and small, brings in witness, gives sentence, yea, in some measure, puts it into execution, and can make hell begin even here, by an inexpressible anguish and horror.

1. Could there be such a power in man to distinguish between the good and evil which is within him, if there were not also some higher power above him, who has thus formed him with such principles? Yea, could there be a judging and witnessing within a man, if there were not a law and rule over him? For it is sure the conscience in all its actings has respect to a higher judgment and law, which even nature's light, though very dim, holds forth, but is express and clear in the Scripture. 2. Is it not very strange to see such a power within, and yet against a man; that the grossest atheist is an enemy to it, yet cannot be without it, or get it shaken off; and whilst men have a strong bias and inclination to evil more than good, they are yet forced to justify the one more than the other? the drunkard cannot drown this conviction, nor the worldling bury it in the earth. 3. Though men may go some length to divert and silence this conscience, so that it cannot exercise its function without some special Divine excitation, yet when once it is awakened, the stout-hearted cannot keep his ground to debate with it; yea, when they run, it follows with as swift a pace. No skill, no arguments, no violence can defend from its force, but whilst they sin without the rebuke of their fellow men, this is continually at hand to tell them that he who is greater than the conscience does regard.

4. Can any thing be more real and certain, than these effects of the conscience? Do you know a place of the earth where this power does not over-awe men, though not exposed to any visible hazard; and can all mankind, through the whole world, in all ages, be in so strange a delusion, if there were no real ground for it? 5. Men are at perpetual work to bribe it, to frame diversions, yea, to find out false grounds of peace, and some such gloss and commentary as may reconcile the rule with their grossest actings and exorbitances. Why is this, but that in outdaring it, they find it stronger than they, and therefore must counterwork by darkening that great light, and find out some show of reason to silence conscience, and promise peace to themselves, though they walk in the wickedness of their heart? 6. Do not those strange extremes which are obvious in men's condition, witness the reality of this power? O what a marvellous thing is it to see a man stupid this day, and des-perate the next; the conscience so raging, that to be rid of its torment the poor man would seek a shelter in the grave! Yea, is it not usual to see some men wear out their time as beasts, yet, at dying, they are seized with an inexpressible horror of God? Is not this something awakened, which was formerly asleep? 7. Do we not see such desperate acts of wickedness in the world, against warnings and convictions, as may even convincingly show some pursuit of the conscience, and horrid attempt to silence its noise, by some violent stroke? 8. Are not those unlooked for outbreakings of the conscience most remarkable, such convictions taking them unawares? The recourse which the grossest of men will, in such an extremity, have to God by prayer, declares the impression they

have upon them of a Deity. 9. How marvellous
a confidence and support does the conscience afford,
when it is a friend, under the greatest misery and
trouble from without; but when it is an adversary,
nothing so insupportable. It will torment one
within, when none without dares to provoke him;
yea, it will cause the oppressor to tremble, whilst
it upholds the oppressed with confidence.

VII. That there is a reward for the righteous,
and unquestionable gain in godliness, are truths of
the Scripture held forth in every age to the view of
the world, Psa. lviii. 11 ; xcvii. 11. Isa. iii. 10.
It is true that the Christian's lot is often followed
with much trouble, and sometimes with loss of his
life ; for the great reward which the man who fears
God has insured to him is laid up in another
world. But there are convincing proofs of this
truth held forth even to the observation of the
world.

1. It is the dictate of a natural conscience, not
only that God is, but that he is a rewarder of such
as serve him ; yea, none amongst men are so gross
or brutish as not, in some measure, to distinguish
between good and evil, with some fear of a punishment to the one, and some hope of recompense to
the other, and also to notice some of the more signal and convincing examples of that kind. 2. Does
not the world see in every age the history of Joseph, in some part, acted over again ? Surely there
have not been wanting many remarkable instances
of an upright and straight walk through a labyrinth
of changes, conducing at last to a happy end. This
is no romance, but a history which in all times and
by many examples may be seen in Providence, and
surpassing the richest fancy that any fiction or romance ever contained. 3. Is it not convincing,

even to the worst of men, what a visible blessing often follows the mean lot of some of the saints, which makes their little reach far, and causes them to abound more in their poverty, than others amidst their abundance? A secret judgment blows upon some men's estate, that no means can prevent, and a secret blessing, which makes things prosper, accompanies the Christian's little, so that it is easy to see where real contentment, with cheerfulness and giving of thanks, dwells. 4. May not the world see there is a feast in a good conscience, how little soever its possessor has of the world: that well-doing, and the practice of godliness, have some present reward in their hands? So remarkable a difference may be discerned between the countenance and carriage of the upright, and of those who trust in falsehood, that when greatest natural spirits fail, the former alone can enjoy themselves, and have calm and composed spirits; amidst the several changes of their life, their peace does not ebb or flow according to outward things, but they are at a seen advantage above others, in the day when men are sore outwitted with their straits; so that it is most easy then to see the good of religion, when the vanity of other things is most discernible. 5. Is it not also seen that true honour waits on humility, but flees from them who most pursue it; yea, that faithfulness and an upright walk will gain credit even amongst enemies, and respect before the world? 6. That those who are faithful and diligent improvers of a small talent, have usually more added; and as the drying up of the parts of some, as a judgment on unfaithfulness, is often obvious, so also such a blessing upon serious diligence, as has made the last first. Yea, it is truly seen how grace helps men's gifts, and raises and sublimates

their spirits.    7. Does not the Lord put some visible difference between the righteous and the wicked
in a time of common calamity, which may convince the world that the righteous have had an invisible hedge of preservation about them, and have
been under some better care than their own?    8.
What a clear witness ungodly men often bear to
this truth at death, or at some other strait, so that
their consciences have forced them to justify the
godly man's choice, and to say that his lot alone
is desirable?    9. That faithfulness and integrity
transmit men's names with more honour, than
either riches or outward preferment; yea, that there
is a great difference between the memorial of the
righteous and the wicked.

VIII.    That verily there is a God who judges in
the earth, Psa. lviii. 11, is a truth which the world
has, in every age, manifested to them.

I shall here point at this truth, as it is in the
providence of God written in such great letters, as
are obvious to the view of the world.    It is true,
much may be laid over to the last judgment; yea,
sometimes we see the most wicked go in peace to
the grave.    The sovereignty of God also appears
very observably in the different measure and kind
of punishment; but this is also sure, that the Lord is
known on the earth by the judgment which he executes, and in every age sets up such convincing
examples before men, that the greatest atheist may
see, and make this acknowledgment, that such
judgments can be no casual thing; while something
of a power higher than man, and a clear verifying
of the word, are so discernible therein.

Now, to demonstrate this truth, I would observe,

1. That the very heathen have yet so much of
a natural conscience, that they not only put some

difference between virtue and vice, but even in some measure can discern that flagitious crimes are punished by a Divine hand. Time could never yet wear out the observation of this truth through the world; and though many things may be received and credited, which, not having a sure ground, quickly vanish, it being truth's privilege still to outlive falsehood, yet, in the darkest parts of the earth, this has been still noticed with a remark, and transmitted from one age to another; yea, the records of heathen writers show that remarkable punishment has followed cruel oppression, covenant breaking, and such other gross sins against the second table, yea, that these have been the usual forerunners of great strokes on kingdoms and families.

2. That in these remarkable judgments which have come on a nation, there is something higher than second causes, in bringing them about; that all must confess they arise not out of the dust, but that a Divine hand is there; and truly, though some desolating strokes are very terrible in themselves, and blood and ruin should be no matter of pleasure, yet we should not only with fear, but even some holy congratulation, consider his work. To clear this point, consider, (1.) That strange concurrence of providences which uses to appear when God is against a people; how all things will then conspire, as by a fatal conjunction, to work their woe and ruin, that men may see, surely this is from a hand against which there is no striving. (2.) How such remarkable strokes are seen to concur with some remarkable height of sin in such a nation, so that it is easy then for all to confess the righteousness of God therein. (3.) When judgment is coming on a land, instruments are quickly

raised, and in a more than ordinary way endowed with all advantages for such a service. (4.) There is then a visible blasting both of counsel and strength ; men are confounded even in the use of their ordinary abilities ; their heart and usual courage are taken from them. (5.) That astonishing success which is usually seen to follow those whom the Lord sends forth to execute his judgment ; they move swiftly and with vigour, they do not stumble or weary; neither rivers nor walled cities can stand in their way; mountains are made valleys, to show it is the Lord who strengthens their loins, and makes the sword and axe sharp for his service. (6.) Amidst the various strokes which come on a land, can men pass the pestilence without some special notice? Where God's immediate hand may be clearly seen in its strange progress in spreading, which like a lightning often goes through cities and countries in a small time; does not this tell aloud to the world that it comes not unsent, and without some special commission? Ordinary means are not effectual in such extraordinary plagues, until he who brought them on, also by his own hand takes them off.

3. The clear resemblance which is often between sin and the stroke is observable ; how justice keeps a proportion, and shapes out the judgment so exactly, both in measure and kind, that it may be easy to see the stroke pointing, as with a hand, to the cause by its discernible likeness, and both to the righteous judgment of God, which thus measures out to men what they have dealt to others. We see how the Lord rewarded Agag and Adonibezek ; how Sodom's burning lust was punished with fire from heaven ; yea, what even David received for his murder and adultery ; the sword did

not depart from his house, and he was punished in his own wives by his own son. (1.) A universal overspreading of sin in a land, has usually some national stroke following. (2.) Blood waits on bloody men, and suffers them not often to live out half their days. One oppressor is punished by another; the unmerciful man is paid home in his own coin. (3.) The proud and insolent are usually met by some humbling, abasing stroke; and such as will not honour God, shall not obtain the honour which they seek from men. (4.) Those who have been most given up to uncleanness are often seen not to increase, but their issue is observably made to fail, yea is rooted out. (5.) They who have chosen sin to shun suffering, have in their sinful way, got as large a measure of the latter, as that man who, in queen Mary's time said he could not burn for the truth, and therefore forsook it, but was burned to death at night by the conflagration of his house. (6.) The treacherous and deceitful are thus dealt with by others; yea, children who have been undutiful to their parents, have from theirs met with the same recompense. (7.) Whilst men have even denied themselves the necessary use of outward things, they are often seen to leave their estate to those who quickly waste and scatter it; and thus the sinful parsimony of parents is punished by the prodigality of their heirs. (8.) The frequent use of some dreadful imprecation, is often punished by the Lord with a suitable stroke. (9.) They who have united themselves against the truth have been visibly broken as to their own private interest.

4. How very convincing and obvious this truth is, may be seen from the ordinary remarks and proverbial sayings which we find in all ages, and

in every part of the earth, concerning the judgment
of God: for truly these are an express witness
how universally this truth is known and received
by men; how much the world is convinced thereof
through a long tract of observation from the fathers
to the children; yea, thence they have had a divinity of their own, even a belief that such sins do
not pass without some notorious punishment. I
shall name some few of these remarks. (1.) How
some families have not thriven, but a secret judgment has been discernible on them since they had
a hand in some gross acts of wickedness, such as
bloodshed, &c. their former prosperity from such
a day visibly declining. (2.) That an evil purchase uses not to be of long continuance, but the
estate is often, in a very strange and insensible way,
made to vanish, which their children, though fru-
gal, can by no means keep up; being purchased by
fraud, and transmitted with a curse cleaving thereto.
There is no warding off the judgment of God. (3.)
How sacrilege has caused a visible waste and consumption in private estates. (4.) That falsehood
does not keep its feet, nor a wicked way prosper
long, whatever it seem to the first view; yea, I
may add, what was an ordinary saying in the time
of Esther, that it is not safe troubling the church,
nor for men to place themselves in opposition to
God's people.

5. Is there not the appearance of a Divine hand
very obvious to the world in the discovery and
bringing to light some gross acts of wickedness?
(1.) By what strange unexpected means these have
been brought forth, even such as have forced not
only spectators to some special remark, but have
even struck the guilty party with wonder and conviction. (2.) How the hand of justice pu suing

men for some known crime, as often brings to light some which they thought the world could never reach; yea, while men have been found out in one sin, it has also brought forth the discovery of some other, and forced them to confess that it was a righteous judgment.

6. Is not the dreadful consternation which men, after some gross acts of wickedness, feel, a very obvious witness to this truth—that there is a God who judges in the earth, into whose hands it is a terrible thing to fall? It shows how great a punishment wickedness is to itself. The horrid cries of many dying men who have most sported with sin, may tell bystanders there is a Judge who can stretch forth his hand on the soul, whereto no outward torments are any way comparable.

7. The extraordinary signs and prodigies which usually go before some judgment on a land, clearly point at a Divine hand. For as these are a solemn forewarning from heaven to alarm men before remarkable changes, so they are a convincing testimony that these judgments are no casual things, it being clear, (1.) That such prodigies have been in every age visible, and the gravest histories, both of ancient and latter times, fully witness them. (2.) That such things should also be previous to great revolutions in the world, the Scripture is express, Joel ii. 30; Luke xxi. 11. And as we should guard against any superstitious respect, we should also beware of stupid atheistical indifference to these strange works of the Lord.

IX. That there are evil spirits, Eph. vi. 12; Rev. xx. 2, 3, is a truth not only witnessed from the experience Christians have of their assaults, but is undeniable by the world.

I confess it may cause fear and astonishment to

think, that spirits so knowing and originally excel‹
lent have fallen into such indignation against infi‹
nite goodness, that it is now their only pleasure to
dishonour God, and destroy his image in man. It
should indeed cause us to fear Him that spared not
the angels who sinned; but the truth itself is sure,
to prove which by arguments, were to light a can‹
dle to let men see that it is day, when it is easy to
discern that power which the prince of this world
has upon the children of disobedience; many are
transformed, even to the very image of Satan, in
desperate prodigious acts of wickedness, at which
we should think human nature, though corrupt,
could not but tremble, yea, look on with horror.
But I principally aim here to hold forth what a
concerning truth this is, and of what great conse‹
quence if seriously considered.

1. That in this the Scripture is truly fulfilled,
which witnesses that these spirits are adversaries
to man, in their nature and inclination desperately
evil. 2. That they pursue something more pre‹
cions than the body, for their actings have no ten‹
dency to ruin men's estate in the world; it is the
soul, the immortal soul. 3. Is it not an undeniable
consequence of this truth, that there must be an in‹
visible world that has inhabitants of another kind
than such as are here, that there is some being
above man, yea, a real correspondence between
men and spirits? Should not man, thus placed in
a middle estate between the angels and the beasts,
partaking in his body with the one, but in his
reasonable soul with the other, raise himself to
thoughts of some more excellent condition for
which he is framed, than a sensual life? 4. Is it
not also sure that there is an invisible guard, and
these desperate spirits are under restraint by a

stronger power, which can bound their malice? This is certain, that they who have so great eumity to man, who are so near, and have such advantages over us, would not keep at such a distance, but that they are kept in chains by a higher power. 5. How is it that now by the gospel, and within the precincts of the church, Satan's power is so much restrained? It is also known that the oracles of old ceased, and the public worship which the world had given them, at the very time of Christ's appearance ; these night-beasts getting to their dens when the day appeared. Plutarch and other heathen writers are witnesses to this. 6. Whence is it that within the church, where Satan is most restrained, his wrath should be more apparent than in all the world besides? There is something seen besides men's natural enmity to the truth, even a fury and violence in their actings, with such an insatiable cruelty against the followers of Christ as holds forth a lively resemblance of the devil. 7. Is it not sure that there is such a party, by this, that he so impetuously tempts men to sin, and incites men to war against Heaven by curses and blasphemous oaths, which have no pleasure or gain?

X. That there is such an enmity between the seed of the woman and the serpent as the Scripture has held forth, is very manifest, Gal. iv. 29. And here let me observe,

1. That no private quarrel among men has ever been pursued with such vigour and malice as this of religion, and which still puts the world more into a flame than any private interest. 2. That this feud could never be adjusted through all the successions of time : it is a strife which is not lately begun, or to be seen only in one age ; no, the

most sage and wise amongst men, the greatest peace-makers, could yet never fall on a way to re-concile these two parties, but the children have still proved themselves heirs to the hatred of their fathers against the church. 3. Is it not seen that they who are more civil, and can bear with the form of religion, yet will break forth in greatest rage against the power thereof? It is indeed here that the inbred contrariety which is in men against holiness betrays itself, even in them who are otherwise noted for a calm and peaceable disposition. 4. What strong natural antipathy is that which causes men to pursue with so much bitterness those from whom they never had any personal injury? 5. This separates between nearest friends and relations, and alienates those who have sometimes been most dear to each other; there is no bond in nature which it will not break; it sets the husband against the wife, and the parents against the children; yea, when once religion appears in a land or a family, it puts all in a flame. 6. When once grace appears in men, they are as a sign and wonder to a profane generation: the world then sensibly changes her countenance, and looks like an enemy; while, on the other hand, the turning loose of professors, and running to that excess of riot with others, causes their old adversaries to relent towards them, and, alas! proves the surest way to gain men's friendship.

XI. That the creature is made subject to vanity because of sin, Rom. viii. 20; Eccles. ii. 11, is a portion of the Scripture that none can be ignorant of.

1. Have not the greatest instances of the glory of the world been usually the greatest examples of its vanity? How few has ambition raised, but it has also ruined; yea, given the sorest fall to those

it had lifted most high ? Surely if the tragedies of princes, and of those who in their condition have been raised above others, were put by themselves on record, it would show that their prosperous estate only made their fall the more observable. 2. What a frail, dying disposition is in all worldly things. Even the greatest kingdoms and politic bodies, to maintain which neither policy nor strength was wanting, yet, like natural bodies of men' have their inevitable periods, their youth and flourishing times, their declining and old age, and at last their grave ; the glory of greatest empires and monarchies is sunk in the dust, yea, scarce a heap of stones is left this day to tell us where cities once famous have stood. 3. What a small distance we see between extremities in outward things, even greatest plenty and poverty, the highest place and a low condition, so that the morning has seen some happy and flourishing in the world, whom the evening has seen miserable. They who were once great have sunk into so little bounds, that men have been put narrowly to consider them, and with admiration ask, Are these they who were once a terror in the land of the living ? Yea, their place has not been found, who a few days before seemed to place themselves alone in the midst of the earth. 4. What is it but the very present moment of time that makes such a difference between the rich and poor, since, as to what is past, men's happiness and misery may be reckoned as though it had never been, and who but a fool would boast of that which is to come ? This only is sure, that a few days will make all conditions equal, when the bones of the rich and the dust of greatest princes will not be discernible from those of the poor. 5. Is there any thing so pleasant which has not a worm at the root thereof, a moth which naturally breeds in the most satisfying enjoyments, and quickly eats out the heart thereof, and blasts our hope before the harvest? How oft is greatest longing in the pursuit turned to loathing and weariness when obtained, because it is not the nature of the thing, so much as the novelty thereof, that makes it pleasant! Hence many sensual men have turned monastic, and greatest monarchs become melancholy; yea, it is usual for many to survive their pleasures, and bury their delights in the world even before themselves. 6. Is it not found that riches and abnndance do load more than fill, and that men's wealth only further heightens their wants? How very poor are some amidst their fulness,whom the world wholly possesses, while they do not at all possess it, neither is it in their power to make use of what they have! Yea, are they not sick, and do they not die, in princes' courts as well as in the meanest cottage; and are not the complaints of the great and rich usually more than those of the poor? The great man oftener wants an appetite and rest, than the poor man wants food and a bed to lie on. 7. Voluptuous men move in an endless circle from one thing to another; still calling for variety, to take off the weariness of one pleasure by another, else the delight they have therein would quickly languish and wear out; yea, the best things are not on a near approach what they seemed to be at a distance; the eye is not satisfied with seeing, nor the ear with hearing, but the more they are pressed the less they yield, neither do they enjoy such things with most satisfaction who take a full draught and steep themselves in their enjoyments; so that sometimes men's attaining their desire has caused their delight in those things to cease. 8. It is also clear, that outward things are incident to the worst without making them the better, and separable from the best without making them the worse; and how can silver or gold suit an immortal soul more than virtue and godliness can suffice to fill an empty chest. 9. How rare is it for men to get their lot in the world accordant with their desire? They are still at some jar with their present condition, so that oft there needs no more to make men discontented, but the thought of some lot which they apprehend more satisfying than their own; yea, many men's disquiet increases with their wealth. 10. Is not the excellency of most outward things only according to opinion, or the institution of men, with but small intrinsic worth from their own quality? What a poor vapour are swelling titles of honour if soberly weighed! The proud man's happiness hangs upon the poor who go by, and is begged from others with the greatest artifice. Would the choicest jewels, or a bag of gold laid upon the heart of a dying man, any way quiet his spirit or ease his pain? 11. Amidst the various changes of the earth princes and great men walk on foot, and servants ride on horseback, the children are often put to ask an alms from those who had served their fathers: fools are loaded with wealth and greatness, while men of the choicest spirit are buried under contempt and poverty. That which, in one age, is raised, is often pulled down in another ♀yea, many are at much labour to undo that which others have done with greatest care and expense. 12. Will not the want of a very small thing oft embitter the pleasantest lot? the smallest touch of pain, the tooth-ache, yea, some melancholy thought, will make men disrelish all their present enjoyments. What torment does a small affront prove to the proud man even in the midst of his glory ? Carnal mirth and joy, and wallow-ing in the delights of the world, have still in the close a bitter sting, which, as the shadow attends the body, is the native and inseparable consequent thereof. How usual is it that when there is too bright a sun shine in outward prosperity, if great sobriety and moderation do not accompany, the same is an ominous and fatal presage of a storm !

XII. That the end of the upright man is peace, Psa. xxxvii. 37, is an undeniable truth, not only because the saints are then entering into perfect peace, but because, however the godly man may have very sharp assaults in the close of his days, yet this truth is generally discernible, that integrity and an upright walk have much peace in the end, and land men in a comfortable harbour. 1. It has not been Balaam's wish alone to die the death of the righteous, and to have his latter end like theirs, but the worst of men are still forced to testify their respect to the lot of a dying Christian, and would wish a share thereof when it comes to their turn. 2. The saints then testify abundant peace, and a present unspeakable complacency that they have valued Christ above all other advantages, and chosen affliction rather than sin ; they cannot smother their joy and peace on this account, but declare to all who stand by what they find ; and truly it has been oft seen that the inward joy which some of these have had has exceeded their outward pain, and has been more sensible to them than their sickness; yea, in leaving the world they have been much more cheer-ful than those whom they left behind. 3. With what a sweet composure have they relied upon the promise l In that hour when they were grappling with the king of terrors, their spirits have been

quiet and calm, they have taken the truth and testimony of God for their sheild and buckler. 4.
Even an untimely and violent death could not frustrate that peace which integrity causes. For innumerable instances can witness what marvellous joy
and satisfaction the saints have shown at a stake
and upon a scaffold, and thence they have had a
more cheerful exit than the rich man stretched upon
his soft bed, or the greatest monarch amidst all
outward advantages. 5. Must not the world grant
that this peace and joy at death can be no counterfeit, as there is no temptation that could thus bias
them to deceive others and themselves in a matter
of such high concernment, and at a time when it
is expected the worst of men should speak truth?

XIII. I add something concerning that great
truth, *The immortality of the soul, and its sub-
sisting after death,* to which this joy has a special
respect. I know this seems so common and uncontroverted a thing, that the naming of it may be
looked on as impertinent; but oh! how unknown
a truth is it. There needs no more to show the
little solid persuasion men have of this truth, but
that it is so usually passed over with so few, and
those very common, thoughts; it is not indeed
much questioned, not because it is believed, but
because men are not in earnest about such a thing.
It concerns the world to keep from a thorough
knowledge of that which would be their torment
to know; and there is cause for this sad complaint
within the church, that the most great and fundamental truths are usually least studied. It may
truly be said, the better part is so buried in the
worst, that until men are dying, few lay this to
heart that their souls must live for ever; yea, must
part fellowship with the body and enter into an-

other world and an unknown state until the resurrection. Consider, 1. How express and clear a
testimony the Scripture gives to this truth. 2. On
what plain and undeniable grounds of reason this
truth is demonstrable to the world. 3. How great
a thing it is to believe and be assuredly persuaded
thereof.

1. It is undeniable that not only the Scripture
holds this forth, but that there only men have a
clear and right discovery of it. It is indeed known
what glances the world has had of this, yea, what
has been written thereon, by some whose sole
guide was the light of nature ; but it is no less evident that though they could not shift some conviction thereof, it was through a dark cloud, and as
some pleasant dream, they looked thereon ; because
they did not know its rise and original, and what
the end was, to which in its actings it ought to be
directed ; they knew not what its after-condition
could truly mean, whence they express their
thoughts with wavering and uncertainty. How
perplexed and uncertain have Aristotle and others
of the ancients shown themselves here ! For they
knew not the Scripture, where this truth is so
clearly set forth, Gen. ii. 7 ; Eccles. xii. 7 ; Luke
xvi. 22, 23 ; Heb. xii. 9 ; 1 Pet. iii. 9.

5. This may be also held forth to the world by
such a clear and rational demonstration, that the
most brutish of men can hardly sink so far into
the condition of a beast, as to deny they have a
never-dying soul. (1.) If you question the being
and subsistence of the soul after death, you must
also deny its frame, that it is a simple, immaterial,
and active substance, which has neither quantity
nor parts. (2.) Consider, if by these diseases to
which the body is subject the soul is not reached,

must it not also have a distinct existence from it? You must grant that the soul does not directly suffer from any outward diseases, but that the body may be under inexpressible pain and anguish, when there is a sweet calm and serenity within. (3.) Docs not this witness that the soul dies not with the body, since it suffers no decay, but is found strong and vigorous in its actings when the flesh is brought low? Yea, is it not at the greatest advantage in its exercise and discernment, the more it is separate from the body and sensible things? Now, that cannot be destructive to the soul in its being, which is so subservient to it in its operation. I think they who have ever observed the joy and peace of a dying Christian, and his excellent frame and composure of soul under a body languishing through many diseases, may clearly see this truth, and there read a lecture on the immortality of the soul. (4.) Can the soul of man have a dependence on the body in its being, when it does no way depend thereon in its acting and exercise? For it is sure it does truly act, yea, has a clear power of reasoning, even when the body sleeps. (5.) If there are spirits and incorporeal beings which act without a body, and yet have a true and real subsistence, can you doubt the existing of the soul, or its exercising the faculties thereof, without the body? And if there be indeed a converse and intercourse between us and spiritual beings, yea, a truth in fellowship with God the Father of spirits, does not this demonstrate the existence and acting of the soul, even when the body is at a distance and in the grave (6.) That which has a dominion and pre-eminence over the body, by its making a rational choice of good when most opposed to the desire of the flesh, yea, which determines it to

endure most grievous torments with a special de-
lighting therein, is it not something truly distinct
from the body ?  Now you will not deny that there
is such a dominion over the flesh, and a captivating
of it to the law of the mind, which the most sensual and brutish will not deny, how little acquaintance soever they have with it themselves.  (7.)
Since there is a discovery of things not only above
the reach and impressions of sense, but even contrary thereto, so that men  rationally judge and
assent to truths which truly contradict their senses,
as the rotundity of the earth, which seems to us a
plain, &c., does it not show that the soul, which
can so far soar above the earth, and exceed the
body, must be of a more excellent mould, and truly
different from it ?  What means that war and strug-
gling between the flesh and the spirit, which to
every Christian is known ; yea, that which is
know  to every man, between  the  passions and
conscience ?  What mean those reflex acts of the
soul on itself, those marvellous products of the understanding ?  Why are men so anxious about their
surviving name, which were a poor airy accident
not worth the regarding, if there were a destruction of the whole ?  What means that marvellous
deportment of so many martyrs for the truth, who
have shown such a joy and satisfaction amidst their
torments, as though they had no bodies ?  What
means so universal a consent to this truth, that they
who hate and fear it, yet cannot be rid thereof ?
How are the choice and the excellent of the earth
so often crushed under the feet of their oppressors,
whilst the ungodly often wallow in all satisfying
outward delights, yea, sometimes go hence without
bands in their death ?  In a word, what is it that
makes so vast a difference between men and beasts,

since these have a sensual life, and want not some natural sagacity, and have their enjoyments by the senses as well as man?

3. How great and astonishing a truth this is! Can we believe that we have an immortal soul, which is of a more excellent nature than the visible heavens, than the sun, moon, and stars; for which no less than the blood of him who was truly God, was paid as a ransom from everlasting wrath, and yet put so small a price thereon? Is it indeed believed by men, whilst they are so hot in their pursuit after the world? since what should it avail a man to gain the whole world, when it is purchased with the losing of the soul? Surely there is no imaginable proportion between that and a piece of red earth, or between a few years of time and a long eternity. I remember a passage of worthy Mr. Blair, who the first time he heard Mr. Bruce preach, said, The fame of so great a man caused him to expect something very extraordinary from him; but his sermon did press this truth of the soul's being immortal, and that it was a great thing to believe it. He confessed it did at first somewhat amuse him, why he dwelt so much upon so known and common a subject. But he soon found it was some other thing than appears at the first look; for men may dispute and toss it as a notion in the schools, who never knew what it was to believe the truth thereof; and a serious impression of it on the heart, is something else than a swimming in the head by some ordinary speculation. Men should consider, (1.) What it is they have thus held out to them, and how great a change is before them. (2.) That this marvellous change is truly near; time making long steps: the vessel under full sail carries men, whether they sleep or wake,

to their port; for it is sure this cannot be long de
ferred, and that this night thy soul may be re
quired. (3.) That this change must be in a moment, in the very twinkling of an eye, and there is
no interval, but a present entering of the soul into that
after state, which shall put the Christian in possession of an inconceivable joy, in the immediate presence of God, in the embraces of the Mediator,
amongst the angels and spirits of the just made
perfect: and one moment also must put others out
of their sensual pleasures and delights, the prince
off his throne, and those who have been wallowing
in the world, into those dark and horrid prisons,
where, with the ceasing of this world's melody,
they are forthwith met with the horrid noise and
howling of devils, and of all the company of the
damned. (4.) Should it not cause us to think
seriously on this, which admits no after change,
but a long eternity is the true measure of the soul's
duration after death? O to be ever, ever blessed
or miserable, where the one has no fear, and the
other no hope, or possibility thereof! The hope
of the hireling is not there, that he may change his
master at the next term, for these gates are ever-
lastingly shut by the decree of him who alters not.

XIV. I offer one instance more, wherein the
world may see the truth of the Scripture; it is this,
That the way of God is perfect, Psa. xviii. 30, and
that " his work is perfect, and his ways are judgment," Deut. xxxii. 4; yea, that " he doth all
things well," Mark vii. 37. This can be said
neither of angels nor men, but to God it has a peculiar respect; even to him alone in whose way
there is nothing crooked, no mistake, no inequality,
nothing too much or superfluous, nothing out
of due time, either too soon, or too late, nothing

incongruous, nothing misplaced; but every part of his work leaves matter of wonder behind, and thus declares him to be God. I know the world pretends to find a visible contradiction, from the great disorder that things here seem to be in; the miscarrying of instruments, the strange emergency of most grievous accidents, the most promising means frequently blasted; yea, good and evil so strangely interwoven, and the present day often undoing the work and labour of the former; yet, whatever the world can say to darken this great truth, it must shine: the sun ceases not to shine when the clouds obstruct its brightness as to us.

1. You may see it clearly verified, that the way of the Lord is perfect, in the whole frame and structure of the church of Christ. It is true, her glory is within, and lies not in the common road of men's observation; yea, some parts of this excellent body oftentimes are in such disorder, as to darken the beauty of the whole; there is such an intermixture of the hay and stubble of human inventions with this choice building, as mars its order and beauty; the carved work also may be spoiled and broken down, as with axes and hammers; yet, with all these disadvantages, there is a glory on the church of Christ, an awful majesty, such convincing marks of its grandeur even under its ruins, as have forced the world and the great men thereof to consider that sight with wonder and amazement. " They saw, they marvelled, and hasted away," Psa. xlviii. 5; and the preceding words give the reason, for " God was known in her palaces for a refuge." Do but consider, (1.) On what a sure foundation it is built, even that of the prophets and apostles, which is the Scripture of God; whereon, as it is manifestly founded, it is no less marvel-

**19**

lously united and joined together in Jesus Christ, the chief corner-stone! (2.) Is it not likewise obvious, that the church thus fitly joined together, and knit by all that the joints supply, in its whole complex frame, grows up as a building to the Lord? Yea, is there not a very close union and correspondence between all the parts thereof in the same faith and worship, that though divided in so many parcels through the world, yet it is still one entire body? The variety of members, the great inequality amongst them in their growth, the remoteness of place, difference of language, exile, or change of countries, cannot break off that near tie that joins the church of Christ together. (3.) It is in the world, yet not of it; it spreads itself among the nations, yet loses not its own distinct being; is mixed with human societies, yet is an inclosure and incorporation by herself; a fountain of sweet waters sealed, though surrounded with this great salt ocean of the world; made up of many particular churches, yet every part of the same nature with the whole; and though it seems to be open to sore assaults, yet is a defenced city, and has both her walls and watchmen, her bulwarks and strong towers. (4.) It is both visible and invisible, yet not two distinct churches, though under diverse considerations it comprehends both without any jar; has communion with Jesus Christ as her Head, standing related to him as his mystical body; and yet as a visible politic body is related also to him, as her supreme Head; receives his government and guidance, and has an express charter granted for her rights. (5.) Though it does not want some spots, they do not so far mar her beauty, but that in all its several administrations there appears a singular grace; it has indeed its blemishes and failings, yet every measure and degree thereof does not forfeit her rights and privileges. (6.) It does not want a corrupt mixture, yet in its rule and constitution allows no corruption; and though many are found dross within, yet does it distinguish between the precious and the vile; yea, is not more tender and easy in admission, than awful and authoritative in rejection. (7.) All her officers have their appointment, and each their work assigned, yet no greater variety of service and employments than of gifts, which from her Head are dispensed and suited to the same. (8.) She is of such a mould and frame that though she can boast of a power within herself, yet she derives it from another fountain. (9.) This is a body, the members whereof are indeed subject to the magistrate, and deny no due obedience to that power, yet without any subordination or subjecting of the church, as such, to a human power, and though it has not its authority or jurisdiction from men, it denies them no just respect; it binds and looses upon the earth, and no human power can make void; and though cast among the nations, yet by peculiar bounds she is kept distinct from all other societies; though her government is truly monarchical with respect to her Head, yet, with respect to the servants and officers, it is a most excellent, well tempered republic. In a word, both tenderness and severity do here concur; there is a healing in her sharpest rebukes and censures, whilst private efforts are to go before a public and judicial procedure; yea, her authoritative determinations are without prejudice to the judgment of Christian prudence and discretion, which belongs to every one of her members. She wears not out, but has still a spring after the winter; and whilst she is losing and in a decay as to particular members, she is still travailing in birth for a new offspring and succession. " Walk about Zion, and go round about her : tell the towers thereof. Mark ye well her bulwarks," Psa. xlviii. 12, 13. Surely the word is herein fulfilled, " His way is perfect, and he does all things well."

2. Is not this clearly demonstrated, not only in the frame, but the whole conduct and administration of Providence about the church ? Through what a variety of dispensations God brings forth his work, and makes his way often break out of the bosom of a dark cloud. I know this is a great deep, and we cannot have such a discovery of the dealings of God about the church, nor so reach the meaning of things in their first mould, as when that great work of Providence, that now is put over in the hand of the Mediator, has its perfect close, and the whole frame and contexture shall be set up together, as one entire piece to look upon, that is now by several pieces, and through a various succession of ages, carried on. Yet the Lord comes so near even in the darkest times, and makes the glory of this truth shine forth in such a measure, as may convincingly witness that the way of the Lord is perfect. I shall here offer some few things that in every time are obvious. (1.) God does nothing in vain, but makes all things congruous to his end ; even things that amongst themselves do most cross one another. He carries on his designs by the miscarrying of instruments, and brings forth his greatest works by means small and contemptible. I know the world can see no such thing, and indeed Providence cannot be understood by one look ; but, do you discern the motion of the hand upon the clock, even whilst it is certainly going

'forward? yet, when it comes to the hour, and strikes, you will then see it was moving. There are such periods of Providence, when its meaning does not clearly appear until it comes to the striking of the hour, and then the most stupid are forced to observe, what once seemed most improbable in the way of the Lord. (2.) Is it not also obvious, how the Lord ensnares men in the work of their own hand, and turns their wrath unto his praise? How he takes the wise, and outwits them by their counsels, makes events fall out contrary to their second causes, frustrates the most promising means, and by things unknown and unthought of, often brings forth the deliverance of the church! (3.) The church is often fed by the rod, yea, under that appears with such advantage, that it may be said, her meat has been brought forth out of the eater. How usually is her mercy and enlargement prepared for her by the sharpest down-casting! (4.) The Lord does at once, and by the very same providence, reach many several designs; yea, bring forth various and contrary effects, so that no human reason could ever anticipate the result by the premises. Severity and mercy are at once brought forth; a more full stroke on the adversary by his further raising, yea, by a long forbearance of that stroke. The church sinking, yet does not perish; in a flame, yet not consumed, but is thereby kept alive; brought under the yoke of the oppressor, to make her grow and flourish; is wounded and smitten for her further healing; has a greater weight and burden put on, to give her ease and enlargement, yea, is chastened with suffering to prevent suffering, that she may rest in the day of trouble. (5.) What strange things do sometimes fall in between the beginning and close of some special providence about the church! Yet, in all these, there may be discerned a remarkable dependence and connexion of things. In such a variety of contrary events, and in a long continued tract of providence, every thing falls in aright, in its own place; yea, every step, every circumstance is so proportioned by a marvellous disposal, to make the whole complex providence beautiful, that, on a serious review, the world must confess that this is a concatenation so strange, that it must be his work, and his alone, who sees things from the beginning to the end. (6.) How perfect is God's way, who can hasten his work by delays; and when he seems to take a long circuit in bringing about his design, yet loses no time, but in such a visible going back does most effectually move forward! Yea, he makes things fall in, that are very unexpected, and remote, to answer his blessed end; and even disposes that, which above all seems most directly destructive to the church, to be of all other things most subservient to her advance; he brings her more quickly to the harbour by a storm than a calm. (7.) What a certain, steady motion Providence has, whilst the world is reeling to and fro; how the church's mercy has by greatest disappointments been more fully answered, than in the most probable way; yea, when her salvation seemed furthest off, with what a strange surprise does Providence appear from under the ground with an unexpected mercy! (8.) He puts a peculiar beauty upon every occurrence of providence, and brings it forth in the very fittest time, so that it could not fall out with more advantage to the church. There is a cause for her sharpest trials, and the necessity thereof is no less discernible, than that of the winter for the profit and advantage of the earth; her reviving never came too late, but in the very fittest time. The world can see this in the revolutions of the year, but not in the changes of the church; yet, I am sure that the church of Christ has her sad, and more comforting times here, with as discernible a succession of the one to the other, as there is of the summer to the winter; yea, that under these vicissitudes of her condition, she is still seen to look forth with a peculiar advantage. I shall add, what a marvellous composition and temperament of contraries is discernible in this excellent frame of Providence! There is nothing here incongruous, nothing here too small, and which does not fall under its reach, and nothing so great that can overreach it; here is no jar or disagreeing with the diligent use of means, yet this rises so far above the same, that no human care can bend it, nor is there any running contrary to such a current.

3. I shall yet further pursue this demonstration with respect to that great and marvellous work of God, in the redemption of the church; a contrivance more wonderful than this whole structure of the universe of the heavens and earth, which are so exquisitely framed. For here the thing itself is not more astonishing, than the way and conduct of infinite wisdom in the whole frame, and all the steps thereof. This is, indeed, so far above nature, that without a Divine illumination it cannot be understood; yet so much is discovered, that they who have only report, and give some ordinary assent thereto, cannot have their reason and judgment in exercise without some conviction upon their souls that this is a contrivance above human reach, and worthy of the great God; yea, that herein his way is most absolutely perfect. Here we may see so

excellent a correspondence between the foundation
and superstructure, that the whole tract of the gospel is but one entire and complete means for glo-
rifying God. Here men may see the greatness of
his power, the inexpressible freedom of his grace,
the holy severity of justice, all meet and join -to-
gether in a sweet agreement; where justice is
maintained, and yet sinners saved; where mercy
rejoiceś over condemnation, vengeance is taken on
our inventions, and the inventors escape: a redemption without price and absolutely free, as to
sinners; yet all that a just God could exact is fully
paid. Here we may rise and pursue this greát
thing up to the fountain head—the sovereign pleasure of God, and thence follow it down to that
infinite satisfaction of the Mediator, the great meri-
torious cause, and see how marvellously well ordered are all the steps of this way, all the parts of
this contrivance: how the elect are made -meet for
inheritance through sanctification of the Spirit;
how faith has its special concurrence and instru-
mentality, without prejudice to the absolute free-
ness of grace, since it is freely given to believe;
how these excellent means are, by a most near connexion, linked with the eternal counsel of God,
and in a most beautiful order joined one with another. Here sanctification flows from an eternal
decree, and, like an excellent stream, runs down
through time, until it loses itself in the great deep
of everlasting blessedness; yea, thus the purpose
of the Lord respecting his people runs under ground,
until it break up at last in their heart by their answering the call of the gospel. Here you may
see that grand plot of the devil to undo man, turn
upon himself, and his head crushed by the seed of
the woman; where so glorious a fabric is raised

out of so great a ruin, and man established by his fall; where the glory of the sovereign God, the freedom of grace, and man's blessedness, at once meet together; where the cure is broad and large as the wound, and the restoration made to answer to every piece of the ruin, not only in man's being ransomed from eternal wrath, but in the marvellous change of his nature by the renewing of the Spirit, which restores him in part to what he lost. By this blessed contrivance we see men brought by irresistible grace, yet without violence; their reason further raised and refined, yet not broken, and its true liberty not taken away, but restored; yea, a notable consistency between moral persuasive arguments and the efficacious power of grace; between men's planting and watering, in the use of means, and the alone increase thereof from the Lord; between a physical and moral concurrence in producing one and the same effect; between those two desires in prayer, *Da, Domine, quod jubes, et jube quod vis.** How marvellous a contrivance is that wherein the blessed majesty of God finds an argument in himself, when man had none to plead; when he was found in the form of a servant, and became our nearest kinsman to redeem the inheritance; where his people's standing is insured oy another surety and strength than their own; not on their apprehending, but their being apprehended; where the Lord obliges himself by bond to make that good, which is only of grace, and is most freely given; where he frames the desire within the soul, and then satisfies it! Here the redeemed have nothing in themselves to boast, and

* Give, Lord, what thou commandest, and command what thou wilt.

the reprobate none but themselves to condemn; for those on whom that door is shut, have therein actively concurred to draw a bar for shutting themselves out.

4. I shall offer one instance more, wherein this great truth may be demonstrated to the world—that the way of the Lord is perfect with respect to the marvellous order of nature, and the disposal of his works. God comes so near, that men may feel after him, Acts xvii. 27; so that it may be said, there is no way to avoid this discovery, but to stop their ears and shut their eyes. O what a wonderful disposal may be seen even in the commonest things, with a mutual subserviency to each other; and in this great variety and throng of the creatures, is it not obvious that each, has its voice and speech to give us something of instruction, and every thing has some matter of wonder in it, so that we may say, it is hard to be an atheist? We cease to wonder, because every day we live and converse amongst wonders. Here the world has a demonstration of the Scripture which they dare not debate, lest they should deny sense as well as reason; and if any will question the glorious Former of all things, why things are thus ordered and disposed, let him but retire within himself, and he will find the defect is truly within, and not in the way of the Lord. In this frame and composure of the universe each thing answers its part, and the conservation of the whole; amidst a great contrariety an excellent concord is manifest in all the different parts, natures, and dispositions. Not only duty, but delight and pleasure, may call men to this study; yea, even to lose themselves, as it were, in so sweet a labyrinth, where it is more easy to enter than to find an end. Do but consider this stupendous

frame of the universe, a fabric that in all parts is most exactly joined, and nothing in it defective or out of order. Here you may see that great minister of nature, the sun, with what advantage it is placed, and fitted to dispense its light and refreshing influences to the earth, so that to move in a higher or lower orb would not answer the advantage of things below. With what a constant motion does its light travel to fulfil its annual course, and in divers parts successively arise, that by turns it may give the several parts of the earth a visit! Should we cease to wonder at the rising and setting thereof, because it is so frequently seen? May not this arrest our thoughts with astonishment, to see with what wisdom it is made subservient all along its course, to cause summer and winter, spring and harvest; yea, how its approaches and withdrawings are gradual: that by its ascent in the spring it may dispose our bodies for the summer, and by its descent in such a degree in the harvest, may prepare and fit us for the winter, that there should not be an immediate bordering between these extremes? Is not the correspondence that it has with things here below also manifest, it not only reaching the surface of the earth, but the most inward bowels and secret caverns thereof? Is it not also evident, that this glorious body of the moon, though of a lesser glory than the other, is for another use than for men to gaze on; how it keeps them from groping in utter darkness through the night, and lights a candle to the world when the sun is gone down? Its influence is known also upon the sea, upon seeds and plants, yea, upon the humours and complexion of men's bodies. O what innumerable employments are there by which it is made continually subservient to the world! The night has its special use, as well as the day; yea, it has its peculiar beauty, and by its darkness commends the light, and makes its approach more sweet and desirable. This gives the labouring world some time for repose, and most observably answers man's weariness, and the necessity of such a rest with so fit a season, that we may say it but draws a curtain about us for that end, and puts us in a sweet and silent composure from the noise and hurryings of the day. Yea, every evening solemnly warns men of their approaching death, and the swift passing away of time, that they may have no excuse of being surprised who have so grave and so frequent a monitor. How marvellous are the various motions of the heavens, the positions of the stars and constellations, where each has its own proper course, yet all are carried about to one general and common end, to show there must be a first mover who is not subject to motion or change, but manifestly determines all these! How does this great body of the earth hang upon nothing! a thing so vast and ponderous lean upon the air as on a foundation! How does it keep its centre, and rest thereupon! How steady is the axis of the earth, so perpetually parallel with itself, that it cannot tumble this or that way! What a marvellous order is seen in those higher motions of the celestial bodies, of which some are slow, others more rapid, some tend to the east, others toward the west, and yet from these, though cross to each other, there results a singular harmony, in which the conservation of the world and the production of things here below are concerned! It is true, the Lord might have made every day a year's length, and might have caused the earth to be that length of time in turning round ; but he divides our life in such short daily stages to make us more frequently mind our change.  We see likewise how marvellously the earth is framed in its various parts and proportions, and the singular advantage it has, both in its posture and figure ; the mountains and high places do not mar its beauty nor want their use.  Is not nature likewise more displayed and laid open to men by the plains and valleys, which are a special ornament to the earth?  How manifold is the use of the atmosphere which is in the vast space between the higher and lower world!  Here the birds find use for their wings, through this the rains find an easy passage, this intervenes between the sun and the earth, yet is no let to the communication either of light or heat, but its scorching is thus qualified by the cool breathing of the air.  How are the winds directed and bounded, so that men can neither cause a storm nor a calm at their pleasure! Can you look on the sea, and not wonder what marvellous things are there; how it is shut up with gates and bars, and has appointed bounds, without which there could be no reason that a bank of sand should restrain the great ocean from breaking forth ; strange that this not only is made passable, but, by the art of navigation, becomes a more easy way for transport and commerce, by which cities and countries are made to flourish !  Do you not see the regular course it keeps in its ebbings and flowings, and the singular use and subservience of the tides; so that though men are stopped in an inquiry about the natural cause of these things, they cannot but observe the special end and advantage thereof?  Do we not also see that those countries which have no rain, as Egypt, have some supply thereof by an overflowing of the rivers?

Do you see any members either of men or beasts superfluous and without use; or is there any poison but has some peculiar antidote provided? The poor have medicinal waters provided without money. What a marvellous use is there of natural antipathies and sympathies, whereon the special improvement of navigation in the use of the load-stone so much depends! The harvest gives a large compensation for the toil of the spring; and the poor man's labours, through the day, make his bed soft in the evening, and his rest sweet unto him. You see the correspondence which the heavens keep with the earth, in sweet refreshing showers, by which its seminal virtue is drawn forth, and thus the rain moistens what the heat would scorch; you see how it is distilled and dropped down, not in violent gushes, but as it were through a small sieve, for otherwise it would hurt more than help; you would not desire to be without rain, nor yet to have it perpetual. The vapours are exhaled from the earth, that by refreshing showers they may return thither again. O how manifold are the works of the Lord, and in what wisdom has he made them all! The pain and travail of the beasts in bringing forth their young is propor-tioned to their condition, and to the lodging they have. "They bow themselves, they bring forth their young ones, they cast out their sorrows," Job xxxix. 3; and as their time and duration is, for the most part, shorter than man's, their growth also is suited thereto. Men have their lodging furnished before they come into the world; the beasts are provided, and by a wonderful instinct they are taught to seek after them. The want of hearing or sight is usually compensated with some special natural sagacity; yea, a want and defect in some parts of the body is often supplied with a greater agility in some other members thereof, such as that woman in Scotland, of whom I have heard, who had no arms from her birth, but could make use of her right foot instead of her hand. The beasts have some natural defence, and are taught self-preservation; and what the hare and hind want of the lion's paw and strength, is made up often by a more swift foot. There is an advantageous antipathy amongst the beasts, lest the earth should be overrun with those which are hurtful. The dog is fitted by a strange tendency to pursue the wolf and the fox, and the cat to destroy the rat; and the ox, whose strength is above many of the wild beasts, is tamed to endure the yoke, and brought under discipline. Those things which are most absolutely necessary are most easy to be had; and whilst there is such a variety of labour and toil attending the lot of man here, does not the earth also afford a variety of delights? The birds need no instructer to build their nests, and choose a fit place, nor do they mistake their seasons; yea, those sweet musicians, by their natural melody, call men to praise, whose debt is much above theirs. There is a marvellous coalition between the graft and the tree, which exceeds human art, if nature did not so wonderfully co-operate therein. The seed thrown into the ground dies and rots there, that it may rise with the greater lustre and advantage, and by such a significant emblem teaches men the certainty of the rising of their bodies; for the ordinary things of nature are great and convincing hieroglyphics, to hold forth more divine things. You see what veins of coal and other minerals go through the earth, whence it is furnished, and has fit materials for daily use, ånd for an improvement of men's faculties. The earth is watered by an intercourse which springs and rivers have with the sea; and what some parts of the world want, is by other things supplied. Every country has some peculiar advantages; the coldest places of the earth do most abound with the warmest furs; the beasts want not their table; and the lily is well clothed. Doth the grass of the ground want its use? yea, is not the very colour thereof notably suited for men's eyes? What cause of wonder is there in the different forms, the virtues, and variety of plants! The little ants have their magazine and storehouse; the bees want not order and government; yea, no human skill can frame such work as theirs. But O man! what a curious and exquisite fabric is that which did come in among the last of the creation? A most rare piece of work, of a strange, various, and subtle composition, in which there is so notable a harmony made up of many contraries. I think they who would learn atheism are not only concerned to stifle their reason, but to shut their eyes from looking on themselves and the frame of their bodies, which is so curiously wrought with nerves, sinews, and veins, with such a variety of parts, and yet not one bone or muscle superfluous.

## THE FOURTH ARGUMENT TO PROVE THE FULFIL-
### MENT OF SCRIPTURE.

ARGUMENT IV, to prove the Scripture's accomplishment, is this—That the most part of it is fulfilled, and may be at this day clearly read in the event, and but a little part remains to be made out.

I would premise some few things.

1. Though the Scripture takes place in every generation as if it were alone directed to that time,

yet a special part has its proper accomplishment in those ages to which in a peculiar way it relates.

2. It is also sure that the whole work of God, and his providence about his church, are comprehended in the written word, where the Lord has fully revealed his mind concerning every interest of the church, though we often are in the dark in finding out the same; but the event will in due time speak for itself, which should cause us until then to pass our judgment with much sobriety on those truths not as yet fulfilled.

3. The prophets of old not only foretold such great changes as were to happen to the church, but they often point at the times, and periods of time, to which they related; and though sometimes in dark terms, yet they clearly show that there was a certain prefixed time for their performance.

4. The full accomplishing of the Scripture and the perfecting the Lord's work about his church, will take place at once, and then there shall be a full discovery of God's way in providence.

I would lay down these two things to be considered.

I. What is already accomplished; and II. What yet remains to have an accomplishment.

I. *What is already accomplished.*

1. Let us go back to those first times after the fall, and see that dreadful stroke which came upon the old world by the flood, and we shall there find the fulfilling of that which Noah, the great preacher of righteousness, had often foretold. (1.) No records of ancient times could ever contradict this truth; yea, some of the oldest writers clearly witness something of a universal deluge, with the wonderful preservation of some from it, though

20 *

they were in the dark as to many circumstances. (2.) This might be brought about even in the way of natural causes made use of for that end ; for we find that the windows of heaven being opened, the air being condensed into clouds, and their reten- tive power loosened, the water falling not in drops, but in a full body, might soon overwhelm the earth with abundance of water ; while the foun- tains also of the great deep beneath were broken up ; that is, not only the ocean let forth over its banks, but a universal vent to all the veins of the earth ; which waters meeting those that were from above, may give men a clear and rational account how such a thing might be.  (3.) This part of history is most congruous to the whole scope of the Scripture, as it points out a universal defec- tion and a universal stroke meeting together; it leads us forward to Christ, of whom the ark was an excellent shadow, in that salvation which in and by him the church has from eternal wrath ; and is a manifest pledge of that last destruction of the world, which will find men in the same condition as this flood found them in the days of Noah.

 2. The confounding of man's language is ex- pressly threatened by the Lord, Gen. xi. 7, as a judgment upon men for their ambition and pride, and is most clearly verified in the event.  (1.) There is such a confusion and variety of langua- ges in the earth at this day ; and by this confusion the earth is divided, and one part thereof rent from another, commerce and correspondence made diffi- cult, and a bar drawn between nations by a diffe- rent speech.  Yea, the most ancient records of the world witness these languages to have originated in ancient times.  (2.) No tradition or history,

but the Scripture, gives us an account how or whence it began. Yea, they who have written most of other things, can give no reason why they write in one language rather than in another, but that it is proper to the country where they had their education; how the race of men, who have such a community in other things, should be thus divided, is a mystery which Divine truth alone can unveil. (3.) There is no language but what is acquired either by long continued use, as children do their mother tongue, or by set rules. It is true, Adam had his by some extraordinary infusion, but this is the case with no others. (4.) This diversity of languages is a most strange and marvellous thing, and in no ordinary way, yea, not without a miracle, could it be brought about, and no continuance of time, or invention of men can account for it, if we consider, [1.] That if man can be traced back to some beginning, there must then have been some one language; so that if you admit the truth of the creation, you admit also but one language to have existed in the beginning.: [2.] That men could not choose so great a judgment on themselves, if they had any use of reason, as it would divide between them and the great part of mankind, hinder trade and interchange with other countries in exporting or importing necessary commodities, would also obstruct human knowledge, and the excellent inventions and experiments of other places; yea, give man, whose days are so few, a sore labour to acquire but a few of the many different languages in the world. [3.] It is above human understanding, how, in an ordinary way, such different languages could have been found out, and afterwards acquired by the body of nations; yea, how there should be such an agreement in this amongst a vast multitude of different tempers and capacities. It is obvious there must have then been an inventing of the first radical languages; I mean, those that are not dependent upon one another; and therewith a vast dictionary of words, with a determination of their significancy and rules to conjoin them in sentences, must have necessarily been framed. The abandoning also of their former language, so far as to the bringing of it into oblivion, would require the universal concurrence of the multitude. I confess this were not so strange if such a difference between languages were but in some peculiar mode or propriety of phrases, as in the alteration of words, according to the various tempers and climates of the earth; but we see different languages, wholly independent, not only in original words, but in the very frame and bulk, such as can be no compound of other languages, as many modern tongues are. The Scripture only can resolve how this is; for besides many commixtures and variations of languages which through continuance of time, conquest, and mingling of nations together, exist in the world, there are many that may be judged mother tongues, of which, whatever minute variation there has been by the adding of some new words, or the disusing of others, the whole bulk remains entire. [4.] What a strange and marvellous thing must this be, if we consider that ancient maternal languages were previous to the use of letters, whence alone rules could be conveyed from one to another, if it had been only human invention; for we know from surest antiquity, how long it was before several nations learned a further way to communicate knowledge and represent their conceptions than by speech, or some significant symbols or hiero-glyphics, which were then in use to supply the want of letters. Little either by pen or printing has been discovered to the world till of late; very little even of the Greek language is upon record before Homer's time. Now this clearly demon-strates that in an ordinary way these languages could not then have been acquired. (5.) The Scripture determines that by these different lan-guages, nations and families were at first divided, Gen. xi.; yea, that this was the first rise of divi-ding them. Thus did the Lord inclose his church in Israel, and by this diversity of languages outlaw the rest of the earth; for in Israel was that venera-ble first language of the Hebrews kept up, by which the sacred oracles of the Old Testament were made known. And as God displayed his power in the first confusion, so in the subsequent gift of tongues. And the latter mercy was as re-markably subservient to the diffusion, as the for-mer judgment was to the preservation of his holy word.

3. The church's delivery from Egypt was fore-told by Joseph at his death, and has now for many ages been fulfilled. (1.) This was a deed known and public, not done in a corner, but in the view of the world, and before all the children of Israel. (2.) It was testified by Moses, an eye witness thereof; one whom even the most ancient of hea-then writers mention with much respect, and in this never disputed his testimony, though a matter of that moment that all the nations about could not but know it. They might easily refute such a thing, if false, and the Egyptians and many others could want no good will to disgrace a people they so much hated, nor be ignorant of that which

Moses published in his own time. (3.) A truth delivered to the Jews, to be kept by them and their children in all succeeding ages, and the record of which they so narrowly looked to and reverenced, that all the syllables and letters thereof were by them numbered, lest in the smallest point it should be wronged. (4.) A thing the remembrance whereof was from that time yearly celebrated by the Jewish church, whence the institution of the passover had its rise; that deliverance being a sign and sacramental pledge of the great salvation by him who is our true Passover.

4. The more full growth of the Jewish church. The prophecy by dying Jacob that the Jews should enjoy a sceptre, and the promise to Abraham that his seed should be as the sand of the sea, and enjoy Canaan for an inheritance, have long since been fulfilled. (1.) For many ages Israel enjoyed that land in a most flourishing condition, as appears from the very ruins and desolation over which they have so long lamented, and from the once famous glory of Jerusalem and the temple, which causes a reverence amongst them to the very rubbish thereof to this day. (2.) They were once a people by themselves, not mingled with the nations, but kept at a distance by their religion and laws from the rest of the world, as a peculiar people to the Lord. (3.) Whilst they enjoyed the land, there was a singular blessing of fruitfulness thereon; that so small a piece of ground was enough for an innumerable multitude of inhabitants; but is at this day a barren sand: an extraordinary curse being no less apparent now, than a blessing in former times. (4.) Something in the way and carriage of this people, even in their low wandering condition, discovers that they have not forgotten their former

grandeur and flourishing, but still keep by themselves, with some hope of regaining the land which their fathers enjoyed.

5. That part of the Scripture written by Jeremiah, which concerns the Babylonish captivity, has now many ages since been fulfilled; a truth attested by sacred and profane history. As to this particular prophecy, consider, (1.) That which Jeremiah foretold concerning the captivity, and its completion, was put on record in a book of the church's lamentations. There this truth may be read in her tears, and besides, is witnessed by a visible monument, even the destruction of the temple, which, though rebuilt, never attained to its former splendour. (2.) This was a matter of fact noted and famous at the time, done in the view of all the nations, a considerable piece of the Babylonian conquest; yea, the testimony of the Scripture was, a few ages after, made public to other parts of the world by the Septuagint translation, so that it had been easy for Ptolemy, or any in those times, to have discovered the falsehood of a thing so lately done. (3.) Though much of human history be lost, and the records we now have are both corrupt and defective, yet there wants not consent from the best of these, to many of the most observable things in the history of the Old Testament. Some of the oldest writers, Berosus, Herodotus, and Xenophon, give some light to us, whose witness the atheist cannot challenge; yea, it is clear that Josephus, not only from sacred history, but from the fragments of former times then extant, though since lost, composed his Jewish Antiquities which give so particular a relation of this truth.

6. What was foretold by Daniel concerning the

.rise and fall of the monarchies, has for many ages
past had a most punctual performance.  (1.) The
prophecy of Daniel was translated into Greek, and
laid up in the great library of Alexandria, long before much of it was fulfilled ; even before Antiochus
Epiphanes, and the rising of the Roman empire,
of which Porphyry could not be ignorant, though
all he could answer to that evident agreement between the prophecy and the event was, that it must
have been written after these things were accomplished ; but it is clear that a part of the prophecy
of Daniel, which concerned the fourth monarchy,
was not fully accomplished even in his times ; yea,
something thereof reaches to the last end of time.
(2.) In these great revolutions of the monarchies
there is a discernible harmony between the Scripture and those ancient records which we have of
those times, so that not only the things themselves,
but some of the most observable circumstances, particularly those mentioned by Daniel, may be read
in Xenophon, Herodotus, and Diodorus Siculus.
(3.) Some things, which in Daniel's prophecy
seem most improbable, such as Belshazzar's death
in the very night when the hand-writing was
showed to him, are particularly attested by Xenophon's history ; as that Cyrus took the advantage
of the Babylonian security, whilst they were in
the midst of a solemn feast, and by diverting the
channel of the Euphrates entered the city without
opposition.   The great horn of the he-goat being
suddenly broken, and the coming up of four in his
room, expounded by Daniel of the Grecian monarchy and the dividing of that empire after Alexander's death, is punctually corroborated by all the
histories of that time.   (4.) There was a very convincing appearance of a Divine hand in the rise

and fall of these monarchies, and an extraordinary providence appears both in Cyrus' conquest of the Babylonians, and the marvellously swift progress and success of Alexander against the Persians.

7. The great scope of prophecies under the Old Testament. The coming of the Messiah is verified; the Lord is come unto his temple, even he whose day Abraham and the saints under the law did see long after. This was the most notable crisis that ever the church was under: the great epoch of time from which she now reckons. God was manifest in the flesh, made his abode for some time in the earth, suffered at Jerusalem before many witnesses, arose from death on the third day, was seen and known by his disciples, and having finished the work for which he came, was received up again into glory. (1.) It is undeniable that the Messiah was to come, to whom all the sacrifices under the law, the ancient types and shadows, clearly pointed, and to whom the prophets bore witness; this was the faith of the ancient Jewish church, of which promise they were persuaded, even whilst they saw it from afar. There is a most clear and exact portrait of the Messiah drawn under the Old Testament, to teach us by what peculiar characters he who was to be revealed to Israel should be known. (2.) The special period of time wherein Christ should come, was shown to the ancient church, though under some figurative expressions; yet, this truth was so far revealed, that upon a diligent search, and particular collation of the times, it was easy to discern the Messiah's coming and near approach. And truly the fall of the monarchies, and the computing of Daniel's weeks, were solid grounds for a clear exposition; thence there was a general expectation of the Mes-

siah among the Jews, at the very time when he
came, so that divers impostors arose, whom the
people were ready to follow; and we see with
what amazement the Pharisees inquired of John
the Baptist, if he were the Christ, or not. Yea,
Josephus shows that the persuasion of this most
excited the people to war with the Romans, from
the prophecies they had in holy writ, that from
Judea one should arise who was to be Emperor of
the world. (3.) It is also sure there was such a
one, who, in the days of Tiberius, and under the
reign of Herod, was made manifest to Israel; who
came with no outward show, but did great and
marvellous things before all the people; was crucified at Jerusalem under Pontius Pilate, and,
notwithstanding the ignominy of his death, was
adored and followed 'both by many of the Jews
and gentiles; whose doctrine did in a short time
spread through the world. (4.) This appearance
of Christ to the world exactly concurred with the
time foretold by the prophets. Jacob's prophecy
was thus accomplished, for the royal line of David's house did not cease, until Herod a stranger
came, by whom it was utterly cut off. The
seventy weeks mentioned by Daniel must be understood of years; for, reckoning from the decree
given out by Cyrus to rebuild the temple, they
amount to 490 years, and answer to the very time
of Christ being in the world, and to his death,
which necessarily falls in the last of these weeks.
(5.) In him who at that time was revealed to Israel, whom the Christian church this day wor-
ships, was exactly accomplished whatever was by
the prophets foretold concerning the Messiah; and
it is no small advantage for the Christian cause,
that it needs but appeal to these records which

have been kept in the hands of her adversaries, where there is so clear a portrait held forth, of his person, his way of coming, the place whence, the entertainment he should meet with, and his death, so that it is a contradiction to acknowledge the Old Testament, and not grant the New; since the Jews look for no other Messiah than such a one as is held out by the prophets, and they acknow-ledge also the Divine authority of Isaiah, Daniel, Micah, Malachi, &c., who by clear marks point him forth, and show the Church how they should know him when he cometh; for it is not moré certain that the Messiah should come, than that Jesus Christ is he. What do the Jews this day miss in our blessed Lord Jesus, which the Old Testament warrants them to expect in the Mes-siah? Should he not be of the seed of the wo-man, Gen. iii. 15, born of a virgin as Isaiah show-eth, his voice not heard in the streets, despised and rejected of men, a man of sorrows, &e? Such a one as should be made a sacrifice for sin, yea, who should come with no outward pomp, but meek and lowly, and riding upon an ass; that he should be betrayed and sold, and his price was noted by Zechariah at thirty pieces; a crucified, dying Christ, and cut off from among the children of his people? (6.) The Jews, in their present case, cannot possibly expect the accomplishment of this promise; the Messiah cannot now come according to the Scripture, except they could be put in such a condition as they were in at Christ's coming. He cannot appear in the temple which is utterly destroyed; there is now a subversion of the tribes, and the family of David is not known at this day. Yea, the gentiles are brought in, who Isaiah shows should be gathered under the standard 'of the Messiah; the daily sacrifice has ceased for many ages, and this was to be after his coming. How was that ever fulfilled, that the glory of the second temple should exceed the glory of the first? This could not be on the account of its structure, or outward magnificence; there is nothing wherein this glory could appear, but in the advent of Christ, and the dawning of that glorious light which was before its destruction. (7.) An innumerable company have embraced the gospel, and received the Spirit by the ministry thereof since the times of the Apostles: it may be said, these were the excellent of the earth in their time, of the greatest outward parts and abilities, whose moral integrity and candour was beyond question, Jews and gentiles, of all ranks of men, of all nations and languages, who not only by a naked profession, but by their walk and sufferings, have shown forth the power and virtue of a crucified Christ; yea, have shone as lights in the world. (8.) We see a manifest agreement between the New Testament and the doctrine of the ancient Jewish church. As the five books of Moses hold forth the sum of the gospel, the covenant of grace, and the mystery of salvation by Christ, so the prophets carry it on with further clearness, and the evangelists complete it, like an excellent edifice, that is founded and advanced in the one, but perfected in the other; all breathing the same spirit, so that we may say, the Jews under the law were in effect Christians, and the followers of Christ under the gospel are in some respect Jews, both being one in the substantials of religion; for it is clear, the poor apostate people now called Jews, have wholly departed from their own doctrine, and will not come to the

light that they may be judged according to the
Old Testament. Can paganism, the Turkish
Koran, or Jewish Talmud, hold forth any such
doctrine as the Christian religion does, such pure
and excellent precepts to restrain the inordinancy
of corrupt affection, backed with arguments becoming an immortal soul; a doctrine so sincere,
solid, and rational, so consistent with itself, where
every page and line breathes forth holiness towards
God, and righteousness and humanity towards
man? (9.) The clear, convincing evidences of
the truth of the gospel, which attended the first
publishing thereof, may force the greatest atheist
to silence; for, [1.] They were Jews, concerned
in the religion of their fathers, who first published
the gospel; none more zealous according to the
law than Paul before his conversion; none could
pretend their deriving an outward interest hereby,
since persecution and bonds, yea, greatest hazard
was that only which they could expect. [2.] They
walked by no rule of human policy, nor by the
ordinary ways of insinuation which the world uses
to engage men and to make a party; but delivered
the truth, a truth most repugnant to the flesh, with
the greatest candour and simplicity, though with a
convincing authority; yea, they came with a message to the world, which had no other persuading argument but the evidence of its own truth.
[3.] What is published concerning Christ by the
evangelists, the great works he did, his dying at
Jerusalem, with all the stupendous circumstances
thereof, were things not done in a corner, but in
the public view of men; but yet, there cannot be
produced one contradictory testimony to the truth
of these relations, by any adversary of the gospel,
either at that time, or since. These things were

21 *

published early by the evangelists and apostles; whilst that generation was alive; yet, though in a matter of such concernment, which made then so great a noise, and was at that time putting the earth all in a flame, none was found, either among Jews or gentiles, who could, or durst pretend to discover the least cheat or falsehood in them. [4.] Whatever different parties and sects opposed the truth in other things, in this they all consented, that he who was crucified at Jerusalem was the Messiah. If there could have been the least ground to challenge any imposture in this great foundation of the Christian faith, surely the bitter contentions and heat of those whom the Apostles and church in that time did pursue with so much zeal, and the sharpest censures, would have engaged them to put all the disgrace upon the truth which they could. Even the arguments and objections which the adversaries of the gospel have brought against it, are a convincing confirmation. The Jews assert that the great works Christ did in the days of his flesh were performed by stealing the name of Jehovah out of the temple; this needs no refutation, and even here they are forced to witness the truth of the matter of fact. The later atheists, such as Vaninus, Cardan, &c. dare not challenge the facts, only they ascribe the great works which Christ wrought to the influence of the stars, a thing so absurd that it needs no answer.

8. The remarkable prophecy of the ingathering of the gentiles, Isa. liv. 1, 2; lx. 3—9, is a thing now clearly written forth in the event. Now to clear this, consider, (1.) That for many ages this truth, the calling of the gentiles, was sealed up in a prophecy, and was so astonishing to the ancient

Jewish church, that they could not comprehend it, until the event explained how the gentiles should be fellow-heirs of the same body, and partakers of the promise in Christ, when the bounds of the church did not exceed Judea, and the whole world besides lay buried in dark paganism. The most pleasant places of Africa, Asia, and Europe, where afterwards many famous churches flourished, were within these 1800 years but a savage wilderness. Britain, Germany, and France, then worshipped the sun and stars, and sacrificed to the gods of the heathens; yea, the eastern parts, on which the sun first rose, did not then know the God of Israel. (2.) This prophecy was not held forth in a general way, but the time was foretold when it should have its accomplishment, even the appearing of the Messiah. Before which time, a bar was drawn in the way of the nations, and a wall of partition between them and the church, until he appeared who should hold forth an ensign to the people and gather the gentiles under his standard, Isa. xi. 10; xxxiv. 1; lx. 1, &c. Then the mountains were to flow down at his presence, nations to be born at once, yea, the light break forth to the east and the west; then should the children of the desolate be more than of the married wife, when this time, even the set time for the gentiles, was once come. And it is most observable, that notwithstanding the more flourishing condition of the Jewish church in former ages, and the neighbourhood and commerce which the nations about had with that people, yet, though they were scattered by the captivity among the Persians and Babylonians, there was no such change in the world until the appointed time came. (3.) The Lord then visited the gentiles with the knowledge of his truth, which caused such a change in the earth, that a great part of it has been brought from heathenish idolatry to worship the God of Israel; and those who were once aliens, are now made to profess the faith of the ancient Jewish church. For not only an innumerable company out of all nations and languages, but the generality, the very complex body of kingdoms and nations, can bear witness thereto; yea, there are but few parts of the world where there has not been some appearance of a church, though the promise has not yet had its full accomplishment. However, the Lord has in a great part fulfilled his promise, so that the church may with astonishment cry out, who hath begotten all these children; who are these that fly as a cloud, and as doves to their windows? O blessed day, in which the light first broke out on the poor offspring of Japhet, who then dwelt in the shadow and region of death! O blessed day that brought salvation with it to the gentiles, when the Lord visited these dark places of the earth, which were full of the habitations of cruelty! (4.) Not only the time, but the very places of the earth, are particularized by Isaiah and other prophets. For the isles, so frequently mentioned as waiting for his law, and the mention of the uttermost parts of the earth, whence he would bring the daughter of his dispersed, may refer to what the Lord has done to Britain and Ireland, with other remote parts of the earth. (5.) This change which was wrought upon the earth by the call of the gentiles, was so great and astonishing, that were it still in the promise, and not yet fulfilled, it would stagger our faith how it should ever come to pass; for it could not be effected without an extraordinary power, if we consider, [1.] The swift progress which the gospel had then; how it ran through the furthest parts of the earth, and like lightning broke forth from one place to another, so that, in the Apostles' time, the Scripture shows that most of the conspicuous provinces of Asia had received the gospel; Parthia, Media, Armenia, Phrygia, Cappadocia, Pontus, and Pamphylia, with much of Egypt, and different parts of Africa; besides Rome, Spain, and other places of Europe, were in Tertullian's time almost wholly Christian. It is indeed clear that the bounds of the church were then of a large extent. [2.] In that solemn day of the gospel's spread amongst the nations, suffering and persecution all the time attended the church; yea, in such a measure, that neither famine, pestilence, nor the sword, destroyed so many of the world, as the persecution of the church. The swift spreading of the church was most discernible in times of hottest persecution, for upon her beginning to flourish with external peace, conversion was at a visible stand. [3.] If we consider the many different languages that then prevented correspondence between the church and the rest of the earth, how could the truth spread among the nations; yea, in such remote places of the world, churches be planted by the Apostles, and have the Scripture translated and made legible to them, without that extraordinary gift of tongues, given for that end from the Lord? [4.] In a short time the gospel enlightened and put a lustre on the most rude and savage places of the earth, where humanity had scarce been, and brought them from the condition of beasts to men, tamed and civilized the greatest barbarians, and caused the lion to lie down with the lamb; yea, these were the results of that gospel, and of that crucified Christ, to the Jews a stumbling-block, and to the Greeks foolishness. The nations were thus led from their old way, and from the religion in which they and their fathers had been so long rooted, and a little spark which broke out in Judea, brought down the idols of the nations, and burned up their temples.

Alas! that there is so little of that primitive zeal and fervour this day among Christians for the enlargement of the church! O that in those parts where the truth is known and professed, the Lord would raise up men of such a spirit, who would make it their work, and lay down solid grounds how to advance the kingdom of Christ in the dark places of the earth, and who would reckon their interest in a foreign plantation upon the account of the gospel, no less than on the account of trade!

9. The destruction of Jerusalem, and ceasing of the Jewish daily sacrifice with the rejection of that people, Dan. xii. 11 ; Matt. xxiv. 2, has many ages past been fulfilled. (1.) This is a truth which needs no other witness than the scattered remnant, and desolate ruins of that once flourishing nation of the Jews, whose present state is so great a monument of Divine judgment, so clear a witness to the Scripture, that I think men cannot look thereon, without the conviction of the finger of God. (2.) What has befallen this people may be an astonishment to the world in all ages ; a stroke that has put them in a more sad condition than any nation we ever yet heard of; that cast them out of their own land, scattered them as vagabonds through the earth, so that for many ages they have had no sceptre nor lawgiver, no part of the earth they can call their own, no privi-

lege or liberties, but a naked permission to keep
their lives and estates during the pleasure of those
under whom they get shelter; a people put by
themselves, with a visible mark of Divine wrath
upon them, like a beacon set up for all the nations
to look on, though once eminently owned of the
Lord, who was known in their palaces for a refuge. Surely Ammianus Marcellinus, a heathen
writer, intended no testimony to the Christian
cause, in relating that the Jews, by Julian's permission, attempted to build the temple again, but
a fire breaking up from the foundation thereof, destroyed many of the workmen, and forced them
with much terror to desist! (3.) It must be some
dreadful provocation beyond the sin of their fore-
fathers, at which so unusual a stroke points. Notwithstanding their frequent idolatry, and their of-
fering up their children to Moloch, and setting up
altars in the groves, rejecting the message of the
prophets, and thrusting some of them in a dungeon, yet they were only punished with seventy
years' captivity, and were afterwards by God's
very immediate hand brought back again, they
who had taken them captive concurring with them
to rebuild the temple. But now how long and
dark has their night been; and though they cannot
for these many ages charge themselves with idolatry, yet no Saviour or deliverer has been raised
up, no prophet sent forth, no sign or appearance
of relief for these 1600 years;* yea, amidst the
frequent changes and revolutions in the world,
there has been no change in their condition! Sure
if that people were on speaking terms with their
consciences, this might put them to a strange de-

* Now eighteen hundred years.—ED.

mur to know, what but the killing of the Messiah can have caused so long, so sore, such an unusual and unheard of stroke! (4.) It is also a singular providence of God that they, who of all the world are most violent enemies to the Christian truth, are also a most convincing witness to the same, whilst, [1.] they clearly attest the Scripture, the Divine authority of Moses, and of the prophets, the true copies whereof they most tenderly preserve; yea, durst never offer in the least to vitiate, but have transmitted them still from one age to another: to which records, the Christian church can with much confidence appeal and demonstrate from the Old Testament the undoubted truth of the New. The Scripture is therefore no imposture of Christians, being witnessed even by the greatest adversaries and maligners of the Christian religion. [2.] The strange hardness of heart of the Jews, who after so long a time cannot see the cause of their rejection. Truly, there is nothing in their judgment more strange and astonishing, than their continued obstinacy against the truth, and their being dark in the noonday; but herein, the Scripture is fulfilled, so that we may even turn a poison into an antidote.

10. That which is so expressly foretold in the New Testament; yea, is the great drift of the prophecies thereof—the coming of antichrist, and revealing of the man of sin to the world, 2 Thess. ii.—has long since been accomplished; and the corresponding of the event with the prophecy is so clear, that this truth is now as obvious, as once it was dark to the church. (1.) The Spirit of God in the Scripture has been in a more than ordinary way particular to point antichrist forth, by such marks that after ages may know him. I con-

fess, it is not strange the popish party should forbid the ordinary reading of the Scripture, since that light would soon make their kingdom dark; for, if men would but compare the history of the church since the times of the apostles with the Scripture, it would be easy to know that antichrist is come. And herein does the Lord's tender respect to his church appear, that he not only, in a very solemn manner, forewarns men of this great trial, but also makes so clear a discovery of the whole fabric, rise, and progress of that party, with such particular circumstances and different characteristics from any other enemy of the church, as may render the world most inexcusable, if they will needs dash themselves against that rock, whereon the Scripture hath set so conspicuous a beacon. (2.) It is sure, that the mystery of iniquity began to work even in the times of the apostles, and that which then for a time withheld his coming—the heathen empire of Rome—has long since been taken out of the way. Besides, we find the church's trial from antichrist should be the most sore and lasting trial under the new testament, being, after her breathing from heathenish persecution, to continue for many ages. The rise and fall of this enemy was to be gradual, and might be traced to the first times of the church, and his close and final ruin near the second coming of Christ, by the brightness whereof he shall be destroyed. (3.) Such a one as the Scripture points forth, who most fully answers to all the marks given of antichrist, has been revealed to the world; a thing so very manifest, that except men will force their consciences, it cannot but be beyond question. Such a one, whose coming should be after the working of Satan, with all power, signs, and lying wonders; forbidding to marry, and commanding to abstain from meats which God had appointed; who sitteth in the temple of God, having a name full of blasphemy, and exalts himself above all that is called God; who bewitcheth the kings and great men of the earth with his enchantments; yea, may be known even by his livery of scarlet and purple; in a word, such a one whose traffic and merchandize is not only gold and silver, but the souls of men; who should be drunk with the blood of the saints and martyrs of Jesus Christ, under whose reign the church must fly to the wilderness and there be latent for a long time; and his seat, the city situated upon seven hills, even that great city which rules over the kings of the earth. O strange, that men can acknowledge this for the Scripture of God, and yet not see in this portraiture of antichrist the peculiar characters of the Pope and the popish hierarchy, such as can answer to no other adversary which Christ ever had under the new testament, either Pagan or Mohammedan! (4.) No age since antichrist was revealed altogether wanted some witnesses, many of whom loved not their lives unto the death, that they might seal this truth; and it may be a question, if more of the blood of the saints was shed under the heathen, than in after times under antichrist. Yea, though we had not such express marks to discover him from the word, it were easy for men to judge who that is who is so directly opposite to Jesus Christ and the great design of the gospel, who assumes to himself what is alone due to God—to forgive sin, and be worshipped with religious adoration; who challenges a magisterial power and supremacy over the whole church as its head, a style too great for any of the angels; who makes void the merit of Christ, and lays down a way of life and salvation on the same terms that it stood in the covenant of works; who destroys the great intent of the gospel, and, in effect, denies Jesus Christ to have come in the flesh; who sets heaven upon sale, and permits none to perish and go to hell, but the poor; who dispenses with the grossest acts of sin, and the express commands of the Lawgiver; makes moral prohibitions void by his authority, yea, hallows the most horrid acts of uncleanness; who takes on him to change the condition of the dead, and insure to their friends the happy state of their souls, if they will make large offerings on that account. (5.) The hardness and blindness of the popish party is no less strange than that of the Jews; whilst the one confesses the Old Testament, and yet knows not Christ, the other grants the truth of the New Testament, and knows not antichrist. I profess, in these latter times, I cannot see how one can be a knowing papist and not an infidel also, for the following truths appear convincing:— [1.] There is a full and particular discovery in the Scripture of this great adversary, in his rise, growth, reign, and fall, by the apostle, 2 Thess. ii. 3, 4, and by John in the Apocalypse; yea, we have through the whole revelation most clearly discovered what he should be, and what a sore and long trial the Christian church was to have under his reign. I profess when I read the Scripture, and there see so express and clear a forewarning, which many ages before we have concerning the coming of this adversary, with such peculiar distinguishing circumstances and marks, as are at this day most exactly verified in the event, I am constrained to admire the convincing and unanswerable witness to the Scripture's divinity, and to think it strange how men can wrestle against the truth, except by getting a victory over their conscience, whilst they own these prophecies of the New Testament to be of Divine verity, and yet evidently distort them against their clear sense and meaning; yea, adventure such a commentary on them as manifestly destroys the text. [2.] Can you possibly expect antichrist's coming to the world now, if he be not already revealed, when his forerunners were even in the times of the apostles preparing his coming? If this adversary should this day begin to appear, could you reconcile the contradiction of the present rise of him who was beginning to discover himself 1500* years ago? For it is so long since the apostle showed this mystery of iniquity was working, 2 Thess. ii. 7; clearly pointing at antichrist who then was hatching. Can he be yet latent, yet in the bud; has there been no further advance after so many ages; has this mystery yet not wrought itself above ground? O where has he been, that such a working thing, so dreadful a spark, could keep so many ages under ashes, and no flame nor fire be perceived? For it is sure if he were then at work he has not yet ceased. Yea, if you admit the Scripture, the rising of the Turkish empire, in the order of the trumpets is clearly after the revealing of antichrist; and this horrid scourge is held forth, Rev. ix. 20, as a remarkable judgment from the Lord on the Christian world (then turned antichristian) for their idolatry, worshipping of images, &c.; abominations not brought into the church till the man of sin was towards his height.

* Now 1700.—ED.

[3.] Is not this manifest, that he who withheld, and restrained antichrist's coming, for a time, cannot now be standing in the way? The Scripture shows expressly there was a bar to be removed, and then was this man of sin to be revealed; and it cannot be doubted that some temporal power was meant which then forcibly withstood, as the original word κατεχων imports; for whilst the Roman empire was heathen, antichrist could not rule in Rome, or as a monarch have his seat in the city with seven hills; he could not then sit in the temple of God, and have the kings of the earth to give their power to him. But can any such bar be yet standing after so great, yea, such innumerable changes of the world? There have been such various successions of states and kingdoms, and such decays of greatest families, that temporal power existing in the days of the apostles cannot exist now in the world. [4.] Can any other party be found to whom all the marks of antichrist held forth in the Scripture do truly agree? O will you be so much in earnest with your conscience, as to examine what there is in the prophecies concerning antichrist's coming in the world, which is not now verified in the event? Admit the Scripture to judge therein, whether there is any such particular distinguishing badge and mark held forth in that blessed record for his discovery. which does not plainly agree with the Pope and his followers. [5.] Is there now, or has there been, under the New Testament, another adversary to the church of Christ, to whom these distinguishing characters of antichrist could agree; one who should be no open adversary, but sit in the temple of God under the veil of a friend, with a show of great wonders and miracles, and yet under

that show exalt himself against God? I am sure,
if you would seriously judge, you could not deny
an assent that such a party, whosoever he be,
bears that great badge of antichrist, in exalting
himself against God, who assumes the titles due
and competent to the glorious God and Mediator
alone, of being head and chief doctor of the catholic church, who calls her his spouse, who challenges infinite power by those words, " All power
is given unto me," &c., Matt. xxviii. 18, which
blasphemy that book, entitled "Pontifical Ceremonies," asserts, (lib. i. fol. 36 ;) who assumes authority to bind men's conscience by his law, and
to free their conscience from those laws which are
Divine and unchangeable; who appoints Divine
worship and adoration to creatures by directing
prayers to them; subjects the faith of the church
to the determination of a man, in which, as infallible, all must rest. Now, besides these distinguishing characters which the Scripture so expressly
gives of antichrist, consider the forbidding of marriage, and the distinction of meats, which the apostle holds forth, 1 Tim. iv. 3. You have in Rev.
xviii. 13, a merchandize with the souls of men
pointed out; and can any one be in the dark, who
they are who have such a peculiar traffic by re-
deeming souls for money, and making a sale of
pardons and indulgences of men's souls? In Rev.
ix. 20, the worshipping of idols of gold and silver
is stated as the character of this adversary. This
is both the doctrine and the practice of the Romish
church, as one of the most learned among them
expressly asserts, saying that the images of the
Trinity are not set up for a show, but for religious
adoration. [6.] The dominion of antichrist over
the kings of the earth is foretold, Rev. xvii. 18.

Now this is convincingly verified, and has been for many ages, in the Pope; and I am sure his followers would be loth to deny a thing in which they so much boast. I confess were it not thus foretold by the Scripture we could not think it credible, that the kings and great men of the earth should be in such a measure bewitched, as to enslave themselves and their interest to that party, and yield so strange a subjection under their yoke; it seems so very irrational, yea, like an infatuation, since they cannot but see under what a terror he keeps them by his interdicts, by assuming a power to loose subjects from any tie to their princes, and thus binding and loosing their conscience at pleasure; what interest he has in their counsels by that subtle device of auricular confession; what intolerable homage and service he requires from princes; what vast treasure he draws for support of his hierarchy from those places where he has power; yea, what a visible tendency his actings have to promote a worldly interest, and make the great men of the earth dependent on him; how easily he can dispense with the greatest breaches of the moral law, whilst most cruel and inexorable in anything that copes with his power and supremacy! O how astonishing would this blind devotion of the great to the support of such an interest be, if we had not a clear discovery from the Scripture that this is from the Lord, who has put it in their heart! [7.] Is not that a convincing witness to the Scripture, and a clear argument for the Protestant Reformed church, even that which some so much object against her, that her condition for so many ages was low and abject, whilst the popish interest was resplendent and flourishing; for such a long continued suffering of the church.

under antichrist is expressly foretold : the witnesses
were to be put to prophesy in sackcloth, and the
woman (which is meant of the church) was to flee
to the wilderness, and be there hid; so that you
cannot say that the church and followers of Christ
have been lower in the worst and darkest times
than the world holds them out to be. [8.] Is not
antichrist pointed out in the Scripture by some
proper mark, some visible sign, which his followers
should receive as a distinction from any other
party? Rev. xiii. 16. Let the world judge if the
many strange ceremonies and rites of the Romish
church, their distinguishing signs and badges,
which they so much own and indispensably require
as visible characters of their profession, do not accord with the Scripture herein, and most clearly
verify the same in the event. The world knows
that frequent use, nay, most horrid and idolatrous
abuse, of the sign of the cross, which not only in
a special manner they take as a distinctive badge
of their party from others, by so frequent a crossing, but ascribe also to it an effective and operative
power, and as a charm or magical sign, make use
of it to effect things supernatural, to restrain sin,
and drive away the devil; by this they conjure
spirits, and they wear it in their rings; yea, it is
by them adored and worshipped, and made use
of for the blessing and consecration of all other
things.

11. What was prophesied of the killing of the
witnesses under antichrist, Rev. xi. 3, 7, 8, has
clearly come to pass; for it is manifest, (1.) That
during antichrist's reign, even in the darkest times,
there wanted not some to seal the truth and bear
witness to it, both by open confession and suffering. (2.) During that dark night those who gave

a testimony in behalf of truth against the grievous encroachments of antichrist, were put to prophesy in sackcloth, there being nothing left but to weep over the church's ruins, and witness their detestation of the growing apostasy. (3.) As the prophecy points at some more remarkable persecution which the church was to meet with from antichrist, beyond all it had endured from that adversary in former ages; yea, a special permission from the Lord to that party to vent their rage and cruelty against the saints after the witnesses had finished their testimony, so did the event convincingly verify the same; for, upon the close of antichrist's reign, when the truth began to appear, then this sorest storm of persecution broke upon the church, even in its budding forth. The adversary not only put forth the utmost of his power and rage against the saints, but seemed, in some measure, to bring his cruel designs to pass, which the dreadful massacres in France, Provence, and the valleys of Piedmont, the sore and violent persecution of the church through the Netherlands, under the duke of Alva, and in England by queen Mary, in Germany, after the defeat of the duke of Saxony and landgrave of Hesse, can clearly witness. (4.) This remarkable storm was, according to this prophecy, to be previous to some eminent reviving of the church, which accordingly fell out in the event, like a resurrection of the witnesses from the dead, to the astonishment of the world; so that when the church's enemies thought they had gained their end, and concluded by such persecutions, and particularly by the French massacre, that the Protestant interest was quite ruined, they were forced to see their labour in vain, and the church more eminently flourishing.

Antichrist has not only been revealed, and his kingdom at its height, but it is clear that this day it is on the falling hand, and his ruin is now begun. We have cause to sing that the " winter is past, the fig tree putteth forth her green figs, the singing of birds is come, and the voice of the turtle is heard in our land," Cant. ii. 11—13.

II. *What is yet to be accomplished.*

Having touched a little upon some of the prophecies of the Scripture already fulfilled, I shall now point at the unfulfilled prophecies which concern the church in these last times, whereby we may have a sure demonstration how far the night is spent, and of the near approach of the liberty of the sons of God ; for this would finish the mystery of God, if once that which remains of the prophecies of the word were fulfilled.

These events we have a sure warrant to expect, 1. The full ruin and downfall of Babylon. 2. The conversion of the Jews to Jesus Christ. 3. A solemn day of the church's flourishing, both among Jews and gentiles. 4. The destruction of the Turkish empire, raised up and established for judgment, with which the Lord shall yet reckon for all that Christian blood so unjustly shed, Rev. xvi. 6. 5. The full and last stroke upon Gog and Magog. Then the Lord is at hand, and the great mystery of the prophecies of the Scripture shall then be finished.

I. We have the full ruin and destruction of antichrist clearly prophesied in 2 Thess. ii. 8 ; Rev. xvi. 10, 17. (1.) That this judgment is already begun is now clear, for the Lord has begun to consume antichrist by the breath of his mouth ; and since the first dawning of the light his kingdom has been mouldering down before the word. It is true the church wants not sore conflicts under the vials; and it is the Lord's way to try his people with such various uncertainties, that when things have been most promising, another providence comes, like a cross wave, which seems to drive them as far back as once they seemed to be forward; yet it is sure that antichrist's overthow is advancing, and the work of the Lord for his church's deliverance is going forward. (2.) This is one of the greatest acts of the judgment of God on his enemies, one of the most eminent manifestations of his glory, wherein the appearance of his hand shall be very manifest by this remarkable stroke, that a place shall be made for that glorious house which Christ is to have for himself in the latter days, and which shall be built upon antichrist's ruins. (3.) Though we are to expect the Lord's immediate hand in this great work, which shall be so convincing that all beholders must with fear and astonishment confess that this is God's own work; yet he will therein make use of instruments fitted and chosen for that end, who shall be raised and actuated with a more than ordinary spirit to execute the vengeance of the Lord, even the judgment written. Yea, the kings of the earth, and the race and successors of those who, in former times had given their power to the beast, shall be raised up to hate the whore, and make her desolate. O blessed are they who shall destroy that accursed city, built up with the blood of the saints and martyrs of Jesus Christ! (4.) We have clear ground to believe that Babylon's ruin maketh haste, and the day of the Lord upon her is near, and that the instruments of his vengeance are making ready. One stroke upon that party is already past; antichrist has begun to fall before the word, and must fall further, until that great stroke which shall destroy his seat and lay waste his land, be accomplished. [1.] The many prayers which are now before the throne and which cannot fail of success, wait for this solemn manifestation of the judgment of God ; and the blood of the saints does not cease to cry, yea, it has as loud a cry as ever. [2.] The preached gospel ripens, and helps to make the harvest more white ; and truly if we consider how long the word has been calling on that party to come out of Babylon, and that for these 150* years they have been acting in opposition to so clear a light, to such a solemn call, to so many warnings, yea, to such convincing discovery of the Lord's being against them in very remarkable providences, it shows at what a height their sin is. [3.] That judgment which was to be poured forth on antichrist under the vials, is in a great measure now verified. [4.] The Lord's work is now hastening ; Providence is swift, and makes great advance ; he will cut short his work in righteousness, for a short work will the Lord make in the earth, Rom. ix. 28. [5.] Antichrist and his followers in this day seem to be at an advantage, the Lord's work being as it were at a stand, yea, rather going back. The late visible growth of popery in Britain and Ireland, and so dark an hour upon the Reformed churches abroad, I think is a promising evidence of the near approach of a further stroke on that party ; for it is clear, both from the word and God's ordinary way of procedure, that a sharp storm is usually previous to some remarkable enlargement of the church, a very

* This book was written in the middle of the seventeenth century.

low ebb before the turning of the tide; yea, that every step of her advance whereby she has gained ground on antichrist, has still had some conflict and wrestling going before, and thus the Lord ripens his people by suffering, for such times of mercy: for which time let us pray and wait, when the smoke of that accursed city shall ascend up to heaven, and his people be made to triumph, and sing that song, "Alleluia; salvation, and glory, and honour, unto the Lord our God, who hath judged the great whore; and hath avenged the blood of his servants at her hand," Rev. xix. 1, 2.

2. We have a clear prophecy of the calling in of the Jews, and their conversion to Christ in the latter days, Isa. xi. 15; Rom. xi. 24; Rev. xvi. 12. (1.) This promise does not concern particular persons, but the body and generality of that people, is clear from the Scripture, Isa. xi. 11; Zech. xii. 10; Rom. xi. 25; where it is undeniable that their gathering must be as full and remarkable as their scattering; and as there is no nation so remote whither some of them are not at this day. so the Lord shall assemble the dispersed and outcasts, and bring them back from the four corners of the earth. The apostle expressly shows that it is all Israel to whom this promise points, for though they are enemies concerning the gospel, yet are they beloved for the fathers' sakes, because of the covenant which was made with Abraham and his seed; and truly we have ground also to expect something further than their conversion, even some temporal restitution and re-collection of them as a nation. See Amos ix. 11—15. (2.) This promise must follow the rejection of that people, and must not take place until the fulness of the gentiles be brought in. The apostle held this

forth as a mystery, which the ancient Jewish church could not well comprehend when it was pointed at by the prophets, and even at that time was not understood, which surely could have been no mystery if their conversion had reached no further than the apostle's time ; and it is known how small a number of that people has since been brought·in to Christ. (3.) This great day shall be a very remarkable and solemn time, which will cause astonishment to the nations, and make a wonderful change on the face of the earth ; a time of God's eminent appearance for that people, when his singular respect shall be as manifest as formerly was his great displeasure and anger. There shall be a large pouring forth of the Spirit, even on the body of that people and all ranks ; yea, the converted of Israel shall then see how far the glory of the second temple exceeds that of the first; and the Jewish church shall be a very conspicuous part of Christ's universal kingdom ; eminent for the power and purity of the ordinances, to which others shall look as to an excellent pattern of a purely reformed and glorious church. (4.) Consider how this people are still kept by themselves amidst all their scatterings, not mixed or incorporated with other nations. Great multitudes· of them are in the eastern parts ; yea, through most of Asia, Africa, and in those places of Europe where the Christian church is ; while their land is possessed by a rabble of Turks, under whose yoke they groan ; and though the genealogies of particular families are lost at this day, yet there is still so much sure as to the genealogy of the nation, as distinguishes them from any other people. (5.) The authority of the word should silence all our thoughts how so great a thing shall be brought about; yet we may judge that the fatal stroke upon antichrist will be one means to that conversion, as removing the stumbling-block of idolatry which has so long hardened them against the profession of the gospel. Alas, that the usual deportment of Christians with whom the Jews converse should often heighten their prejudice against Christianity!

3. There are many prophecies which clearly point at a great flourishing and prosperity in the days of the gospel, Isa. lxv. 25; lxvi. 12; Mic. iv. 1, 2.

I confess the event will be the surest commentary, and until this appear men should be cautious that they darken not the counsel of God with any wild fancy, and not aim to be wise above that which is written; yet I think that there are great things laid up in these promises for the church that we cannot now well reach, until the appointed time unveils their meaning. (1.) These promises of the enlargement of the church, point to some particular features of the church's condition common to other times. (2.) This flourishing condition concerns both Jews and gentiles; and the word clearly points to some further increase of the gentile church by the calling of the Jews, and has a peculiar respect to that solemn time of Israel's restoration and antichrist's ruin; so that, as Isaiah and other prophets refer this great flourishing of the church to the days of the gospel, the apostle, Rom. xi., points to a more precise time, wherein this in a larger measure shall be fulfilled. (3.) The Christian church never enjoyed so great an enlargement as these promises import, for persecution and suffering have mostly been her lot; first from the Jews, next from her heathen adversaries, and lastly from antichrist. (4.) The full accomplishment of this promise must answer to that remarkable day of Satan's binding, and the saints' reign with Christ, when the kingdoms of the earth shall become the Lord's; which we find immediately precedes Satan's last loosing, and his going forth to gather his broken forces to that great battle, which is to be very near the end.

We may judge that the Lord will usher in that glorious and everlasting state of the church by some preparative degrees; the latter times are therefore to be reckoned the more blessed, the nearer they approach to the dawning of glory.

Now, in this place, I shall point out some things which, with a safe warrant, we may expect in the accomplishment of these promises. It is very clear they hold forth a great enlargement to the universal church, both of Jews and Gentiles. Particular churches may be in a sad and withering condition, whilst other parts flourish; but these promises seem to point to a day which will concern the saints in all corners of the earth. Some bright sunshine of the gospel is held forth, some remarkable spring tide of the Spirit, which shall be as discernible as the church's low ebb was formerly; a day of the great power of God, in which his presence shall be manifest among his people beyond former times, so that the name of that place shall be called Jehovah-shammah—The Lord is there, Ezek. xlviii. 35. Yea, in that day Christ's visible kingdom shall more eminently flourish, and there shall be a flowing in of the nations with much fervour, accompanied by purer ordinances, a more universal oneness amongst the worshippers of God, a discernible lustre of holiness, Christ's goings full of majesty, and the shout of a king among his people. Though we see no sure ground to expect a time wherein the church militant shall not have trouble and persecution from the world, yet there are clearly intimated a great calm, and a more favourable gale of outward prosperity; yea, this in some longer continuance than in former ages; a day wherein the haters of the Lord shall be made to feign subjection, with much of the countenance and concurrence of magistrates and of the civil authority in behalf of the church; yea, a time of much holy fear amongst the people of God, and of much terror and awe upon his enemies, to which the great works of the Lord shall then effectually contribute.

4. There is a special prediction of Satan's restraint, and of some remarkable reign of the church with Jesus Christ, Rev. xx. 2. This seems one of the most abstruse prophecies of the Scripture, on which there have been many strange thoughts and glosses. I shall only offer some things to be considered, which seem most clear and obvious. (1.) This solemn time of the saints' reign with Christ concerns the militant condition of the church, and must be expected on the earth, not in heaven; for we find immediately after it there is a very sore assault of the devil mentioned as a new trial to the church. (2.) Since the Scripture is the best interpreter of itself, we must understand this rising of the saints and martyrs of Jesus Christ to reign with him, in a figurative sense—in such a sense as that in Rev. xi. 11, to wit, a rising of the witnesses in the same spirit and power. Compare Mal. iv. 5, and Matt. xi. 14, concerning John's coming in the spirit of Elijah. (3.) The greatest enlargement of the church under the new testament until the second coming of Christ, is held forth in the reign of the saints; so that it manifestly points at a more sweet, refreshing interval, remarkable

both in measure and duration beyond all she formerly had, and shows that there is no other such
happy time for the church, till she be triumphant
in heaven ; therefore, it is called the church's reign,
considered comparatively. (4.) This remarkable
time cannot be previous to antichrist's coming, nor
under his advance and growth, since this points
expressly to those who were beheaded for the witness of Christ, and who had not worshipped the
beast and his image, nor received his mark, who
should thus be raised to reign with Christ. But
it very immediately precedes the last assault the
church shall have, upon Satan's gathering the nations to that great battle, and so must concern the
times when the Lord is pouring out his vials upon
the throne and kingdom of the beast. (5.) This
great restraint of Satan is no such absolute binding
as will put the church wholly beyond trouble ; no,
this belongs to heaven, and is there only to be expected ; but the Scripture very evidently shows
that Satan shall not deceive the nations, nor have
his wonted power to darken the face of the church
by any great or universal apostasy during this time;
and it is undeniable, that since the church's rising
from under antichrist, Satan has been thus restrained, and by all his violent assaults he has not fully
withdrawn any one nation which was brought
under the yoke of the gospel, whatever may be said
of poor Bohemia, for this once famous church is
scattered in various other places, where there are
yet considerable numbers ; yea, it is not altogether
without hope that the great Avenger of blood will
yet visit her cruel usage on her persecutors, and
return yet her captivity. I shall but add, that the
resurrection mentioned in the prophecy must be
understood in a spiritual sense, and can be no bodily

rising of the saints, since it is so expressly there
called the first resurrection, to distinguish it from
the second, and is spoken of in opposition to the
first death.

5. Rev. xvi. 12, compared with Rev. vi. 13,
seems clearly to point at the fall and destruction of
the Turkish empire; for this drying up of the river
of Euphrates must relate to that party which in
Rev. ix. 13—15 is raised up from about that river,
a part where the Turk has so considerable a portion of his dominions. (1.) Such a party was
foretold by John, in Rev. ix., and a solemn warning given to the church; the time is also restricted
to the period when antichrist should be at a great
height; yea, the portraiture of that adversary is
most evidently held forth, a cruel, destroying party,
with breastplates of fire; their number is there
said to be that of a very great multitude, which the
huge armies usually brought by the Turk to the
field attest. (2.) It is also expressly declared that
this was in judgment, and for a plague on men for
antichristian idolatry, which then had so much
overspread the earth. It was no wonder, when so
much of the visible church was turned almost brutish in their religion, and from the pure worship of
God was carried after idols of gold and silver, the
work of men's hands, that so brutish and barbarous
an adversary should be sent for a scourge: truly,
as antichrist and the abominations of that party
have been hitherto the hinderance to success against
the Turks, so we are not to expect their fall and
ruin, until the cause be removed. (3.) It is very
clear that such a party was raised up according to
the prophecy, yea, at the appointed time thereof,
who like a mighty deluge overflowed a great part
of the earth, and with strange prodigious success

overran much of Asia, some parts of Africa, and entered Europe to give work to those kings and great men, and be a scourge to them who had given their power to uphold the throne of the beast. (4.) The Lord will as eminently appear in the fall and destruction of this adversary, as in the raising of him up; and by his fall will make way for the accomplishing of his promise concerning the church's further increase, and the calling of his ancient people, to be ushered in by the drying up of that great Euphrates; a miracle as great and as strictly relating to the Jews, as the division of the sea, and making Jordan a dry chaunel for his people to go through.

6. There is yet one great assault which the church shall have before the end, and then her warfare will be near finished. Satan for a little must be let loose, and the perfect victory which the church in the close of time will get over all adversaries, shall be ushered in with a very sharp trial; and once again this ungodly world will show its rage, and rally its broken scattered forces with as much fury as ever, Rev. xx. 8, and then shall the Lord eminently appear, and by one full stroke for ever decide that long-continued war between the church and her enemies; a deliverance which as it will be the last, so one of the greatest that ever the church had; the Lord thus finishing his work of providence by a stately and magnificent close. After this we know no more of canonical Scripture to be fulfilled, but the coming of the Lord, when the poor, tossed, afflicted church shall enter into a triumphant state, above all the violence and oppression of men.

O blessed and long looked-for day of Christ's return to judgment, when the dust of the saints, that for some thousand years past have been resting in hope, shall awake, and this earth and all the glory thereof disappear, like a poor vain show! O blessed and comfortable time, in which the saints shall then fully know what that heaven is, which they have so often admired at a distance; behold his face in whose presence is fulness of joy, and need no further confirmations of the word, when once this great promise of the Lord's return is verified!— a promise, wherein all the precious truths which concerned the church in her journey, as so many streams, shall empty themselves in this great deep. Then there is no more to do, the work of the gospel is finished, the redeemed are all brought in, and the bride is made ready to go forth to meet him, who shall fully satisfy and comfort his people according to the days of their former affliction, and be for ever their exceeding great reward.

## THE FIFTH ARGUMENT TO PROVE THE FULFILMENT OF SCRIPTURE.

ARGUMENT V. That the Scripture not only is for the most part already accomplished, but is a thing whereof we have sure confirmations, yea, a great pledge in our hand from the Lord, that what yet remains shall be certainly fulfilled.

I shall here point at some grounds whence we may be thoroughly confirmed in this belief.

I. The being of the world, yea, the heavens and the earth, with the continued course of nature, are given from the Lord as a witness to his truth. When we look upon the heavens or the earth, we may there read a visible seal of the certain performance of the whole Scripture of God : this is clear in Jer. xxxiii. 20 ; the covenant with the day and the night is there given to the church to confirm the covenant between the Lord and his people: so also in Jer. xxxi. 35, "Thus saith the Lord, who giveth the sun for a light by day, and the ordinances of the moon and of the stars for a light by night, if these ordinances depart, then the seed ,of Israel also shall cease from being a nation." It is also clear from Psa. lxxxix. 2; "Thy faithfulness shalt thou establish in the very heavens." And these are given as a special pledge, to confirm the faith of his people in the performance of his word. The rainbow, also, in Gen. ix. 13, is given as a visible sign of the covenant of God, to seal unto men the assurance of his word and promise.

I think it strange, that we do not consider this world, and look on the frame thereof, with more astonishment; yea, that we do not think seriously whence it is, and how it came to have a being. Let us suppose that one were brought forth into the light from a dark place, where he had never seen it before, and let his eyes wander a little upon the heavens and the earth, what a dazzling and amazing sight would it be! But though we look on these objects every day, we know not how to read or understand what is written therein; this great universe is for the most part as a sealed book.

There are two things we should consider. 1. That these visible heavens and earth are the very work of that God, whose word we have in the Scripture; for otherwise there can be no reasoning from them to the truth of his word. 2. The pledge contained in them for confirming our faith in the Scripture, and of the sure performance of all that is to be accomplished.

1. As to this, it might seem unnecessary so much as once to mention it, since it is so little questioned; but it is too clear, that many truths

are easily admitted which are not really believed.
I know the world would find it hard to shun so
manifest a demonstration, that this universe is the
work of the great God, when there is in it so
bright a discovery of infinite power and wisdom;
and truly it is strange, how men can admit its
being, who deny its beginning; which not only by
faith we understand, but is most evident from solid
grounds of reason; and though men are undone
with a mere implicit faith and a common assent to
the greatest fundamental truths, without any solid
persuasion thereof, yet the greatest atheists cannot
keep from the discovery of this, except by keeping at a distance from it. Aristotle, and others of
the ancients, did not so much deny the fact, as
doubt of the manner of its commencement. Thence,
Epicurus, and others of his followers, finding they
could not solve the phenomena of nature, and shun
unanswerable absurdities, if they admitted an eternity of the world, fell on the irrational fancy of the
fortuitous concourse of atoms; yea, some believed
an eternal pre-existence of the first matter; which
pitiful notions may show the sad case which men
are in, who grope after the truth by the twilight of
nature, and are strangers to the Scripture. But I
leave this, and shall only touch some most clear
and satisfying evidences of the beginning and original of the world. (1.) If you confess there is
a Deity, you must necessarily admit a creation and
beginning, since eternity is a thing that is only
communicable to the first cause, and you cannot
conceive that the earth could produce itself; for to
exist and not to exist at the same time is a contradiction. (2.) You cannot deny that there is such
a thing as a beginning of time, since there is no
judging of days, years, and ages to be infinite, or

how one thing in a continued order should go before another, without coming to some first and beginning. (3.) The gradual advance of human
knowledge in the earth, and the continued improvement in the arts and sciences, witness very clearly
a beginning and original of the world; for you
cannot conceive a perpetual succession of mankind,
with a constant essay after further knowledge, with
such a continued progress in experience as an eternity would produce, and yet the most useful arts
and sciences, yea, the choicest experiments and
inventions we have in the world, so late in their
rise and date; such as the use of printing, and of
the mariner's compass by the load-stone, the improvement of minerals in medicine; yea, the very
motion of ·the blood in man's body, all which are
but of late discovery. (4.) The short history
which we have of the world witnesses its late original, and that it is not of eternal duration, since
the most ancient records of time do not exceed
some thousands of years; and can it be possibly
conceived that infinite ages preceding, if such had
been, should give no account nor leave a remembrance to posterity, when these late ages give so
much? (5.) The rise and increase of nations,
and the advance of a great part of men from a
rude and savage estate into society, under laws and
government, are facts well known from records.
(6.) You cannot judge that men have begotten
each other eternally, without going back at last to
some first man, who could not beget himself. (7.)
It is manifest what an· increase a few men may
have in an ordinary way, to people a vast country
even in some· ages; now, if you suppose that
every age in this eternal duration should but add
to the race of man two or three, it would come at

last to this, that the earth could not bear them; since we must thus suppose some infinite increase from an infinite continuance of the world, which no wars or consuming strokes could in any considerable degree diminish. (8.) Can you conceive that should be eternal which is wholly made up of corruptible and perishing things; for it is evident that the things of the world have all their set times and seasons, wherein they appear and are quickly gone?

2. Having premised these few evidences of the original of the world, I shall now show how great a pledge this is to the faith of the godly, that the Scripture must have an accomplishment. (1.) That the world now is, is a sure and confirming witness to its last close, and of the accomplishment of that promise of its dissolution. It is not long since there was no earth, nor sun, moon nor stars; now, upon no less security than that word by which it was formed, we must believe it shall ere long cease to be what now it is, and thus, when we look upon the world, and see such a thing before us, we ought to read that promise of its after-dissolution clearly written thereon. (2.) It is a very clear consequence, that God can bring his word to performance, and his power therein cannot fail, yea, that his counsel has no dependence on means or instruments. We truly mistake the meaning of the heavens, with the marvellous order of the great celestial bodies, when we cannot read the faithfulness of God in all his promises written there, for they are held forth to men as a confirming pledge of the same; this were indeed an excellent improvement of astronomy. (3.) Since it is undeniable that this earth hangs in empty space, supported by a marvellous Divine power, and so

established that it cannot be moved, there is clear ground for adventuring of the church with its weight, and every Christian's burden whatever it may be, on the promise of this God, on whose word the great bulk of the earth leans ; no mathematical demonstration follows by a clearer evidence, than this consequence from such premises. (4.) We see that the Lord keeps covenant with the day and the night, yea, the summer and winter do not fail, according to his promise; and these are a visible witness for God, that his truth and covenant with his church shall not fail. (5.) The Lord clearly witnesses by the strange contrariety amongst the elements, and the different qualities whereof he serves himself in this great frame and component parts of the world, that this promise shall not fail; but it is easy for him to make all things work together, were they never so opposite, and disagreeing among themselves, for the accomplishment of his design. (6.) When we see the rage and violence of the great ocean bounded by a bank of sand, for which there could be no reason given but the faithfulness of God, who by a perpetual decree has thus bounded it; is there not thence a visible confirmation of his truth that he can also restrain the rage of men, and turn it to his praise, and for this end serve himself by most improbable means ? It was a notable saying of a grave minister of Christ, when he was upon the sea in a storm, " Shall I fear the face of a tyrant, I who serve Him who can restrain and tame the rage of this swelling sea ?" (7.) If we consider the earth and its original, and look aright on that so often repeated discovery of the seed time and harvest, and of the earth bringing forth such innumerable kinds of vegetables in the spring after a dead winter, as out of their graves—may we not thence have a very clear confirming seal of that great truth, of the resurrection, and of the raising of the dust of men's bodies buried under the earth? Does not God thus set before our eyes the continued course of nature, to assure us that his truth shall not fail, though there were no appearance how in an ordinary way it could be accomplished?

II. The ground whence we may be confirmed in our faith is, that not only the most part of the Scripture is already verified in the event, but also, that those truths which of the whole Scripture are most strange and marvellous, yea, which would have staggered our faith if they were yet still in the promise, are this day accomplished. I shall only instance the coming of the Messiah, that God should be manifest in the flesh, and a virgin bring forth a son whose name should be Emmanuel, one that was to die, and be cut off out of the land of the living, not for himself, but for the transgression of his people. This is the most astonishing thing that ever was or shall be, and should fully silence our thoughts respecting any other Scripture truth ; for we know that the great business of redemption is closed, the ransom fully paid, the doctrine of the gospel sealed and attested by blood, even by the blood of the Testator ; the promised Messiah has come, and this is he who in the days of Pilate suffered at Jerusalem, in whom all things which were written by the prophets were truly accomplished. Is not this a great pledge to assure us of the fulfilling of every other promise? It is sure he died, his blessed side was pierced with a spear, and upon the cross he cried with a loud voice and gave up the ghost. Here lies the greatest cause of wonder, not what yet remains of the Scripture, but that which is already fulfilled; not that Christ should come again to judge the world, but that once he came to the world, and became man; for God to be found in the form of a servant, and die, this is beyond expression wonderful! For the other must necessarily follow as a consequence, that he who has redeemed the church, and paid her ransom, should see the travail of his soul, and be satisfied; that having made such a purchase, he should also have possession and finish the building, the foundation whereof was his own blood. I confess what we yet expect are great and astonishing truths, even the final overthrow of antichrist, the resurrection of the Jewish church, but specially Christ's return to judgment. How great soever they are, yet how small comparatively are they with that which is already accomplished—the incarnation of the Son of God! a mystery hid from ages, whereon the angels with wonder look! This is unspeakably greater than to create this world, and turn it again to nothing. Is it not this day much more easy to believe the Scripture, and the fulfilling thereof, than it was for the Jewish church before Christ's coming? And may we not with as much assurance wait for the second coming of the Lord, and a full perfecting of his word, as for the return of the sun after it is gone down, and for the breaking of the day when once the night is past?

III. The ground of confirmation is this, that Jesus Christ is come to action against the enemies of his church; yea, that he is now gone forth in the greatness of his strength, conquering and to conquer.

It is true, the church is now low, and the work of God meets with very sad interruptions, needful both for trial and rebuke; but this also is sure, that the Lord has eminently appeared, and done great things for his church; yea, he has, by a confluence of very remarkable providences, thus condescended to strengthen his people's hands, to confirm those who are ready to stagger on account of the greatness of those things promised.

For consider, 1. How very consonant it is to the Scripture, that in the last times the Lord will thus appear in his great strength and set up his standard against his adversaries; yea, will then, in a special way, call forth his people to glorify him by an active testimony. 2. That the Lord has thus begun to appear is a truth undeniable, and should much help to confirm our faith.

1. That this is manifest from the word, observe, (1.) That though the church militant will ever have some persecution from the world, even in her best estate; yet we have a safe warrant to expect that the Lord will glorify himself in a peculiar way in his people in those latter days, by doing and acting for the truth as in former ages. (2.) In the last days, when Christ is to raise his church from under the power of antichrist, he shall appear in a warlike posture, Rev. xix. 13—15. He is represented as one at the head of his forces, with his vesture dipped in blood, to show that when the war is begun against his adversary, and this Lion of the tribe of Judah begins to rouse himself up, he will have a terrible appearance in that undertaking. The Lord has declared in his counsel, that his Son, Christ, should in the latter times take unto himself his great power and reign, Rev. xi. 17; yea, God will cause the world to know him as Head of principalities and powers, as well as of his church; for his glory as a King, which former ages seemed in so great a measure to darken, must then clearly

shine forth. (3.) The Scriptures point at the last times as that special time of recompense for the controversy of Sion, to which the Lord has reserved a solemn triumph of his justice, when he shall inquire for the blood of his saints shed upon the earth since the days of Abel, at Babylon's hand, Rev. xviii. 24; for that great adversary has made herself heir to all the violence and cruelty done in former ages, and in her hand must that cup be found full, which the enemies of the church from the beginning have been filling up. (4.) In the last times, when the Lord shall bind up the breach of his people, and heal the stroke of their wound, who for so long a time have been trampled under by antichrist, he shall by some signal providences roll away this reproach and scandal of meanness, contempt, and persecution, and shall put some glory on his church proportionable to her former abasement; yea, comfort her according to the days wherein he had afflicted her, and cause his people's rising to answer in measure and kind to their low and suffering state from antichrist. In the last times the Lord shall make them appear with the face of a lion; the feeble shall be as David, and as the angel of the Lord, Zech. xii. 8, which promise clearly points to the church's rising and delivery from antichrist. (5.) The Lord shall gloriously appear in bringing his church out of Babylon, and in executing his judgment on that adversary, as in the day when he brought his people out of Egypt; and therefore shall they sing the song of Moses and the Lamb, Rev. xv. 3; his great power and outstretched hand being no less discernible therein, than if they had been standing with Israel at the Red Sea when they saw their enemies lying dead upon the shore.

2. That the Lord has thus begun to appear to the world in these last ages is a thing very easy to demonstrate; for, (1.) In these last times he has met his enemies upon their high places, and in their greatest strength; by a strong hand he has made room for his truth, when both law and force withstood the same, and made the marks of his wrath, on those who would oppose the spreading of his kingdom, as visible as was their rage and violence against the church. Yea, since the Lord began to lift up a standard for the truth, and call forth his people to act, they have lost their ground more by underhand treaties, and turning aside to carnal politic shifts, than by open force, which the French massacre,* with other sad instances, can witness. (2.) By what dreadful shakings and alterations of the earth the late glorious Reformation of the church from antichristianism has been ushered in! Has not the Lord caused the nations to shake, and the earth to reel like a drunken man, to show men that, though he suffered long in the former times of the world's ignorance, he will not now bear an opposition to his truth? (3.) That universal deluge of blood, which for a hundred years past† has overflowed Europe, is a witness that the Lord has taken peace from men who would not embrace the peace of the gospel; and has given his enemies, who had shed the blood of the saints, blood to drink in great measure. Germany was for twenty years together a field of dead men, and France from the days of Henry II., to the establishment of Henry IV. How long were the Low Countries made a stage of war, where many a

* Of Bartholomew's day.
† In the seventeenth century

cruel Spaniard fell under the sword of an avenging God; besides the late bloody wars in Britain and Ireland!

How wonderfully has the Lord appeared in delivering his church at the greatest extremity, turned his enemies' counsels and designs upon themselves, brought about the great works of these last times, by means so unexpected, that his judgment already executed against antichrist has been no less marvellous than that Jericho's walls should fall at the sound of trumpets of rams' horns, or a cake of barley bread tumbling into the host of Midian should smite and overthrow it!

IV. The ground to confirm the faith of the saints in the full accomplishing of the Scripture is, that the prophesied victory which the church shall have over antichrist is not only begun, but in a great measure advanced.

We wonder at the greatness of the things promised; but why should we not also wonder at that which God hath already done for his church in our days? The Scripture shows that antichrist's ruin must begin by the word, that this stroke shall be gradual, and though that great work of God shall meet with much opposition, yet it shall no more go back.

Now, consider, 1. How far the church's victory over antichrist is advanced. 2. How the Lord's very immediate hand has been most discernible therein.

1. The first I need but name, for we have seen kingdoms and nations subject themselves to the truth, the kingdom of antichrist grow dark with the breaking in of the light, and many of his followers made to gnash their teeth, being scorched with the heat and power of the gospel. In how

great a measure is that interest now shaken in Britain and Ireland, through much of France, Germany, Sweden, the Low Countries, Poland, Den-
mark, yea, even in Hungary and Transylvania!
That antichristian empire, contrived with such wisdom, underpropped with so great strength, whose
commands, not long since, were received as oracles, with an awe and respect only due to God,
has in a wonderful measure begun to fall before the
power of the word. An adversary has been overcome, whose little finger has been sorer than the
loins of all who went before, if we consider his
cruelty over men's bodies, his tyranny over their
conscience, and the long continuance of that trial;
in respect of whom it may be said, Pharaoh was
an easy taskmaster, Antiochus and the Roman em-
perors mild; he having for near 1200* years carried
on a desperate and bloody war against the church.

2. How the Lord's hand and an extraordinary
providence has been no less discernible in this late
rising of the church, and her begun victory over
antichrist, than in the first planting of Christianity
by the apostles.

The *first* witness to this truth is, that wonderful success which the gospel has had in these last
times. For, (1.) From what a small spark did so
great a fire break out, which in a short time put
Europe in a flame, and made so great a change
therein—even Luther's appearance against Tetzel
upon the account of indulgences! (2.) What a
swift progress did the gospel have! We may say
with wonder, Can a nation be born at once? Yet
we have seen many nations and cities in one and
the same age, yea, in less than forty years, brought

* Reckoning to the end of the seventeenth century.

into subjection to the truth. (3.) We have seen religion propagated by martyrdom no less than in the primitive times, and men's efforts to ruin the church, helping its growth. What but a Divine power could thus bring gold out of iron and clay; bring a flourishing church out of ashes, and turn her poison to a preservative? Whilst men were burned for the truth, and for reading the Scripture, their affection also burned in reading the same; but, alas! it is sad that now with our liberty there is a great decay of devotion. (4.) The wise politicians of the world must confess that this late increase of the church is a thing above their reach, contrary to all their rules, and which, in an ordinary way, could not be brought about. (5.) Instruments most unlikely for so great a work, if we judge as men, such as Luther, Zuinglius, Melancthon, Bucer, &c., went forth to confront that power which then made the earth to tremble; a means as unlikely to succeed, as the sending forth of the fishermen to convert the nations. (6.) They were none of the rabbies of the time, whose repute and fame might have purchased easy access for their message; nay, they were loaded with all the reproach which their adversaries could devise, with novelty of doctrine, deceit and falsehood in their dealing, and represented to the world as monsters. Luther was forced to answer a printed relation of his death, which asserted that he was carried away soul and body by the devil. (7.) The message they carried was most opposite to men's carnal inclinations, to the principles they had sucked in from their infancy, to the religion of their fathers; yea, in a word, had no outward encouragements, the whole world seemed to combine against them. Luther at his first appearance was excommunicated by the Pope, and proscribed by the Emperor; and good Melancthon was often made to faint when he thought on the expected opposition; so that, with-out an extraordinary power, nothing could have looked more improbable than their success.

The *second* witness is the sharp assaults which the church met with from a party no less cruel and powerful than any adversary which the church had in the primitive times. No ordinary means was wanting to crush the gospel in its first budding forth; counsel and force, and the authority of law, backed with greatest rage and violence in its exe-cution, yea, the power of the princes of the earth, were put forth to the utmost to withstand this great work of God. (1.) We find a Spanish emperor devoted to the popish interest, more powerful than any who went before, brought in on Germany with the very first breaking out of the light. (2.) The rise of the boors and the German Anabaptist party, who were so gross, and destructive to civil order, looked like a sad concurrence, and a probable means to beget much prejudice against the truth. (3.) The sad overthrow of the duke of Saxony and the landgrave of Hesse, who were such great friends to the church, threatened the very ruin of the Protestant interest in Germany. (4.) The council of Trent, where the popish party had all their politics on foot in a strong combina-tion to ruin the church. (5.) The "interim" of Germany, a most subtle contrivance to divide, and thus break the strength of the Protestants, was also a sore assault, a snare to some and a cause of persecution to others. (6.) The Spanish Inquisi-tion, established through Spain, Italy, and the Low Countries, a horrid cruel engine which attempted to prevent the smallest glancings of the truth.

(7.) The French massacre on Bartholomew's day, where not only the admiral de Coligni, but most of the considerable Protestants through all France, were in a few days cut off; this, with the Catholic league, which quickly followed, was a very strong and formidable combination to root out the Protestant interest. (8.) The taking away of Edward VI. of England, and establishing of a cruel persecutor, Queen Mary, looked like a stroke that would root out the church, and destroy that famous plantation of the gospel in its tender growth. (9.) The grievous difference which, at the commencement of the work of reformation, began between Luther and Zuinglius, about Christ's presence in the sacrament; yea, which came to such a height, and was followed with so great heat and animosity, as seemed calculated to frustrate the work they were about.

The *third* witness is that wonderful patience and resolution of the saints manifested in their greatest sufferings in these latter times; yea, no less manifested than in the sufferings of the primitive church from heathens. Sure no times, even those of Nero, Domitian, &c., can show more horrid, more strange engines of torment and cruelty, than in these last ages the church endured from the popish party, whose savage and barbarous usage of the poor flock of Christ witnesses a cruelty more than human. The number is almost beyond reckoning who in France, Germany, Britain, and the Low Countries, beside other parts, were slain within these 150 years,* for the word of God and the testimony of his truth. It is also known what a Divine and invincible courage and resolution appeared

* This work was written in the seventeenth century.

in the carriage of the people of God under this sore persecution; how they triumphed over their oppressors, and cheerfully met death in its most terrible shape; a thing which the schools of Socrates and Plato, with all their rules, could never reach. (1.) Something more than nature, a resolution above the ordinary rate of men, yea, something much above their natural temper and disposition, often appeared in their most extreme sufferings, and this without the least shadow of affectation. (2.) Many of the most soft and tender disposition, yea, many women, in this late antichristian persecution, endured the greatest torments, and by suffering triumphed over the fury and rage of their adversaries. (3.) The world has been also witness how serious and deliberate the saints were in this; they made suffering their choice, which they could easily have shunned at the rate of yielding something in the truth; but rather than do this they chose to embrace death, and go to the stake for Christ, even when they wanted not most persuading offers to turn them aside. That excellent man in queen Mary's time, Julius Palmer, had not only life, but preferment offered, if he would recant, to which his answer was, that he had quitted his living in two places for Christ, and now was ready to yield his life also on that account. William Hunter, whom bishop Bonner urged with many offers to recant, told him it must be by Scripture, and not persuasions of that kind, for he reckoned all earthly things but dross and dung in respect of Christ; and at the stake, when a pardon by the sheriff was offered upon such a condition, he peremptorily rejected it. Antonius Riceto, a Venetian, condemned for the truth, had an offer to have his life and his patrimony, which was much mortgaged with debt, restored, if he would but yield a little : his son, with weeping, entreated him to accept the offer, but he answered that he was resolved to lose both children and estate for Christ. (4.) Those who were of great repute in the world, and had a large share of outward things to tempt them, did in these times most cheerfully part with them, and prefer suffering for the truth. We may instance those two great witnesses, John Frederick of Saxony, and the landgrave of Hesse, who under that long imprisonment by Charles V., endured many sharp assaults, both by threatenings and offers, without yielding in the least to the prejudice of the truth; yea, on this account the duke of Saxony chose to forego his estate and dignity. Annas du Burg, counsellor of the parliament at Paris, in the presence of Henry II., made an excellent speech in parliament for the Protestant party, and being imprisoned for it, gave up all his honours and interests in the world, and embraced death for Christ. The prince of Conde, at the massacre of Paris, when the king expressly showed him he should die within three days, if he did not renounce his religion, told him, that his estate and life were in his hand, but before he renounced the truth he would quit both. Charles de Zeroton, a Moravian baron of great interest and authority, in the Bohemian persecution quit all his possessions for the gospel, notwithstanding many large offers and persuasions. The duchess of Suffolk, a lady who lived in the fulness of the world, in queen Mary's time quit both estate and country for the truth, and on that account chose a very hard lot in other parts. (5.) Those who had been ready to faint with discouragement, yet at death, showed a marvellous resolution in the extremity of their sufferings, a thing which shows God's very immediate support.  Mr. Glover was cast down, and could feel no joy or comfort after much wrestling, but no sooner did he come in sight of the stake but his soul was filled with the joy and strength of the Lord, which forced him to clap his hands and cry forth to a friend who knew his former discouragement, "O Austin, He is come!  He is come!" and thus cheerfully he went to death.  Thomas Hudson, a choice Christian, who suffered in queen Mary's time,' when at the stake slipped suddenly from under the chain, to the astonishment of the people, but not from fear of death, but from the want of feeling of Christ, which made him full of heaviness; but after his turning aside, and pouring out his soul to God, he returned, as one raised from death to life, crying out, "Now I am strong, and do not care what man can do;" and thus, with much joy, he yielded up his spirit.  Annas du Burg, whom we before mentioned, being through fear drawn to recant, had no rest in his spirit until he retracted the same, and then cheerfully underwent death.  With what marvellous resolution did that excellent man, Dr. Cranmer, put his right hand into the fire, when he came to the stake, and suffer it to burn without shrinking, to punish it for subscribing a recantation which was the cause of so much grief to him!

That marvellous joy and resolution which the saints in these times in their greatest sufferings showed, is well known to the world; for their sufferings were not in a corner, and did not come short of those of the primitive martyrs.  Let us hear blessed Bradford at the stake, speaking to his fellow-sufferer, "Be of good comfort, for we shall have this night a merry supper with the Lord."

Latimer to Ridley; " We shall this day light such a candle in England as I trust shall never be put out." Mr. Saunders: " I was in prison until I got into prison;" and at the stake he cries, " Welcome the cross of Christ, welcome everlasting life." Doctor Farrer to a gentleman who bemoaned his death and the painfulness of it: " If you see me once stir in the fire, believe not my doctrine;" and he stood without moving in the midst of the flame. John Ardley: " If every hair of my head were a man, it should suffer death in the faith I now stand in." Elizabeth Folks, embracing the stake, cried, " Farewell world, farewell faith and hope, and welcome love." The son of Robert Aguires, when he suffered, with his father, for the truth in the year 1556, at Lisle, in the Low Countries, cried out at the stake; " Behold millions of angels about us, and the heaven opened to receive us!" and after he had some time fixed his eyes on heaven, and when the fire was kindled, he said to his father, " Yet a very little, and we shall enter into the heavenly mansion." Mr. Tims, an English minister, in queen Mary's days, thus writes to his friends: " I am going to the bishop's coalhouse, but shall not be long there before I be carried up to my brethren, who are gone to heaven before me in a fiery chariot; follow you after me, where you shall find me singing merrily at my journey's end, Holy, holy, holy, Lord God of Sabaoth." Algerius, an Italian martyr, thus writes from his prison a little before his death: " Who would believe that in this dungeon I should find a paradise so pleasant; m a place of sorrow and death, tranquillity and hope of life; where others weep, I rejoice. O how easy and sweet is this yoke!" And this he subscribes " from that delectable orchard of the Leoline prison." Guy de Bres says, " The ringing of my chain has been sweet music in my ears; all my former discourses were but as a blind man's notion of colours, in respect of my present feeling. O what a precious comforter is a good conscience!" Lord Henry Otto, a Bohemian, who suffered in the late persecution, said to the minister, " I was troubled, but now I feel a wonderful refreshment. O now I fear death no longer, I shall die with joy." And on the scaffold he cried out, " Behold, I see the heavens opened!" and thus died with great cheerfulness. I shall but add the last words of that holy and great man, Mr. Wishart, who thus spake amidst the fire: " This flame doth torment my body, but no whit abate my spirits."

The *ifourth* witness is, the great and remarkable judgments of God, which in these last times have befallen the adversaries and persecutors of the church, most notorious for their opposition to the truth.

This is a subject wherein we should be very serious and sober, for the judgments of God are a great depth, nor can we determine from events, but so far as they answer to the word. It may sometimes happen to wicked men according to the work of the righteous; but, on the other hand, it is a sure truth, that God is known by the judgment he executes; and in every age there are some great examples of judgment, which, as beacons, are set forth for men to observe. And truly these remarkable instances of the judgment of God, since he began to sound a retreat to his church from Babylon, are far beyond other preceding ages. I would be sparing to repeat what is published by others, but I cannot pass in a general manner, whilst there are so many instances wherein the Lord has made himself known ; and I dare with confidence assert that there is not any passage or matter of fact set down here, without clear and satisfying grounds of its certainty.

I shall first instance in Charles V. whose undertakings were followed with success, until he set himself to persecute and oppress the church, and bathed his sword in the blood of the Protestants, from which time his affairs began visibly to decline ; he was forced to fly before Mauritius, and to seek a retreat in the furthest confines of the empire; and, broken with melancholy and discontent, like another Dioclesian, he finally resigned his empire, and turned to a private life.

Philip II., of Spain, one of the greatest persecutors of the church in these last ages, whose work was to root out the Protestant religion in his dominions, and who to that end set on foot the horrid engine of the Inquisition, at last found all his attempts frustrated ; and after the loss of many millions of treasures, of some 10,000 lives by war, and of a considerable part of the Netherlands, and finally by the breaking of his great armada at sea by the English, was at last smitten in his body by a strange disease, or rather a complication of diseases, which his physicians could neither understand nor cure, his body falling out in grievous boils, whence issued such abundance of vermin, that bystanders could hardly endure the horrid smell thereof; and he who had put so many of the saints to cruel torments by the Inquisition, was himself tormented for two years together with inexpressible pain and anguish.

Henry II., of France, a most violent enemy to the church, when he had sentenced Annas du Burg to death, solemnly used these words, "These eyes of mine shall see thee burnt;" but a little before the appointed time of the execution, running in the lists with a spear against count Montgomery, he was pierced through the eye with a wound that in a short time sent him to his grave, and frustrated his expectation of seeing the death of that martyr.

Henry III., who, whilst duke of Anjou, assisted at the horrid council of St. Cloud, near Paris, where the massacre was determined, was some years after stabbed to death by a Jacobin friar in that very chamber; a thing which Du Serres twice mentions as a marvellous instance of the judgment of God.

The duke of Guise, the great executioner of that massacre, and his brother, the cardinal, a special contriver of the same, were not long after killed by Henry III., at Blois, with whom they had often joined in counsel to root out the Protestants; and by a specious show of friendship, and with solemn oaths, were as treacherously circumvented as the Admiral and Protestants were at Paris by Charles IX.; and these, also, who were his great counsellors, had blood measured out to them for blood, and treachery as they had dealt treacherously with the saints.

The duke of Aumale, who was a joint actor with the duke of Guise in that massacre, fell by a shot off the walls, at the siege of Rochelle, which not only Du Serres, but also Davila, who was a warm Papist, particularly relate; where we may see what a bloody end the great contrivers and actors of that horrid massacre had.

Henry IV., a prince of excellent parts and great natural accomplishments, was followed with marvellous success whilst he owned the truth; yet,

after many victories, and the breaking of the Catholic league, turned a Papist, and abjured the Protestant religion, but within a little he was stabbed
in the mouth by a Jesuit; on which a Protestant
gentleman used this freedom with him : " Sir, you
have denied God and his truth with your mouth,
and he has given you there a stroke; take heed
you deny him not also with your heart, lest the
next stroke be there;" which accordingly fell out,
when he was stabbed by Ravaillac through the
very heart; and it was very evident that some time
before his death he had turned zealous for the
Popish interest.

Ferdinand II., a great persecutor of the church
in Germany, after his victory over Frederick and
the Bohemian states, made it his work to root out
the Protestant religion there, and turned that country to a slaughter-house, not sparing any who would
not abjure the truth; but the Avenger of blood
raised up the Swedes for an adversary, who turned
Germany and the emperor's countries into a field
of blood, and broke that great army which for
many years had given law to Germany; so that,
as some historians mention, an army of 24,000
captains, because all old expert soldiers, was broken
in the plain fields with a huge slaughter. Yea, vio-
lenee and cruelty were thus measured out to them,
as they had measured to the poor church of Bo-
bemia and the Palatinate; and Ferdinand was
broken with breach upon breach, that men might
see the judgment of God pursuing a cruel persecutor.

The barbarous Irish, who of late carried on the
horrid massacre there, sparing no Protestant, whatever was their age or rank, without compassion to
women or children, were visibly met by the judg-

ment of the Lord; their chief leaders, Macguire, Machone, and Philomy O'Neale, were taken and publicly executed, and others of them consumed by the sword; their spirits so debased, that a few English or Scotch soldiers would have chased multitudes of them.

Sir James Hamilton, natural brother to the earl of Arran, was, in the time of king James V., supported by the Popish clergy in his vigilance against such as were suspected of favouring the Protestant religion; and truly he was most terrible and cruel against all he could reach: yea, so violent, that some of his near kinsmen were by him brought under the lash of his power: but lo! when at his greatest height, whilst he was making it his work to crush the gospel in its budding forth, he was accused of treason by one of his friends, whom he pursued on the account of religion; and notwithstanding the solicitations of the Popish clergy for him, he was presently arraigned, beheaded, and quartered in the public street of Edinburgh.

The violent persecutors, cardinal Beaton, and his successor, bishop Hamilton, were no less conspicuous instances of the judgments of the Lord in that time. Friar Campbell, who bitterly railed on that excellent man, Mr. Patrick Hamilton, when he was burnt at St. Andrew's, and to whom Mr. Hamilton at the stake in great vehemency said, " Wicked man, thou knowest the contrary, and hast professed the same; I summon thee to answer before the judgment seat of Christ;" within a few days after fell sick, and died in great horror of conscience.

It is known how the judgments of God pursued those three great apostates from the truth, Olivares, chancellor of France, Latomus, and Francis Spira;

who after they had quitted their profession, and denied the truth, died with great horror of conscience, telling the bystanders what a hell they found within them. Du Serres says, that the chancellor of France, through the torment and anguish of his mind, caused the very bed to shake under him.

The *fifth* witness which holds forth the Lord's extraordinary power in the reformation of the church from antichristianism, is, that large measure of the Spirit which convincingly followed the gospel and ministry of the word in these last times.

This is God's own seal, which is not put to a falsehood; thus he bears witness to his work in the hearts of his people, and by this also the Lord attests the doctrine of the church and commission of his servants. Yea, at some special seasons, when the truth has least encouragement from without, when men will not receive its testimony, then has this in a more full and large measure been discernible. Thus did the Lord eminently confirm the Christian religion in the days of the apostles, and for some following ages, by so great a down pouring of the Spirit, by such visible and extraordinary effects, as then astonished the world, and forced men to confess something above nature. And we have also cause to say, that the Lord has borne a very solemn testimony to the work of the Reformation, and the doctrine of the Reformed churches. (1.) The marvellous success which the gospel had in Germany by the ministry of Luther, Melancthon, Bucer, Martyr, Musculus, and a few other excellent instruments, whom the Lord then sent forth, was a day of the Spirit, a day of the gospel's triumph; not, indeed, by might or by power, yet such as before it the world could not stand. Cities and countries might then be said to be born at once; the arm of the Lord so revealed, that men were either confounded or truly gained thereby. That marvellous power and efficacy of the Spirit also attended the ministry of Zuinglius and Œcolampadius, in Zurich, and Basle, when so thorough a reformation followed to the throwing down of images, abolishing of the mass by public authority, notwithstanding of its long continuance, and this accomplished in a short time. The Spirit and power of God very eminently appeared also in these famous plantations of the gospel by the ministry of Calvin, Farel, and Viret, in Geneva, Lausanne, and other adjacent provinces. It is written in the life of Viret, that at Lyons, which was a populous city, he preached in an open place, where thousands were converted to the truth; yea, some who came with no purpose to hear, but stepped in, only out of curiosity, were so wrought on, and overcome with the power of the word, as for that time to neglect their other business. (2.) The great success which attended the ministry of Mr. Wishart in Scotland, can also witness this truth; whence a marvellous change quickly followed in Angus, Lothian, and the western parts: but this being a thing so known from the histories of that time, I only name it. (3.) Besides these which are known, and upon public record, I must here instance a very solemn and extraordinary outpouring of the Spirit which occurred about the year 1625, in the west of Scotland, whilst the persecution of the church there was hot. By the profane rabble of that time it was called the Stewarton sickness, for in that parish it began; but afterwards it spread through much of that country, particularly at Irvine, under the ministry of Mr. Dickson, of which it may be said, (which divers ministers and Chris-

tians yet alive can witness,) that for a considerable
time few Sabbaths passed without some being evidently converted, and some convincing proofs of
the power of God' accompanying his word ; yea,
many were so affected, that through terror and conviction of sin in hearing of the word, they have
been made to fall down, and were thus carried
out of the church. These individuals became
most solid and lively Christians, and some of the
most gross, who used to mock at religion, being
induced, upon the fame that went abroad of such
things, to go to some of those parts where the gospel was then most lively, were effectually convinced and changed. And truly, this great spring-
tide of the gospel was not of a short time, but for
some years' continuance ; yea, the power of godliness advanced from one place to another, and put
a marvellous lustre on those parts of the country,
the savour whereof brought many from other parts
of the land to learn the truth. (4.) At the solemn
communion in Scotland, held on the 20th of June,
1630, there was so convincing an appearance of
God, and down-pouring of the Spirit in an extraordinary way, especially after that sermon on the Monday 21st of June, that I can assert on sure ground,
that near five bundred had at that time a discernible
change wrought on them, most of whom became
afterwards lively Christians. It was the sowing of a
seed through Clydesdale, so that most of the eminent Christians in that country could date either
their conversion, or some remarkable confirmation
in their case, from that day ; and truly this was
the more remarkable, because after much reluc-
tance, by a special and unexpected providence, a
certain individual was called to preach that sermon
on the Monday, which then was not usually prac-

tised, and the night before was spent in prayer by most of the Christians convened together, so that the Monday's work might be discerned as a convincing return of prayer. (5.) That solemn and great work of God in the church of Ireland, about the year 1628, as many grave and solid Christians yet alive can witness, was one of the largest manifestations of the Spirit that has been since the days of the apostles, where the power of God sensibly accompanied the word to the conversion of souls to Christ; as a judicious old Christian there present expressed it, "It was like a dazzling beam and ray of God, with such an unusual brightness, as even forced bystanders to astonishment." A very effectual door was opened, with more than ordinary enlargement in preaching the word, whilst the people attended with much tenderness of spirit. This was a convincing seal to the truth and ministry of his servants then suffering persecution; yea, a thing which had an awful impression on their adversaries. I remember a worthy Christian told me, that sometimes in hearing the word, such an evidence of the Lord's presence was with it, that he has been forced to rise and look through the church, and see what the people were doing; thinking, from what he felt on his own spirit, that it was a wonder how any could go away without some change upon them. It was then sweet and easy for Christians to come thirty or forty miles to these solemn communions, and there continue from the time they came until they returned, without wearying or making use of sleep, yea, but little either of meat or drink; and as some of them professed, they did not feel the need of them, but went away most fresh and vigorous, their souls being so filled with a sense of God. (6.) The period of

1638 was also remarkable, wherein the Lord let forth much of the Spirit on his people, when this nation solemnly entered into covenant; the spirits of men were raised and wrought on by the word, the ordinances were lively and longed after, for then the nation owned the Lord, and was visibly owned by him; much zeal and an enlarged heart appeared for the public cause, personal reforma-tion was seriously set about, and there was a re-markable spirit that attended the actings of his people which astonished their adversaries, and forced many of them to feign subjection. Alas! how is our night come on, for the Lord has in anger covered the face of the daughter of Zion with a dark cloud! (7.) Since the land was engaged by covenant to the Lord in these late times, what a solemn outletting of the Spirit has been seen; a large harvest with much of the fruit of the gospel discernible; which has been proved in the bring-ing thousands to Christ, a part whereof are now in glory, and many yet live who are a visible seal to this truth; of whom I am sure some will not lose the remembrance of those sweet refreshing times which the land for several years enjoyed, when a large blessing, with much of the Spirit and power of God, was felt accompanying the ordinan-ces; if it were expedient to set down circumstances, I could here point at many such remarkable times and places which would clearly demonstrate this.

Besides these more public and obvious proofs, what a great testimony the experience of the godly in these late times could give to this truth! This would indeed make a great volume, but I shall name these only.

Mr. Welsh, and Mr. Forbes, two great witnesses

of Christ in this land, when they were prisoners, gave this account of their case in a letter to Mr. James Melvin and his uncle, then in London, which under the said Mr. Melvin's hand is set down in a manuscript of his. "Dear brethren, we dare say by experience, and our God is witness we lie not, that unspeakable is the joy that is in a free and full testimony of Christ's royal authority, unspeakable is the joy of suffering for his kingdom, (for on that truth was their suffering endured.) We had never such joy and peace in preaching of it, as we have found in suffering for the same; we spake before in knowledge, we now speak by experience, that the kingdom of God consists in peace and joy." And in another letter, "Our joy has greatly abounded since the last day, (which was after passing sentence of death on them by assize at Linlithgow,) so that we cannot enough wonder at the riches of his free grace that should have vouchsafed such a gift upon us, to suffer for his kingdom, in which there is joy unspeakable and glorious; and we are rather in fear, lest they (to wit the sufferings) be not continued, and so we be robbed of further consolation, than that they should increase. Surely there is great consolation in suffering for Christ: we do not express unto you the joy which our God had caused to abound in us."

The letters of that great servant of Christ, Mr. Rutherford, can witness what solemn days of the Spirit, and sensible outlettings thereof, he often had in his experience, though books can tell but little what he really felt and enjoyed. I shall only set down some of his last and dying expressions, which I had from those who were then present, that may show how lovely he also was in death, and how well that corresponded with his former life. "I shall shine; I shall see him as he is, and all the fair company with him, and shall have my large share.—It is no easy thing to be a Christian; but as for me ·I have got the victory, and Christ is holding forth his arms to embrace me.—I have had my fears and faintings as another sinful man, to be carried through creditably; but as sure as ever he spake to me in his word, his Spirit witnessed to my heart, saying, "Fear not." He has accepted my suffering, and the outgate should not be matter of prayer, but of praise.—Thy word was found, and I did eat it, and it was to me the joy and rejoicing of my heart." And a little before his death, after some fainting, he said, "Now I feel, I believe, I enjoy, I rejoice;" and turning to Mr. Blair, then present, he said, "I feed on manna, I have angels' food; my eyes shall see my Redeemer; I know that he shall stand at the latter day on the earth, and I shall be caught up in the clouds to meet him in the air. I sleep in Christ, and when I awake I shall be satisfied with his likeness. O for arms to embrace him!" To one speaking of his labours in the ministry he cried out, "I disclaim all, the port I would be in at, is redemption and forgiveness of sins through his blood." Thus full of the Spirit, yea, as it were overcome with sensible enjoyment, he breathed out his soul; his last words being "Glory, glory dwelleth in Emmanuel's land."

The *sixth* witness is that appearance of an extraordinary and apostolic spirit on some of the instruments whom the Lord raised up in these last times, for the service of the church, and for the overthrow of the kingdom of antichrist.

It is clear that extraordinary gifts have been

given to the church under the New Testament, for with the first dawning of the gospel there were both apostles and prophets raised up; it cannot be denied also that since the canon of the Scripture was closed, yea, in these late ages, there have been very extraordinary men given to the church.

What extraordinary instruments, how wonderfully called and qualified, were Luther, Zuinglius, Calvin, Wishart, Knox, Melancthon, Beza, Bucer, Martyr, Latimer, Ridley, Bradford, &c.! These were burning and shining lights in their time, mighty in the Scripture, fervent in spirit, clothed with the power and authority of God, before whom the world could not stand. But besides these famous witnesses, of whose lives we have something on public record, I must here record a few late instances now but little known to the world; men truly extraordinary, eminently serviceable in the work of the Lord, yea, of a prophetic and apostolic spirit, and who, through grace, not only equalled those before mentioned, but also some of those great lights of the first age of the church.

I shall instance Mr. John Welsh, whom the Lord called to the ministry at Kircudbright, in Galloway, and afterwards in Ayr; whom Mr. Rutherford calls that heavenly, prophetical, and apostolic man of God; and shows that from the witnesses of his life he had this account, that of every twenty-four hours he gave usually eight to prayer, if other necessary and urgent duties did not hinder; yea, that he spent many days and nights in fasting and prayer, for the condition of the church, and sufferings of the Reformed churches abroad. I can also add, from very sure information, that it was his use, even in the coldest winter nights, to rise for prayer; and oftentimes his wife, who was an excellent woman, has risen to seek for him, when he has been found lying on the ground, weeping and wrestling with the Lord, yea, sometimes he would be much of the night alone in the church of Ayr on that account. One time especially, his wife finding him overcharged with grief, he told her he had that to press him which she had not, the souls of 3,000 to answer for, whilst he knew not how it was with many of them. And at another time when she found him alone, his spirit almost overcharged with anguish and grief, upon her serious inquiry, he said, that the times which were to come on Scotland were heavy and sad, though she should not see them, and this in consequence of their contempt of the gospel.

Whilst he was prisoner in the Blacknesse, in a letter to a Christian lady he stated, " what large joy he had, to suffer for such a truth, that Jesus Christ was a King, and had a visible kingdom in the world, even his church; which was as free to keep its courts and exercise discipline, by virtue of an intrinsic power from Christ, as any kingdom on the earth; for which he was ready to lay down his life, yea, would rejoice to be offered up a sacrifice for so glorious a truth."

After his banishment, he, in a very short time, acquired the French tongue, with such a facility therein, as was thought strange by those who knew it. Trochrig, in his commentary on the Ephesians, relates, that Welsh being called to preach at Saumur, a famous university, before one of the most learned auditories in France, preached with as much boldness and authority, as though he were before the meanest congregation; whereat Trochrig asked him, whence he had such confidence and was so little moved in preaching before strangers, to so grave and judicious an auditory, and in a strange tongue; to whom in a humble way, as one more dejected than lifted up, he answered, that when he considered his standing before the Lord, and that he was delivering his message, he could not regard either great or small, but all flesh then went out of his mind.

Whilst he was minister at St. Jean d'Angeli, a Protestant town in France, where his ministry was much blessed with success, the civil wars commenced, when that city was twice besieged; during which time, the town being sore straitened and ready to be taken, the enemies having raised a battery, and made a great breach in the wall, Mr. Welsh, who had much encouraged the people that their adversaries should not then prevail, went himself with the cannonier upon the walls, and desired he would charge such a piece of cannon, and shoot, for God would direct the shot; and accordingly, to the astonishment of lookers on, it dismounted the battery, and the Lord so ordered things, that the king granted the city favourable terms, and only came in with his court without doing any violence. The following Sabbath, some of the godly in that place fearing Mr. Welsh's hazard, seriously advised him that he would forbear to preach, the court being there; from which he by no entreaty would be hindered, but showed them he would adventure to preach the word to his people, and trust the Lord with what concerned himself, being grieved at their fear and despondence. That day he had a very great auditory, both of friends and others, who came upon the fame of such a man, but in the time of sermon, a great man of the court, with some of the king's own guard, were sent to bring him before the king; and whilst he was entering

the church with difficulty, by reason of the multitude, Mr. Welsh turned himself toward that entry,
and desired the people to give way to one of the
great peers of France that was coming in; but
after, when he was come near the pulpit to execute
his commission, by putting force on the servant of
Christ for his desisting, Mr. Welsh with great authority spoke to him before all the people, and in
the name of his master, Jesus Christ, charged him
not to disturb the worship of God; wherewith that
man was so affrighted, that he began to shake; yea,
was forced to crouch down, and make no further
trouble.   Upon the close of the sermon, when Mr.
Welsh with much submission went to the king,
who was then greatly incensed, and with a threatening countenance asked, what he was, and how
he durst preach heresy so near his person, and
carry himself with such contumacy? he answered,
with due reverence, "I am sir, the servant and
minister of Jesus Christ, whose truth I preached
this day, which if your majesty rightly knew, you
would have judged it your duty to have come
yourself, and heard.  I this day preached these three
truths to your people.  '1. That man is fallen, and
by nature in a lost condition; yea, by his own
power and abilities is not able to help himself from
that estate.   2. That there is no salvation or deliverance from wrath by our own merits, but by Jesus
Christ and his merit alone.   3. I also preached
this day the just liberties of the kingdom of France;
that your majesty owes obedience to Christ only,
who is the Head of the church, and that the Pope,
as he is an enemy to Christ and his truth, so also
to the kings of the earth, whom he keeps under
slavery to his usurped power.'"   Whereat the
king, for a time keeping silence, with great aston-

ishment turned to some about him, and said, " Surely this is a man of God ;" yea, he conversed with him afterwards, and dismissed him with great respect. The year following the city was again besieged, taken, and in part sacked, as Mr. Welsh publicly foretold; at which time the king past a solemn order, that none should in the least wrong Mr. Welsh, or anything that belonged to him, under the highest pains, and afterwards gave him a safe-conduct for transporting himself to England, where he died. During his sickness he was so filled and overcome with the sensible enjoyment of God, that he was sometimes overheard in prayer to use these words, " Lord, hold thy hand, it is enough; thy servant is a clay vessel, and can hold no more."

Mr. Robert Bruce was called to the ministry in a very extraordinary way, having for a long time followed the study of the law both in this country and in France; yea, he had some ground to expect a place among the lords of the session, his father being then a considerable baron; but a more press- ing and irresistible call from God otherwise deter- mined.

Whilst he was in the ministry at Edinburgh he shone as a great light through the whole land, the power and efficacy of the Spirit most sensibly ac- companying the word he preached. He was a terror to evil doers; and the authority of God so appeared upon him, and there was such a majesty in his countenance, as forced fear and respect from the greatest in the land, even those who were most avowed haters of godliness; yea, king James once gave him this testimony before many, that Mr. Bruce was worthy of the half of his kingdom.

He was a man that had much inward exercise

about his own personal case, and had been often assaulted respecting that great foundation of truth, the being of a God, which cost him many days' and nights' wrestling; and when he has come up to the pulpit, after being some time silent, which was his usual way, he would say, " I think it is a great matter to believe there is a God ;" telling the people that it was a more difficult thing to believe than they judged.

The great success of his ministry at Edinburgh, Inverness, and other places whither Providence called him, is abundantly known. Whilst he was confined to Inverness, that poor dark country was marvellously enlightened, many were brought to Christ by his ministry, and a seed sown in these places which even to this day is not wholly worn out.

He was deeply affected with the worldliness and profanity of many ministers then in the church, and the unsuitable carriage of others to so great a calling, and expressed much fear that the ministry of Scotland would prove the greatest persecutor of the gospel that it had. If there were a full collection of the remarkable passages which have been known to others in his life, it would further witness what an extraordinary man he was. I shall only conclude with the learned Calderwood's testimony : " Robert Bruce, a man noble by family and virtue, and venerable by a majesty of appearance. He won many thousand souls to Christ, and now, I may say it boldly, his soul is with his master. And truly were it lawful to trust to man at all, I would say, let my soul be with thine, O Bruce !"

Let me also notice concerning that walker with God, great master Bruce. Besides that blessed frame of spirit which appeared in the whole of his converse, he endeavoured, especially whenever he was to appear in public as an ambassador of Jesus Christ, to have his spirit deeply impressed with the majesty of that God of whom he was to speak, and of the high importance it was to the souls of men to have the mysteries of salvation unfolded to them, not with enticing words of man's wisdom, but in demonstration of the Spirit and power; without which, this preached gospel, though in itself the word of life, will never prove the power of God to salvation: and therefore, though he was known to take much pains in searching the Scripture, that he might know the mind of the Spirit of God, by comparing spiritual things with spiritual, and in preparing apposite matter for the edification of his hearers, which he durst not neglect, and wherein he durst not be indifferent, knowing he was to speak of God, and being afraid of the curse threatened for doing his work negligently, yet this was the least part of his preparation work. The main part of his business lay in having his soul wrought up to some suitableness of frame for preaching the unsearchable riches of Christ, and making manifest the mystery of the gospel as he ought, that so his Master by his service might see of the travail of his soul, and be satisfied. And knowing that the success of preaching depended wholly upon the presence of God accompanying the dispensing of ordinances, his manner was to be much in prayer and supplication in private before his public appearances, pouring forth his heart before God, and wrestling with him not so much for assistance to the messenger as the message. One instance whereof take as follows. Having to preach on a solemn occasion, he was long in coming to the congregation, some of the people beginning to be-weary, and others wondering at his stay, the bells being long rung, and the time far spent, the beadle was desired to go and see what was the matter; who, coming to his house, and finding his chamber door shut, and hearing a sound drew near, and listening he overheard Mr. Bruce often with much seriousness say, " I protest I will not go, except thou go with me."  Whereupon, the man supposing that some person had been with him, withdrew without knocking at the door, and being asked at his return the cause of his delay, he answered, he could not tell, " but I suppose," said he, "there is some one with Mr. Bruce, who is unwilling to come to church, and he is so pressing and peremptory to have him come along, that I overheard him protest most seriously, he would not go if he went not with him."   However, a little after, Mr. Bruce came accompanied with no man, but he came in the fulness of the blessing of the gospel of Christ, and his speech and his preaching were in such evidence and demonstration of the Spirit, that by the shining of his face, and that shower of Divine influence wherewith the word spoken was accompanied, it was easy for the hearer to perceive that he had been in the mount with God, and that he had indeed brought with him that God whom he had met with in private.   He preached ordinarily with so much life and power, and the word spoken by him was accompanied with such a manifest presence, that it was evident to the hearers, he was not alone at the work, but that in his strivings to urge the things which belong to the kingdom of God, and to present every man perfect in Christ Jesus, he laboured, striving according to his working who wrought in him mightily.   For though he was no Boanerges as to his voice, being of a slow and grave delivery, yet he spoke with so much authority and weight, that some of the most stout-hearted of his hearers were ordinarily made to tremble; and by having those doors, which formerly had been bolted against Jesus Christ, as by an irresistible power broken open, and the secrets of their heart made manifest, they went away under convictions, and carried with them undeniable proofs, of Christ speaking in him, and that God was with him of a truth.

The other passage which I present thee with, is concerning his death.. Being aged, and through infirmity of body confined to his chamber, where he was frequently visited by his friends, and being asked by one of them, how matters now stood between God and his soul, he, with that sincerity of soul, which is the effect of the love of God shed abroad in the heart, and that full assurance under which such walkers with God, and workers of righteousness as he was, are frequently taken off the stage, made this return; " When I was a young man, I was diligent, and lived by faith in the Son of God; but now I am old, and am not able to do so much, yet he condescends to feed me with lumps of sense."

And the morning before the Lord removed him, he came to breakfast at his table; and having, as he used, eaten an egg, he said to his daughter, "I think I am yet hungry; you may bring me another egg; but instantly falling into a deep meditation, and having mused a while, he said, "Hold, daughter, hold, my Master calls me;" with these words his sight failed him; whereupon he called for the Bible, but finding his sight gone, he said, "Open to me the eighth chapter to the Romans, and set my finger on these words, 'I am persuaded that neither

death, nor life, &c., shall be able to separate us ·
from the love of God which is in Christ Jesus
my Lord.' Now," said he, " is my finger upon
them?" When they told him it was, he said,
" Now God be with you my children; I have
breakfasted with you, and shall sup with my Lord
Jesus Christ this night;" and so gave up the ghost,
death shutting his eyes that he might see God.
Thus that valiant champion for the truth, who in
his appearing to plead for the crown and interest
of Jesus Christ, knew not what it was to be daunt-
ed by the face and frowns of the highest and most
incensed adversaries, was by his Master taken off
the field as more than a conqueror; and as the reward of much faithful diligence about the souls of
others, and much pains and seriousness about
making his own calling and election sure, had "an
entrance ministered unto him abundantly into the
everlasting kingdom of our Lord and Saviour Jesus
Christ."

The following relation is translated from a letter
of the famous Rivet, printed since his death in the
French tongue. James Faber, a most faithful and
eminent minister of the gospel in Picardy, in the ·
persecution of that time, fled for security to the
queen of Navarre, then in Albert, in Gascony,
who held him in high esteem. On a certain day
the queen apprized him, that she purposed to come
and dine at his house, and for that end invited some
learned men, in whose conference she took much
delight. At dinner, Faber became exceedingly
sad, and now and then fell out in bitter weeping;
at which the queen complained, and inquiring the
cause why he wept, when she had come to be
merry with him; he said, " Most serene queen,
how can I be glad, or make others glad, who am

as wicked a man as the earth bears?" "And what," says she, "is that wickedness you have committed, who are known from your youth to have lived so holy?" He answered, "I am now the age of an hundred years, and remember not that I have committed what would burthen my conscience, or make me afraid to leave the world, except one sin, for which I am assured propitiation is possible. How can I stand before the throne of God, who, having taught others in purity and sincerity the holy gospel of the Son of God, many of whom having followed my doctrine, have constantly suffered a thousand torments, and death itself; while in the mean time, I, an unconstant teacher, fled; and though I had lived long enough, and should not have feared death, but rather desired it, did yet withdraw, and thus cowardly transgressed the command of my God?" Whereupon the queen, as she was most eloquent, both by reason and example showed him this had befallen others of the holy servants of God; and others there also added such considerations, that he became more cheerful, and said, "There remains nothing but that I go from hence to God, and after I have now made my testament, I have that impression that I must delay no longer, knowing the Lord calls for me." He then fixed his eyes on the queen, and said, "Madam, I make you my heir, and to your preacher, Gerard, I leave my books and my clothes; the other things I have I leave to the poor." Whereupon the queen smiling, asked, "What then, Mr. Faber, shall I have?" "The care," said he, "madam, to distribute this to the poor." "It is well," said she, "I solemnly profess this legacy is more acceptable to me than if the king, my brother, had named me his heir." He then became more joyful, and said, "I have need of some rest, be you merry and joyful, and in the mean time adieu." And having spoken this, he turned himself over on a bed that was near, where, as they judged, he lay sleeping, but he was indeed fallen asleep in the Lord, without the least sign of a previous indisposition; and when they were about to awake him, they found him to their astonishment, dead. Such was the end of this personage, indubitably holy, as the queen of Navarre herself related it to the elector Frederick II., of Palatine, when he was sick at Paris, in his return from Spain, from the emperor Charles V., and it was communicated by a worthy gentleman, Hubertus Thomas a counsellor of the said Frederick, who was present at this relation of the queen, from whom Rivet wrote it.

I must instance this remarkable providence occurring to a grave and famous Christian in our country, John Stewart, provost of Ayr, who from his youth witnessed a respect to godliness. He had a considerable estate left him by his father, but having so great an impression on his spirit of the straitened condition of many good people whom he knew, and love to Jesus Christ and his truth having got the command over him and all his interest, he deliberately called them together in Edinburgh, and having spent some time in prayer, he took their solemn promise not to reveal, while he lived, what he was about to do. He then said, he knew in what straits many of them were to hold up the credit of their profession, and therefore he had brought a little money to lend each of them, yet they should never offer to repay it till he required the same. This was not known until his death, when some of them felt themselves obliged to make it known. Some time after he had bestowed this money, the plague having been sore in Ayr, and trade being much decayed, he himself fell under some straits, and some of the profane in that place began to say that religion had made him poor, and that his giving much to others, like a fool, made him now want himself. The credit of the Christian profession was always this godly man's darling, which made him quit the country at that time; borrowing, therefore, a little money, he went over to France, that he might the better conceal his strait. When he came to Rochelle, the salt and other commodities were become exceedingly cheap, because there had been no trading for a long time, on which he adventured to freight a ship, and to load her upon credit; he himself came over the nearest way to England, and thence to Ayr, with expectation of the ship's return; but after long waiting, he was informed that his ship was taken by the Turks; which became matter of great exercise to him, not because he knew not how to be abased, as well as how to abound, but fearing lest the mouths of wicked men might so much the more on this occasion be opened to reproach his profession. For many days he kept his chamber; at last, a maid, who had heard amongst the people that John Stewart's ship was arrived in the road, came running, and cried at the door that his ship was come. He being at prayer could not be moved from his Master's company till he was satisfied, and then went forth and saw it was a truth. But as a further ground of present exercise to him, a worthy Christian, and great intimate of his, John Kennedy, who for joy had gone forth in a small boat to the ship, by a sudden storm was carried past the ship, and in the judgment of all that looked on, he and the boat were swallowed up; yea, the storm so increased that they feared the loss of the ship also; which so deeply affected this gracious man, that for three days under the weight of such a trial he would be seen by none.    But at last, having gone forth to visit the widow, as then supposed, whilst with that family they were mutually grieving, John Kennedy comes in, who had not been cast away, but by a strange providence, the boat had been driven far away to another place of the coast.    Stewart vended the commodities of the ship, which having paid all his debt, returned him twenty thousand marks more to himself.    Thus the bread cast upon the waters, and to appearance lost, after many days returned, and that truth was confirmed, that by liberal devices the liberal man doth stand.    Isa. xxxii. 8.    In the last sickness of this worthy man, when his friends came to see him, he often used this word, " Be humble;" and said of himself, " I go the way of all flesh, and it may be some of you doubt nothing of my well-being; yea, I testify, that except when I slept, or was on business, I was not not these ten years' without thoughts of God, so long as I could be in going from my house to the cross;* and yet I doubt myself, and am in great agony, yea, at the brink of despair." But a day or two before he died, he turned his face to the wall for two hours, and then Mr. John Ferguson came in, a grave and godly minister of that place, who asked him what he was doing; upon which he turned himself, with these words, " I have been fighting, and working out my salva-

* The market-place.

tion with fear and trembling; and now I bless God it is perfected, sealed, confirmed, and all fears are gone."

I shall mention a memorable instance known to many in the north of Ireland, of a choice and godly gentlewoman. During the rebellion there, she fled with some other persons, and her three children, one of them upon the breast, but they had not gone far till they were stripped naked by the Irish, who contrary to expectation spared their lives. Afterwards, going on at the foot of a river which runs into Loch Neagh, others met them, and would have cast them into the river, but this godly woman, not dismayed, asked a little liberty to pray, and as she lay naked on the frozen ground, she resolved not to go on her own feet to such an unjust death; upon which she was dragged by the heels along that rugged way to be cast in with the rest of her company; but she then turned, and on her knees, said, "You should, I am sure, be Christians, and men I see you are: in taking away our miserable lives you do us a pleasure; but know, that as we never wronged you nor yours, you must remember to die also yourselves, and one day give an account of this cruelty to the Judge of heaven and earth." On this, an Irish priest, then present, said, "Let us not take their lives, but put them on this island in the lake." A boat being at the river, all the eight, naked and without meat, were put upon that island, where, after four day's staying, some of the company died from hunger and cold, but not this woman nor any of her children; for she lived by faith upon the word of God, and not by bread only. A day after, the two boys having crept aside, found the hide of a beast, which had been killed, at the root of a tree, which the mother and they endeavoured to get cast over them whilst lying upon the snow. The next day a little boat went by, to which she called, to induce the men in it to take her off; but they would not: she desired a little bread; they said they had none; then she begged a coal of fire, for she had seen smoke in the boat, which she obtained, and thus with some fallen chips she made a little fire, and the boys taking a piece of the hide, laid it on the coals and began to gnaw the leather; but without an extraordinary Divine support what could this do? Thus they lived ten days without any visible means of help; and that good woman professed it was by faith and joy in God that she lived: nor had she any food but ice or snow, nor drink except water; but she thought God put substance into it. She at last got to the side of the water, but here she was no nearer to help. She could not suffer to see her children die in her sight; and though the two boys were young, and so starved that they had no strength, she pressed them to go out of her sight, under pretence of seeking some fire, though in that desolate country she knew they could have no fire. The poor children had not gone far when they saw two or three great dogs eating a man, who had been killed; the children were afraid at the sight of the dogs, but one of them came running, and leaped upon one of the children without doing him the least hurt, but fawned on them both, and would run a little before, and then tarry till the children came up, and so led them on to a house where smoke appeared. . It was the house of an Irishman, protected by the English in Antrim, by whose means they were marvellously preserved,

and the mother sent for and succoured by a party
from Antrim.

The *seventh* witness to this truth is, the great
and marvellous providences by which the Lord has
witnessed his truth, and confirmed the same, since
the late rising of the church from antichrist.

We here understand that these were something
above the ordinary way of the Lord's working,
which evidently witnessed his great and immediate hand. It is true the Lord does not use such
a solemn testimony but on weighty grounds;
when the necessity of the church calls for it, when
he is about some extraordinary work, or when the
gospel comes first to a land long overspread with
darkness, when ordinary means of conviction are
wanting; or in times of great opposition, when
the commission of his servants needs some extraordinary seal; as in such a time as that of Ahab,
when the people are made to halt between truth
and a false way. Thus the Lord confirmed the
first preaching of the gospel, and spread the Christian church through the world. And does it seem
at all strange, that in these latter days, when he
was to raise her up from so long a ruin and desolation of antichristianism, he should thus appear,
and give some signal demonstration of his power
in behalf of his people?

It is not miracles nor any extraordinary providence on which men should resolve their faith,
nor do we here mention them for laying stress
thereon in believing the truth; no, the Protestant
doctrine leans on a stronger ground, it can with
confidence appeal to the Scripture. This, even
this is the reason of our hope, which we offer to
all that ask for the same; and there let the God of
truth, who has revealed his will, and answers men

by the written word, be Judge; and we shall de-
mand no greater advantage at the hand of our enemies. We know that miracles cannot authorize
a lie, nor be a seal to anything repugnant to the
Scripture. And truly the lying wonders which
have been so frequent in the world, and which the
apostle foretells, as an engine that the devil will
make use of to turn men aside from the truth, besides other marks of their falsehood, have this one
most discernible, that they are the support and
warrant of that which cannot stand alone by the
word. Hence the popish miracles are made use
of to confirm tenets, which of all their doctrines
most directly contradict the Scripture, as the merit
of works, purgatory, praying for the dead, &c.
But as we will not boast of such as the authority
or proof of our doctrine, so we judge it a grave
and important duty to observe the wondrous works
of the Lord in our times, that we may tell posterity some of the great acts of our God for his
church, in bringing her again from Babel.

I would desire to be very cautious upon such a
subject, for I judge it horrid divinity to make a lie
for God; it is not the truth, but a false way which
requires such a help; and truly in the following
instances I dare appeal to the Lord, that I have
not knowingly set down anything false, yea, nothing
without satisfying grounds of its certainty.

I shall first mention that solemn testimony of
Mr. Baynam, in queen Mary's time, who in the
midst of the fire, whilst his body was all in a
flame, his arms and legs half burnt, cried out to the
bystanders, "O papists, ye look after miracles;
lo, here is one! I am now burning in this fire,
but feel no more pain than if I were in a bed of
roses." This was the testimony of one upon the

borders of eternity, declared before a great multitude, and attested by Mr. Fox, that holy servant of Christ, who in things so extraordinary was most cautious, and searched out the truth and certainty of what he set down, and by him was published whilst many who might have been present were alive.

Charles IX. of France, author of the cruel massacre of St. Bartholomew's, where the blood of many thousand Protestants at Paris and other parts was shed, a very little after died in the strength of his years by an extraordinary effusion of blood from all passages of his body ; so that as Du Serres and other French writers of that time show, he was made to wallow in his own blood before his death.

God wonderfully appeared in the raising of the late king of Sweden, with that astonishing success which attended him in breaking the power of the house of Austria, whilst at so great a height, and their hands reeking in the blood of the Protestants through Bohemia and other places of Germany. The Lord's hand might be clearly seen in fitting the Swedes for such a service, even in a more than ordinary way.

The breaking of the great Spanish *armada*, in the year 1588, which had been three years in contriving, convincingly witnessed a Divine hand opposing the same. All the counsels, expense, and cruelty, which Philip II., had made use of to bear down the gospel in the Netherlands, came to a similar end. It is notorious, that after many attempts, the loss of 100,000,000 in gold, with near 400,000 lives, the reckoning of all his gain and purchase was only the loss of a considerable part of those countries, and the forwarding the establishment of the United Provinces. Truly the Lord by his great and outstretched hand wonderfully appeared in raising that commonwealth, so that they may date their flourishing in outward interest from their owing of the interest of God. Religion raised them, and no people this day has more cause, and are under greater engagements, to be zealous for the truth and defence of the Protestant cause.

The breaking of the formidable league of the Catholics in France for rooting out the Protestant religion, was very wonderful; all their counsels and designs resolved in their own ruin, so that the most ordinary observers could not but see a Divine hand counteracting the same. Davila, though an adversary, in setting down that history gives a large account of this. .

The great deliverance of the town of Leyden from the Spaniards should be mentioned with a special remark; for if the enemy had made use of cannon in battering the walls, they could not have come short of their design. In an extraordinary way the winds concurred to raise the waters, in order to the town's relief, when they were at the utmost extremity, and again to drive the waters back when the town was once delivered; and, what was very marvellous, the same night wherein the Spaniards were forced to retire, a part of the walls fell down, which, if it had fallen out a little before, that city had been utterly lost.

What wonderful providences attended the actings of that poor handful of Protestants in the valleys of Piedmont. I shall here only touch some passages mentioned by Mr. Moreland, in his history, who was then near that place, and from sure knowledge and information very gravely relates the same; and truly they are providences so marvellous, that men cannot but see the Lord, in an extraordinary way, helping that poor people to do exploits beyond any-- thing that can be mentioned of those great heroes whom the world in former years admired. After that bloody persecution enacted by order of the duke of Savoy, a small number was in a remarka- ble way raised up, at first amounting to but seven, or eight, under the conduct of that worthy gentle- man, Joshua Gianavello. This band met three hundred soldiers sent to exercise further cruelty in, that place, and killing many of them, pursued the rest for a considerable time. Afterwards, a party of five hundred being sent by the marquis of Pia- neza, who then commanded the duke of Savoy's forces, were opposed by eleven of the Protestants, and six others, with slings, and after a short con- flict, were forced to flee with considerable slaugh- ter, the terror of the Lord upon the one, and a spirit of courage and resolution in the other, being very manifest. After these things there was another party of seven hundred soldiers sent forth to seize on all the passages, upon which about seventeen, masters of families, whose hearts God had in a sig- nal manner strengthened to the battle for their poor brethren's preservation, resolved to cast themselves upon the Lord for the success of their undertak- ings; and with such marvellous boldness faced their adversaries, as to put them in amazement, and to make them draw off, resolving to take another way, but they were pursued by this little handful, who killed many without the loss of one man. At another time, the Protestants, being three hundred, under the conduct of the forementioned captain Gianavello, were assaulted by 2,500 of the adver- saries; but the Lord so ordered, that this little party,

getting the advantage of the place, after some con
flict forced them to retire, pursuing them into the
woods and steep rocks with great slaughter; and
thus with a marvellous courage, in a continued fight
for eight hours together, drove the enemy before
them. Divers other remarkable passages of this
kind are mentioned in that history; and truly it
might be much cause for wonder, that through the
Lord's eminent appearance, and his blessing on his
poor people's endeavours for the interest of religion
and their own preservation, they disputed the matter
with such a prosperous success against all the forces
which the duke of Savoy sent, till their enemies at
last began to fear what effect it might produce, and,
therefore, were glad, by a treaty of peace, to get
the sword out of their hands.

Vergerius, the pope's nuncio for many years in
Germany, whilst writing against the truth, was
converted, became a Protestant, and a zealous
preacher of the gospel even to his death.

Carraccioli, an Italian marquis of great place and
estate in the world, was so taken by the heart in
hearing Peter Martyr, as not only to quit all his
hopes of preferment, and a most pleasant and great
inheritance, but to withstand the most pressing en-
treaties and insinuations of his friends, the cries of
his lady and children, and go to a strange place,
quitting all that he might preserve his conscience
and enjoy fellowship with the church.

How marvellous was it that poor Luther, against
whom so much of the world opposed itself with
great rage and violence, should yet live to an old
age, and go to the grave in peace. And truly the
spirit and appearance of this great and first witness
to the truth was a convincing evidence that the
Lord was then about to raise up a people to him-

self, in whom he would be glorified by an active testimony, as well as by suffering.

. Worthy Mr. Forbes whilst banished for the truth, sets down under his hand the following passage. In the year 1607, being at Rouen, in France, and meeting with monsieur Figureus, that ancient and famous divine, then pastor of the Reformed church in that city, he had from him this following relation :—After the close of the council of Trent, in the time of Pius V., there was a consultation in Italy by the pope and cardinals, for an utter extirpation of the Reformed churches in Europe, and to this end every prince of the Romish religion had a certain part assigned where this great project should be put in practice: the death of Pius hindered an immediate prosecution of this design. His successor, Gregory XIII., suffered it to lie dead, having no heart that way ; and until the time of Clement VIII., it was not revived ; but then this bloody resolution was again ratified by him and his cardinals, under their hands and seals ; the only difficulty was to find a fit and trusty person, whom they should make use of to the princes of the Romish religion, for engaging them to subscribe the said ordinance, and set about the execution thereof. At length, a gentleman of good parts, near in blood to the cardinal Baronius, was chosen, which to him was a matter of much grief and sorrow, for, unknown to them, he was of the Reformed religion ; but this grief in his countenance and carriage put his friends to strange thoughts, and especially as he expressly declared to some, that what to them seemed a cause of rejoicing, was to him a just occasion of grief; yet at last finding his danger, he judged it his wisdom to dissemble, telling cardinal Baronius, who pressed him to the office, that his unsuitableness to so great an employment could not but be ground of trouble and fear. He' was, however, forced to engage, getting his commissions, the decree of the conclave, with letters to the foresaid princes, sealed and subscribed. But, however, whilst this poor gentleman was on his journey, having found ways to free himself of his servants and other company, his spirit was in great perplexity between these two grievous temptations, either to be an instrument of utter ruin to the truth and churches of Christ, or to forsake his country, inheritance, and all he had in the world; upon which he resolved to retire by himself out of the highway to an obscure village, where for three days he gave himself to fasting and prayer for direction and resolution from the Lord, and after this had his heart so strengthened against the care of his worldly estate, that he resolved to forsake all, and to reveal this bloody conspiracy to the churches of Christ, and cast himself on God's hand for his future estate. So he turned his face from Spain, and took journey to France, and to Paris, where at that time remained the sister of Henry III., a religious princess, afterwards duchess of Lorraine, to whom the foresaid monsieur Figureus was preacher. To him did this godly man make his address, (after divers refusals of admission, upon suspicion,) showing him the whole business, and delivered the sealed decree with his letters of commission for that effect, and likewise showed him, astonished at such a wonderful providence of God in fostering some of his own children in the midst of Babylon, that there were many others in Italy, yea, in Rome itself of the Reformed religion, who had their secret meetings; and even Gregory XIII. before his advancement to the papacy, was tho-

roughly clear in his judgment on that point whereof he gave him divers evidences. This foresaid
relation so affected Mr. Forbes, that he showed a
marvellous desire to see the man who had done so
worthy and gracious a work for the glory of God
and good of his church, and by a recommendation
from monsieur Figureus, he afterwards went on
purpose to Heidelberg, where this gentleman was
then retired for his further security, where he saw
him, and from his own mouth received the assurance of this former narration to his great satisfaction. This is both written and subscribed by Mr.
Forbes' own hand.

I must here also set down a very singular instance both of judgment and mercy, which in this
land, not many years ago, occurred to a gentleman
whose name was Westraw, a most bloody man,
and notorious for profanity, but most for this, that
it was his great pleasure to put differences between
men, and to engage them in blood. When he had
thus stirred up a neighbouring gentleman to kill
another, finding him afterwards in sore trouble of
mind, he told him that more of that practice would
be the best cure, for he himself had killed six, and
that the first time he was much disquieted, but the
longer he continued, it became the more easy.
But one day, whilst he was riding to a place where
two gentlemen had agreed to decide a private quarrel by fighting, his borse stumbled on the side of a
steep rock, and he fell a great way down, his
sword falling out before him, yet without any hurt;
and by such a strange piece of providence the Lord
so touched his conscience, that he returned home
with great trouble and remorse, a most kindly
change following; and for some years after, he
witnessed much tenderness and repentance, and

28 *

spent much time alone mourning before his death.
On the day that he died, having no visible appearance thereof to those who looked on, he was heard
in his chamber wrestling in prayer; and after long
continuance, the inmates of the house were forced
to break open the door, having no answer after long
knocking. They found him dead in the room,
upon his knees in a praying posture, and the whole
blood of his body swimming about him on the
floor; a most astonishing instance, declaring to the
world that though the Lord pardons the iniquity of
his people, yet some sins he will not pass without
a visible mark of his anger.

An observable passage is that also, known to
many yet alive, of a notorious robber in the south
parts of this land,* called John of the Score; who
for many years having driven that woful trade, one
day met a poor man travelling with two horses,
which he, according to his custom, took away: the
poor countryman falling down on his knees, earn-
estly begged, that for Jesus Christ's sake, he would
give him one again, for he had nothing to maintain
his poor family but what he could gain by them.
But it was in vain; the robber carried them home
with him, leaving the poor man in that desolate
condition. But a little after John of the Score became melancholy, and could get no rest or quiet, not
knowing the cause; but, as he professed, the words
that the poor man had spoken to him, though he
understood not what he meant when he spake of
Christ, were lying like a heavy weight upon his
spirit. When he was sought after for his robberies,
he desired his sons to shift for themselves, for he
could not get out of the way, there being a restraint

* Scotland.

upon him, and something within him that bound him. Thus he staid at his house until he was apprehended, brought to Edinburgh, and put in prison; upon which a godly minister, Mr. Henry Blyth, with a Christian gentleman, William Cuningham, tutor of Bonnytown, who had sometime known him, made him a visit, holding forth to him his miserable estate and the hazard of his soul; and amongst other words, showing him the necessity to flee to Jesus Christ; when he suddenly cried out, "O! what word is that, for it has been my death? That is the word that has lain upon my heart since the poor man spake it to me; so that I had no power from that time to go out of the way;" and being told who Christ was, without whom he could not be saved, he cried: "O, will he ever look on me, and show mercy, that for his sake would not show mercy to that poor man, and give him back his horse?" After further instruction, a most real and gracious change appeared upon him; he gave most convincing evidences of the reality thereof, attained to great assurance before his death, and upon the scaffold, in the public streets, where he was executed, spoke so wonderfully of the Lord's dealing with him, and with such knowledge and judgment, as left a conviction on all present, and forced them to see a truth and reality in the grace of God.

Another notable instance of grace I shall here mention, respecting Patrick Muckelwrath, in the west parts of Scotland, whose heart the Lord touched in a remarkable way; and who, after his conversion, was so affected with the new world wherein he was entered, the discoveries of God and of a life to come, that for some months together he scarce ever slept, but was still taken up in wondering. His life was very remarkable for near converse with God; and one day, after a sharp trial, having his only son suddenly taken away by death, he retired alone for several hours, and when he came forth looked so cheerfully, that when some asked him the reason, and wondered at the same in such a time, he told them he had got that in his retirement with the Lord, for which he would be content to lose a son every day. It had been long his burden that he could retain hardly anything of what he heard from the word; and bitterly complaining thereof to worthy master James English, minister of Daly, his counsel to him was, when he heard any truth which he desired to remember, he should present it to the Lord, and desire Him to keep it for him, and give it back to him according to his need; which accordingly this blessed man did with much seriousness practise. On his death-bed, he solemnly declared to his minister, and divers other Christians, how wonderfully the Lord had answered him in that particular; for as they knew how much formerly the want of memory had been his burden, now the Lord had given him back all the truths which he had put in his keeping, so that what for many years he had heard, was now most clearly brought to his remembrance; this he witnessed by repeating many particular truths and notes of sermons which he had heard.

We have truly cause to say even from late experience, since this dark night came upon the church in these nations, with so sharp a storm of persecution, that there have occurred some very signal and convincing providences, witnessing the Lord's appearance for his people and against their enemies: for it is manifest,

1. How eminently the Lord appeared in over-coming those who had been the great instruments, both in counsel and action, to break the government of the church of Christ in this land, and to lay so much of his vineyard waste and desolate; and this in the height of their power and greatness, whilst they seemed most firmly rooted. Those who made it their great work to oppress the poor church, and like a violent tempest carried all before them, in a moment, when they could have least expected, were made to fall; yea, in a short time they were out of their places and offices, who but a little before had turned out so many of the faithful ministers of Christ.

2. It is known with what marvellous resolution and cheerfulness the Lord's persecuted people have been carried through, being called forth to resist unto blood in their adherence to the truth; witnessing to the conviction of even their greatest enemies, something above Roman gallantry, yea, something above nature, in the staidness and elevation of their spirits.

3. It may be truly matter of wonder by what a marvellous providence so many suffering and desolate families have been carried through, now for these divers years, with such convincing cheerfulness; yea, the experience of many being made to witness that they never less knew a strait, than since they were put from the ordinary means of their support; and others who have been more sharply tried, could not reckon any such plunging strait and difficulty, but they have also found a suitable mercy. I am very sure, that amongst other advantages of these times, a large register of experience and remarkable confirmations of the truth of the word and promise which the godly

have had under this sharp trial, will be sweet matter for an after-reckoning, and a greater gain than
any loss their former sufferings occasioned. We
have seen that what in an ordinary way seemed
irrecoverable, and a stroke which a generation could
not have made up, has been a means to promote
God's glory. He has made us see how easy it is
for him to turn the sharpest storm to the great advantage of his church; that he can act in desperate
cases above the skill both of angels and men,
though we should be brought yet lower, even to
the place of dragons. This may uphold the shaking hearts of his people, and be a solid ground of
confidence, that Christ's power and faithfulness are
this day engaged for his church and truth. He
must increase; his kingdom is upon the rising hand,
and shall yet have a more glorious appearance in
the world, whatever may become of instruments;
and since the Lord has solemnly declared war
against antichrist, and all who will oppose the
spreading of the gospel in these last times; yea,
has passed his word to the church for the fall and
ruin of that adversary—fall he must, though the
dust of the earth should arise against his cause.
We have much ground in these times to believe
that the Lord will yet appear and make himself
known in the earth, by as great and convincing
providences, both of judgment and mercy, as in any
former ages; and thus vindicate his glory, and refute the atheism of this generation, by an argument,
which shall force iniquity to stop its mouth.

Now since this is sure, that the Scripture falleth
not to the ground, for "God's way is perfect, and
the word of the Lord is tried;" it is also sure, and
a conclusion well grounded, that "He is a buckler
to all those that trust in him," Psa. xviii. 30.

None need fear to venture his interest through time on the word; yea, if there could be anything greater than heaven or eternal salvation, the testimony of the God of truth might be sufficient security for the same. It is a small matter how this world reels and staggers, or what are the changes of outward things; it is enough, that the promises of the word shall certainly take place, and the expectation of the saints shall not make them ashamed.

## CONCLUSION.

THE demonstration of Divine truth held forth in the Scripture, is the greatest discovery that ever came to the sons of men; which with a more excellent light and greater lustre enlightens those parts of the earth on which it shines, than the sun in its noon-day brightness. This is the word of life, even the "hidden wisdom of God in a mystery," which most of the world do not understand, but flee from as their plague and torment. But hereby the followers of God know they are of the truth, and assure their hearts before him; it should be matter of astonishment, if by this means the Scripture were not confirmed, to see what rage this light causes amongst men; not against some particular truth only, and the uppermost houghs, but by a remarkable assault against the very being of truth and godliness. Whilst superstition, in times of greater ignorance, overclouded and darkened the visible church, atheism has taken up its room to wear this generation out from under the awe of God, and weaken their assent to the truth; for men everywhere make it their work to load his way with reproach, and put discredit on his faithfulness, who is the God of truth. As a witness thereto is this essay directed. If a subject of so great an import suffer no prejudice from such an unfit pen, I should desire to look on the favourable testimony or the censures of men as at a distance, and far below that solid peace of the soul, which is alone to be found in the acceptation of God. What access it may have to many of this generation, who are taking all advantage to strengthen their prejudice against the truth, and unsettle others therein, I know not: they may pass their judgment thereon at the first look, and throw it aside. But, as a minister of Jesus Christ who believes in an appearing before the Judge, and would desire to be found faithful in that day, being pressed in some measure with the horrid appearance of the atheism and blasphemy of the time, and with that avowed indifference now within the visible church in the great interests of religion and godliness, I lay this witness to the truth at their door; and shall here offer a few thoughts further on this subject, in some clear inferences from the great truth of the verification of the Scripture.

*Inference* I. is the great advantage a Christian has for his establishment. His security is indeed greater than his interest, or anything he has to adventure thereon; and surely, that is not small, since the matter is of no less importance, besides his concernments through time, than an eternity, a heaven, or the hazard of hell for ever. This must require a solid and sure foundation; yea, the furthest degree of certainty, where the superstructure is so great; for it is not opinion, nor a probable conjecture, that can be a suitable basis to bear up that weight: but here, to answer such an interest, and give thorough quiet and repose to the soul, we have the truth and testimony of God, with this great witness thereto, that it assuredly takes place, and not one syllable falls to the ground without performance.

There are two things which, I am sure, men could not think of without amazement, if they made it not their choice to keep at a distance. One is, that there is such a thing this day in the world as the very word of God, that is more sure than an audible voice from heaven, to declare his whole counsel and hold forth to men the true way to that country; and thus marvellously discovers itself, 1. To be his word and testimony who speaks from heaven, and to come with a solemn appeal to men's sense and feeling. 2. Which commends itself upon the nearest approach, and is found the more invaluable the more it is searched into. 3. That though clear and plain in itself, yet by a supernatural light and evidence it can only be known, which no human sagacity, no reason in its highest elevation, without this, can reach; but rises far above the greatest capacity which by nature the most excellent spirits of men boast. In a word, when once it shines in upon the soul, it discernibly stamps the very same image thereon, and begets such a marvellous likeness between itself and the soul, as proves it to be a living thing. We may also consider with astonishment, how great a thing it is to be a Christian. Suppose there were but one or two to be found in the world who were certainly known to be partakers of the Divine nature, to have a real converse with God; would not the report thereof give men a strange alarm; yea, put them upon an impatient search and inquiry to know if this be sure? Is it a small thing to be the son of a king? But the hope of a Christian rises higher, and has another reach. Such a character, within a short time, though now in so mean a garb, shall

assuredly enter into glory; into the immediate enjoyment of God, and of the fulness of joy, among
the triumphant society of the angels, the prophets,
and apostles, and all those who are before the
throne, washed and made white in the blood of the
Lamb, and thus continue through the ages of eternity. Yea, in the very instant of the soul's quitting
the body, he must realize that great change, and
enter there, where heaven only can make us know
what heaven is. It is a strange sleep that men are
in, who in so important a matter are not awakened
to a further inquiry. It were well if some would
but allow reason its true use, and whilst they travel
between the poles, and can adventure to the furthest parts of the earth, to pursue that which they
must so shortly forego, consider seriously what a
greater prize than the gold and treasure of the
Indies, offers itself to them, at an easier rate, in the
gospel. I say, the professed atheism of some gives
not more cause of wonder, than the strange stupidity of others, and that common and easy way
men have in giving an assent to Divine truth.

I must further point at two or three things which,
seriously considered, seem a strange contradiction
to reason. 1. How men can find a pillow to rest
on, who certainly know that their breath for the
few hours of night is not made sure; but if by a
sudden arrest of death it should be stopped, which
is no strange thing in the world, they know not
what is next; but every night they sleep with the
possibility of being before the next day in an irre-
coverably lost estate. Yea, is it not wonderful,
that whilst we see time make such swift dispatch,
dying men can be in that measure estranged from
the thoughts of death, though they hear its sound
by the bell tolling for others; yea, by previous

assaults discern its approach on themselves, which when once come, then man goes off the stage to return no more, nor shall he for all the ages of eternity ever act the scene of life over again? 2. How strange it is that the mere supposal of the truth and certainty of the Scripture, that such a thing *may* be, does not more alarm men and mar their quiet; that they can so much as think of an eternal estate without trembling, whilst they have no solid determination in such a matter; yea, when the Scripture of God does not only witness a heaven and immortality, but shows the world that there is such a thing as the first fruits and earnest of it. I would know if such an atheism is to be found, which puts the atheist beyond fear and doubting, even in his most professed confidence and scoffing at the truth, or which can sufficiently prevent that heart-aching and continued anxiety he is under that such a thing may be true. 3. I shall add, it is matter of wonder that men should admit the report and attestation of others of the truth of godliness, who yet live strangers to it themselves; yea, should be at some toil and pains, and come to be almost Christians, without pursuing this in greater earnest.

*Inference* II. There is a special debt on each Christian on whose soul the truth and faithfulness of God is sealed, to bear witness that God is true. Thus there is a mutual sealing: in 2 Cor. i. 22, the Lord puts his seal; and in John iii. 33, the Christian's seal is expressly called for. This is indeed a duty which the meanest of the saints who has that witness within himself can perform. He does not more clearly see the truth written in the Bible before him, than he knows and can read by another character and engraving this within him, though none else can read the same. There is a debt due to the least Scripture truth, when a witness and confession is called for. But this is something else; it concerns the confirmed Christian as a peculiar debt he owes to the truth and faithfulness of his God, to give unto Him the glory of his faithfulness. So David speaks, Psa. lxxxix. 1; and though some have a more special call to this than others, yet the confirming and sealing of the truth is like a great and public treasure, wherein the meanest Christian should cast in his mite.

1. He who receives the testimony of Jesus Christ thus sets to his seal that he is true, and subscribes to the truth of the gospel, John iii. 33. 2. The showing forth of the power of godliness is, through the course of a Christian's life, a living and visible witness thereto. 3. The converted man, upon that new and marvellous discovery he has of the truth upon his first entering into a Christian state, when he has passed the great step, and is as one come into another world, has a special call and advantage for such a duty; and the first service due from him to the truth, is to commend by his zeal and testimony to others what God has so marvellously commended to his soul. He is then to answer that call, " When thou art converted, strengthen thy brethren," Luke xxii. 32. 4. When a Christian is confirmed after some remarkable staggering, and has got a new seal of the faithfulness of God, he is under a new debt to restore with advantage what he had taken from the credit of the truth, and give that good report and witness thereto, which may obviate any reflection he might have caused by his fainting. Thus we see Hezekiah, after such a remarkable plunge and fainting, comes in with his witness, 'What shall I say? He hath both spoken unto

me, and himself hath done it," Isa. xxxviii. **15.**
And David, "I said, I am cut off from before thine
eyes, nevertheless thou heardest the voice of my
supplication," Psa. xxxi. 22. **5.** When we see
atheism abounding, when it is not a particular
truth, but the whole truth and faithfulness of God
that is challenged, it then calls, and calls aloud to
the godly man for his appearance, by some more
obvious testimony than at other times. When
the lot of a Christian is cast in such a time, and
amongst a generation of mockers, he has a special
call by a grave and prudent witness to own the
truth, as that which he is obliged to seal, though
there were none else. Yea, this should be such a
call and incitement, if zeal for Jesus Christ has
got a command over his soul, as might burst his
tongue-strings, which before were tied, when the
faithfulness of his God, which he so oft has proved,
is by men brought in question. This to David was
like a sword that thrust him through, when they
said unto him, "Where is thy God?" Psa. xlii.
**3.** **6.** Upon the close of some sharp and remarkable trial, when the Christian after a storm comes
safe to land, the new discovery he has of the faithfulness of God lays a new debt on him to bear
witness thereto. He is thus concerned not to
leave the cross of Jesus Christ at a loss, which
has left him at so great an advantage. Thus
afflicted Job, after a long-continued storm, comes
in the close to pay the truth's rent by his seal and
testimony; "I have heard of thee by the hearing
of the ear, but now mine eye seeth thee," Job
xlii. **5.** I hope this debt, in a large measure, will
be found to press the spirits of many of this generation when this storm is over, and that they will
be compelled to bear a testimony that "they

thirsted not when he led them through the deserts," Isa. xlviii. 21. 7. The experience of a Christian respecting the faithfulness of God, is a special trust put in his hand, and calls for his seal, as a rent due to the truth. None of the saints want their peculiar engagements, even beyond others; yea, such singular confirmation they have had of the way of the Lord, and with such astonishing circumstances, that to smother the remembrance of their mercies, without some gain and advantage paid to the truth, might be reckoned a stealth from their generation. Such a thing pressed David's soul, Psa. lxvi. 16; and truly this practice, managed with humble prudence, in a grave intercourse and communication, were a choice improvement of Christian society and fellowship. I confess to manage this well seems one of the most difficult and necessary pieces of Christian duty. What a special improvement of Christian fellowship is held forth, Mal. iii. 16. I could wish so excellent a means were more directed to this end; nor should it prevent such a duty that there may be an empty show and counterfeit of it, and that the shallowest brooks sometimes make the greatest noise. 8. There is a special call for the Christian's witness to the truth under some remarkable exigence and strait, whilst thronged with manifold temptations; then he is concerned to show forth the faithfulness of God, that others who in such times will be great observers of his way, may know that he is satisfied with God and with the security of his word, when he has no resting-place elsewhere; that he thinks not his burden too great to roll over on the promise, but can say in behalf of the truth, "Persecuted, but not forsaken; cast down, yet not destroyed,"

2 Cor. iv. 9. You see the apostle paying such a debt on this account, "Having nothing, yet possessing all things," 2 Cor. vi. 10. 9. A call to this duty waits the Christian in a special manner at the close of his day; then is he concerned to acquit himself of that debt, by commending the way of the Lord, and confirming others therein. It would be a choice appendix to the testament of a dying Christian, to seal with his last breath the faithfulness of God; and then, when his words are of more weight than at other times, to bear this witness, that through the various steps of his life he knows that God is true, and has helped him. Each remarkable time of life has some proper work; this seems to be the last service of a dying Christian to his generation, to deliver the truth off his hand with his seal and testimony. This were to bequeath a choice legacy to others.

Particular rules cannot be given for the practice of this duty. Christian wisdom is profitable to direct as occasion offers; but sure it is, each Christian is thus a witness in behalf of that attribute, the faithfulness of God, to attest by his seal as a confirmatory sign that God is true. And as there is always an implicit seal by believing, there is something more explicit now called for, when the reality of godliness is so expressly impugned by the adversary under the name of fanaticism. 1. We see through the whole Scripture how much the saints have been thus occupied; and in those times of the church when there was no other way to keep up a remembrance of the faithfulness of God, and to transmit a testimony thereto, we find a pillar and stone of witness erected, 1 Sam. vii. 12. 2. The discovery of this faithfulness, to an observing Christian, has sometimes a greater joy and satisfac-

tion than the mercy in which it appears.   3. **The**
Christian has an occasional call thereto whenever
it lies in his way to bear his witness.   The truth
and faithfulness of God never came in David's way
but we find him speak honourably thereof, from
the sense of his peculiar engagements.   4. There
is no part of a Christian's suffering for a particular
truth, but a confession is therewith called for of the
faithfulness of God.   He should thus bear witness
before the world that he is not ashamed of the cross
of Christ; whilst others, by choosing sin rather,
than affliction, do what in them lies to make God
a liar.

*Inference* III.   As there is a personal debt on
the Christian, there is a public debt also on the
church, and a special trust reposed on every age
thereof, to seal the truth to the ages to come, with
a witness to the faithfulness of God.   The Scripture herein is clear, Psa. cxlv. 4—6.   Each time
has some peculiar debt, which it should pay to
posterity, from a new addition of the great and remarkable works of the Lord; and his more eminent appearance for the church in one age beyond
another, adds to this debt, and puts some further
engagements upon it, to transmit the works of the
Lord, and the memory of his goodness, to after
times.

This has the greater call, when it is so much the
work of the time to shake and unsettle men as to
this great foundation; yea, when so much is written that has a visible tendency to this end.   One
thing particularly may be wished, that the public
records of every age, as they concern the church,
contained more clearly some history of the verification of the truth, by transmitting these great and
conspicuous remarks of the way of God with the

church to posterity.  Thus should one age declare his faithfulness to the next.

That part of the truth of God which has endured the greatest opposition from the adverse party, should be especially commended with all care and circumspection, yea, with some peculiar testimony thereto.  It is true, there are in every age some who appear for the truth; yea, it is the duty of each Christian when called, to give a confession of the same: but as no private appearance can be substituted for a public record and monument in a time of great encroachment on the truth, when a remarkable breach is likely to be made, and the assault is not from a private adversary, but a public formidable combination of a party, some more solemn, authoritative, and united concurrence is called for, that may witness to ages to come where their fathers stood, how they held out and wrestled to keep their ground in defence of the gospel.  This is like the casting up of a bank against a further breach when the enemy comes in like a flood; and the confessions of the church in every age, with such a public testimony to the truth, when followed with visible hazard and suffering, have been more effectually subservient to the truth's conservation, than all the disputes of men: thus did they overcome by the blood of the Lamb, and the word of their testimony, Rev. xii. 11.

A special debt is also upon the church to contend for the truth once delivered to the saints.  O how blessed a debate and strife is this, though resisting to the blood should be called for!  But whilst I mention this duty, it cannot be understood with respect to the great interest of religion only, or the weightier matters of the law, whilst under a professed zeal for these, a latitude and indifference in other concernments of the truth is sheltered.  **Let** me ask, can any part of truth held forth in **the** Scripture be of that low value as to warrant the yielding it up when brought in debate, when one line of this is of more worth than the crowns and sceptres of all the monarchs of the earth?  **The** God of truth has prized it at another rate, who declares heaven and earth shall fail, before one tittle of his word shall perish.  Can they be faithful in greater things, who are unfaithful in a little?  It is too clearly seen how small a yielding makes a great breach.  Truths comparatively small may be great in their season, when they are the word of his patience; yea, the smaller the debated point seems with many, it makes the Christian's adherence thereto a greater testimony.  It is clear there is a close connexion amongst the truths of God held forth in the Scripture; one part thereof cannot be reached without a prejudice to the whole; yea, every corruption of the truth has an aim at the very soul of religion.

The great duty of the church at this day is the transmitting of truth and godliness, not in a naked form only, but in the life and power thereof.  Surely it is now too obvious, that through a large part of the Reformed church, and in those places where the truth has brightly shone with much state and warmth; yea, where religion in its purity is yet professedly countenanced and the worship of God owned, even there the power and spirituality of religion is a strange and unknown thing; and by many within the church, and of some repute therein, it might be questioned, is there indeed a Holy Ghost, and an inward teaching of the Spirit, who by his working and efficacious influences is known upon the soul?  Is there such a thing as real fellowship and converse with God in the secret and public duties of a Christian? O what cause is there to fear that the shadow and form will be quickly gone, when the power thereof is so great a mystery! I profess it is not to reflect on any place or particular church that I speak, but this want and decay is too great and universal to be hidden; the tide seems so far spent and gone back, yea, so small appearance of its return, and the church of Christ is at that pass, that if the faithfulness of God were not a surety which stands good for all, we might judge that nothing else is left, but that each one should shift for himself, and give over the church. But sure I am, upon a better warrant than appearance, our safety is this day to keep by the vessel, and not to part interest with an afflicted and almost sinking church; a public spirit may yet be found the best way to secure a private interest. O! what do we see? Almost every where men's hands are upon their loins, and there is little inquiry in this extreme exigence, what part of duty can yet be essayed to get religion up again. Some things are to be wished which would be of singular use to promote this interest: I shall very briefly point at them.

1. It is to be wished that the great means of prayer yet left to the church, were improved with more singleness and fervency, both by the Christian alone, and in converse with others. It is well known, in the most dark and dismal times of her condition, what marvellous help prayer has brought. Here the meanest of the saints has access to do a great piece of service, even to the church universal.

2. It is to be wished that a greater correspondence through the Reformed church were more

effectually pursued, to know what eminent hazard appears to the truth, or what sore trial and assault some particular church may have beyond others. for witnessing mutual sympathy, communication of counsels, obviating prejudices and mistakes, and as a serious incitement to the duty of the times, in promoting the great interest of the gospel. Since the Reformation began how little of this has been practised! · Sometimes the great concerns of neighbouring churches, and the more remarkable occurrences of Providence, are but little known.

3. It might be a notable and useful help, and one of no great difficulty, now when there is such plodding in religion by airy notions, as if that great interest were the essay of men's wit and invention, to translate into other languages some of our choice English pieces, which do most nervously hold forth the truth of godliness, both in its simplicity and in its life and power—such as are most fit to bring the naked speculation of truth down to a near feeling and soul-converse therewith; yea, such as with great clearness may show the world how well godliness suits with, and is a singular help in, every calling and condition of men, to make their way easy and pleasant amidst the trials of life; but especially that may hold forth the indispensable necessity thereof. It is sad to think in what measure holiness is wounded and darkened, by so great a cloud of prejudice, through the Reformed church; through the means of the extravagance and unsuitable practice of many professors; and yet that so little care is taken to obviate and prevent it.

4. It calls now for much prayer to see a spiritual and faithful ministry given to the church, of whom it might be said, These are the ambassa-

dors of Jesus Christ, with their Master's authority
impressed on them, who in earnest do travail in
birth to have Christ formed in their hearers, and
who preach with feeling to themselves as well as
to others; who truly watch for men's souls, with
an awful impression lest their blood be required at
their hands.  How great a blessing would this be
to a decayed church, and what a ground of hope
were it of a recovery! for it is seen what a close
connexion there is between the church's case and
the ministry thereof.  At the breaking out of the
gospel, after the long darkness under antichrist,
how choice and excellent a ministry was then sent
forth; yea, what a remarkable constellation of
great lights appeared, who both burned and shone
in their time!  O! these are gone, and but a few,
comparatively with their spirit are to be found.
The greatest plague the Christian world and the
Reformed church are under this day, is from the
watchmen, by whom the truth has been more
wounded than by its most professed adversaries.
I know there are some in this time who take advantage to reflect on and decry that excellent office
and appointment of Jesus Christ for his church,
because of the abuse thereof, whom I dare not,
from the awe of God, answer in their dialect,
which is only railing; but the Lord rebuke that
evil spirit now abroad in the world!  The present generation owes it as a debt to posterity, to
witness a particular care and respect to those who
are aiming at this great calling, that in so sad a
day they may be encouraged to follow their aim,
and not to faint when difficulties seem to grow in
their way; but, especially, that they take along
with other studies that more excellent study of
sanctification, which is so indispensably necessary

to make able ministers of the New Testament.
Surely they have now a special advantage to witness their love and respect to Jesus Christ, who
keep their faces that way, when there seems no
other incitement but the service of such a Master.

*Inference* IV. It is a duty of special use to a
right understanding of the fulfilling of the Scripture, to discern the times; since in particular ages
and periods of time the Scripture must be fulfilled,
and the prophecies which relate to each period of
time have their particular and exact accomplishment therein. There can be no doubt that such
a duty is called for in so dark an hour of the
church; yea, the greater the darkness, the more
pressing is the call. When we see the clouds
gathering, which are like to cover the face of the
sky; the church universal so sore benighted, that
she has almost lost her way amidst these mists
and among the multitude of these by-paths; then
it is not only incumbent on the public watchmen,
but it concerns the godly every where, to know
the time, and what Israel ought to do. Every
Christian has his watch-tower, where he may go
up by near converse with God in the Scripture,
and thence, as from a great height, consider the
present time; yea, have a clear view of the most
strange and perplexing occurrences thereof; and
see that amidst these, God's work about the church
keeps its way, and moves still forward without
losing ground.

I shall offer some thoughts for a right discovery
and understanding of the time.

1. It is of great importance to know from the
Scripture, " What of the night?" Isa. xxi. 11;
how far it seems to be spent, and in what watch
thereof the church is fallen; for thus we might

know to what period of her condition these great and remarkable things which fall out in the world relate. This, I confess, would be a perplexing business, if the appearance of things were our guide, and if we had not that blessed conduct of the written word. One thing is sure, that the Lord has founded Zion, and is now building her up; which marvellous work is in all ages in a continued progress: the great builder loses no time. These things seem clear and manifest.

(1.) That as the whole election must obtain, so there are a great many of that elect church already entered into a triumphant condition, and safe on shore. There is at this day perfected and before the throne, a great and innumerable company of all nations, tribes, and languages, who were of old committed to the Mediator's trust, and to be brought forth under the times of the New Testament, after whom the gospel followed, and made many a long step to bring them in from the furthest corners of the earth.

(2.) That the church militant has now passed that long-continued and most dismal trial which was to go over her head, even that sore bondage from antichrist. It is true, this adversary does not cease or give over the quarrel, for he wants not wrath even when his power is abated: we see him in a great stir to have that accursed interest set in its own place, that has so remarkably been brought down before the gospel; but a step further of that judgment, which assuredly is not sleeping, will end the business. The winter is past, and the church's spring is begun, yea, in a large measure advanced, whose growth and tender blossom neither the cold nor storm can blast, but must be subservient thereto and hasten the summer's approach.

(3.) I think there are clear and convincing symptoms by which some notable erisis in the church's condition may be discerned; that after many conflicts and sore wrestlings since her victory was begun over antichrist, this time of the church seems to fall under that more remarkable assault from this adversary before the pouring out of the fifth vial on his throne and seat; which, as the prelude of so great a victory, may be more dreadful and sharp for a time than any we have seen. I humbly judge the Scripture points clearly at a continued war between antichrist (even in his falling state) and the Lamb, until the last decision puts him off the field; "For the Lamb shall overcome, and they that are with him are called and chosen and faithful," Rev. xvii. 14. And since the church's interest is advanced by the renewed assaults of that adversary, is it strange that the several steps of her rising should have some conflict and opposition proportioned thereto? This the Scripture witnesses, "Be in pain, O daughter of Zion; for thou shalt go forth even unto Babylon: there shalt thou be delivered," Micah iv. 10. So formidable an approach of antichrist at this day, and the advantage he seems to have, with the sore strugglings of the church of Christ as in an extreme between life and death, have more of promise than of threatening, and are a hopeful presage of a further enlargement, and the bringing forth some great and important truth to a performance; yea, they have a direct tendency, under the wonderful conduct of the blessed Disposer of these things, to help forward such a mercy.

(4.) Though now it seems a contradiction both to sense and reason, the church's interest is on a present advance, and at this day is on the prevailing hand. Under all the changes of her condition, and through the whole time of the New Testament, this truth must be made out, that Jesus Christ in his kingdom must increase, John iii. 30. Even when choicest instruments wear out, that interest flourishes as the palm tree, the more it is depressed; nor has the church bounds set to its continued increase until it come to the perfect day, when the kingdom shall be delivered up to the Father, and all powers shall be subdued and brought under the Mediator's feet. It is true, such hours may fall in with some sad intervals, in which success and advantage appear on the adversary's side; for thus the Scripture points forth antichrist's ruin, and the progress of his judgment, in the various steps thereof, with a special resemblance to the Lord's way with Pharaoh, who appears to have been a type of the great antichrist. We find the same judicial strokes of hardness of heart on both; a gradual procedure, by one plague after another, with the same effect and product, to give the church a new assault on any favourable interval; until the great God makes his power known as he did at the Red Sea. Is it not strange to see the truth brought down to the grave, yea, as it were buried, when even this, by the overruling providence of him who makes all things work together for her good, is turned to her advantage, and tends to her rising with a greater lustre and brightness?

(5.) That blessed, much longed for, and glorious day of the second coming of our Lord Jesus Christ, which for ever puts a triumphant close to the church's warfare, when the soldier's sword and helmet shall be laid aside, and give place to the victor's harp and crown, hastes apace. O let him who writes and him who reads say, "Even so,

come Lord Jesus," Rev. xxii. 20. God, who has
appointed man his time, and with whom is the number of his months and years, has set time its glass
also, and has bounded the duration of this world,
that it cannot continue one minute longer than he
determines; and though the particular time, which
the majesty of God has concealed from the angels,
falls not under our inquiry, yet this is clear, there
are signs given of its near approach, which in their
season will be discernible, though little noticed by
the world. It is in such a lethargy, and men are
so thronged with the cares of this life, that these
grave forewarnings will not rouse them up. But
such signs are not given in vain, for therewith the
church may discern what appearance there is of the
approach of that day; yea, on such an account may
lift up her head with a solemn congratulation. O
what a marvellous truth is this, the serious thoughts
of which might give men new subjects for wonder
each day! The time is hastening when the Redeemer
of the church shall appear in the clouds of heaven,
in flaming fire, with an innumerable company of
the angels; and now the dust of the saints has
not long to sleep until they be awakened with that
unspeakably sweet and rapturous sound of the last
trumpet. Faithful is he who has promised. It is
long since John gave this warning to the church,
"Behold, he comes with clouds," Rev. i. 6; and
thus did the primitive Christians solace themselves
on these grounds. Some few evidences of this
day's approach we may discern, which, as the
blossoming of the spring, witness that the summer
is near. [1.] If the whole days of the gospel
since the glorious triumph of the Mediator in his
suffering for the church, and his resurrection, be
the last times by the Scripture reckoning, we must

then judge that the night is far spent, and the day is at hand. [2.] If the last stroke and utter abolishing of antichrist shall be by the brightness of Christ's second coming, 2 Thess. ii. 8, is there not solid ground to judge that this blessed day makes haste, when his falling is so far advanced? We have seen his kingdom, in a great measure, darkened; his consuming and mouldering down by the breath of Christ's mouth in the preached gospel; and now we wait in hope for that more remarkable step of his judgment, which the Scripture gives as a near sign of the coming of the Lord; even such as the white sky and the morning brightness is to the watchman, of the day being near; and thus, as we see the ruin and downfall of the man of sin advance, there seems to be a proportionate ground of certainty to conclude the near approach of the day of Christ's second coming.

2. The next particular for a serious inquiry is, what the present appearance and signs of the time seem to point at; for these are of special use to give a clear discovery of its temper and disposition. This is a prognostication which the Scripture only can make us know. I confess this day they seem sad, and every where look with a threatening aspect on the church. We see not now those tokens for good, which sometimes have appeared. There are presages which concern this time, that if we be not asleep, might make us regard the same with an awful and humbling impression, for truly they threaten; yet I must say, with reference to the Scripture, that we have a safe warrant to conclude, that whatever may befall a particular church, yet nothing thence can be concluded of mortal prejudice to the universal church; for though this or that particular church may be cut off, yet he and his

kingdom must increase. Yea, when the Lord seems to lose ground in one place, it is made up with advantage in another place; and often out of the very ruins and dispersion of that church which he casts off, he carries materials to build him a house elsewhere; in which case we should, instead of complaining, adore and bless the glory of the Lord, and justify his procedure, and be glad that they to whom he was not spoken of shall see, and they who had not heard shall understand. Even a particular church, which has death-presaging symptoms, and scarcely a token for good, can be recovered by him who heals backslidings and loves freely. He can make dry bones flourish as a green herb; for the issues from spiritual death belong to him. He can make those who have fallen from their first love, repent, and do their first works, whereby the departing of the glory, and the removing of the candlestick out of its place, shall be prevented. I am so much the more pressed to touch this, because the very few serious Christians who are yet left, or are delivered from that spiritual stupidity which has seized on others while they lay to heart the things which concern the kingdom of Jesus Christ, are ready to cast away all confidence and abandon themselves to despondency, through the frightful aspect of affairs, and the consideration of what they observe in the temper of men and tendency of things. They almost question whether they ought to entertain any hope that we shall any more be called by that blessed name, Jehovah-shammah, "The Lord is there," Ezek. xlviii. 35; seeing nothing appears at present in the disposition of men, or in the dispensations of God, which does not seem to portend a final departure. I would desire such to beware, lest in their heart:

lessness they limit the Holy One of Israel, and circumscribe the sovereignty of grace. For their establishment and excitement to a serious wrestling with him, in order to his abode with us, let them consider these particulars.

(1.) This is one of the signs of the time, that the devil is now bestirring himself against the church to beget every where a prejudice against the truth. [1.] His appearing with great wrath shows his time to be short, Rev. xii. 12. [2.] His being let loose, with a more than usual liberty to trouble the church, is previous to some great and remarkable restraint, Rev. xx. 7, 8. There he is in a more special way let loose; but we find, verse 10, his being chained up for ever follows. [3.] The devil rages with a more remarkable noise, when some great thing from the Lord is to be brought forth for the church. When the solemn and blessed time was now come of completing for ever, by one sacrifice, the work of redemption, this same hour and power of darkness introduced an everlasting sunshine upon the church; and Satan, by pursuing the Prince of life unto death, had a most fatal over-throw; for by death he overcame him who had the power of death, that is, the devil; and by being lifted up upon the cross he spoiled principalities and powers, triumphing over them openly; and thus dying, he sung the victory, and said, "It is finished," John xix. 30. Yea, it is clear what a hot alarm the church may expect from him upon the approach of that great victory, and the decision of the last battle between Michael and the dragon, Rev. xii. 7—10.

(2.) We see almost every where the most united and formidable assault of the adversaries of the truth at the kingly power and supremacy of the

Mediator, as head over his church. At this great truth the opposition of the time seems most directly to be levelled; yea, the crown of Christ, which it becomes him alone to wear, is now divided between antichrist and the princes of the earth, each contending for his share. At present the adversary seems to prevail, even to the bearing down of that great interest of our blessed Master. But there is no ground to fear this; nay, being well understood, it is a most hopeful and promising sign to the church: for if Christ must reign until all his enemies be brought in subjection, then the greater the opposition and assault, the greater the victory; and if Jesus Christ will take unto himself his great power and reign, we must expect that he will take it in a more eminent and conspicuous manner, when men are seeking, in the height of their rebellion and rage against the Lord and his Anointed, to seize on his sceptre, and snatch it from him.

(3.) It is a strange sign of the times, that we now see most promising appearances for the church's good remarkably blasted; things which seemed grounds of encouragement made to fail. We see human props almost every where removed or broken; the truth deserted by great men; yea, the families of those falling off this day from the Lord, whose ancestors for a long time had been zealous for his interest. This is a threatening appearance, but I would humbly reason on Scripture grounds, that it is no bad sign, but has therewith some comfortable aspect on the church; it being clear, [1.] That there is often a connexion in the Bible between an extreme exigence of the church's case and the Lord's eminent appearing; see Isa. xxx. 18; li. 20—22; lxiii. 5. Yea, it is hard to find any great mercy and remarkable deliverance

of the church which has not come at such periods.
[2.] Such a disadvantage and forsaken case is expressly held forth as one of God's opportunities of doing good to his people, Jer. xxx. 14, &c. When there is none to plead her cause, and Zion is called an outcast whom no man seeks after, then does the Lord allow his people to be encouraged, and to take it as a ground of hope that he will appear.
[3.] It is clear from the word, that a people at such a disadvantage may be then made use of for the greatest service. The saints mentioned in Heb. xi. 34, were made strong out of weakness. There can be no cause to fear the church's ruin, from the withdrawing of human help, when it falls under the Lord's hand, who by things most destructive can serve his interest, and bring salvation at such a time when none but he could save, Hosea vi. 1—3; Mic. vii. 8—10.

(4.) We do indeed see much of that holy fear and tenderness gone that formerly showed itself amongst the godly; corruption abounding, prejudice easily taken, a spirit of jealousy poured out, yea, very strange and unusual outbreakings in offence and scandal: on which account if God should make us a generation of his wrath, we are called to adore and justify the unspotted way of the Lord; yet I must adventure, with respect to the sovereignty of grace, to offer some discovery from the Scripture of what he has done in like cases. [1.] When the church has had no argument to make use of, no confidence to plead, but is broken and confounded under the sense of horrid guilt, he finds one in himself; "For my name's sake will I defer my anger." Isa. xlviii. 9. [2.] We find the covenant made use of by the Lord to stop a judicial procedure against his people; "Nevertheless he regarded their affliction, when he heard their cry, and remembered for them his covenant," Psa. cvi. 44, 45. [3.] We find the rage and violence of the adversaries, and their taking advantage to blaspheme, made use of by the Lord as an argument to own his people, who had otherwise forfeited all former grounds of confidence, Deut. xxxii. 26, &c. [4.] We read how sovereign grace has marvellously stepped in when the rod did not humble, and smiting would not do; "I smote him, and he went on frowardly in the way of his heart;" yet, "I have seen his ways, and will heal him," Isa. lvii. 17, 18. "O Israel, thou hast destroyed thyself, but in me is thine help," Hos. xiii. 9. Yea, grace has rescued those on whom mercy must be forced, and while departing from God, Hos. ii. 7, 9. [5.] Thus has the freedom of grace, marvellous grace, shone forth in former ages of the church; but they sadly mistake its meaning who are thus made secure, and not thereby led unto repentance.

(5.) There is a great wearing out of the godly, yea, the choice of them, by a more than usual despatch; and this is a sad Scripture presage of coming evil, when such are hastened away, that they may be hid in the grave from a further storm. Yet, [1.] Consider what a remarkable consumption almost wore out the church in the wilderness, when even then there was a hastening of her enlargement; yea, we find Moses and Aaron, with many who had been most eminent instruments in Israel's coming forth out of Egypt, taken away on a near approach to Canaan. [2.] Some of the greatest promises of the Scripture wait on the church when brought to a very small remnant, Ezek. vi. 8, 9; Isa. xxxvii. 31. [3.] The Lord has said in such a case, "The consumption decreed shall overflow with righteousness," Isa. x. 22. The next tide can bring in as many with a marvellous increase, as the former consuming strokes have taken away; yea, the declining of religion in one part of the world, where many have been called, often concurs with its spread in another; and thus the gospel recovers that interest which it seemed to lose.

(6.) The present appearance of the times threatens some sharp storm to come upon the world, some remarkable work of judgment to be brought forth; and though the earth seems this day in a strange measure quiet, yea, to enjoy an extraordinary calm, sure it is, there is a sound of great wrath and judgment in the ears of many who know what it is to discern the times. It is well the Scripture is near, a prognostication that can answer all the ages of the church; on such an appearance that awful impression, Hab. iii. 16, is called for. We should be in a trembling frame when God threatens, and thus utters his voice; yet it is clear that from these threatening signs, there is a comfortable sound of much good to the church; for, [1.] We find days of vengeance on the world held forth as necessary for the accomplishing of the Scripture, Luke xxi. 22, and made subservient to the bringing forth some special truth unto performance. [2.] In times of greatest judgment the church's interest is secured, with a large warrant to the godly not to fear, even whilst his garments are dyed with blood, Isa. lxiii. 1 ; Ezek. ix. 4; Rev. iii. 10. [3.] The church's enlargement and greatest mercies are thus ushered in, Isa. lxiii. 4; Zeph. xxxviii. 8. The putting the earth in a flame, and overturning the nations, are the very steps to an accomplishing of some great promises for the church's advantage, yea, a prelude to the same. We find a dreadful winter storm on the world pointed out as a spring time to the church, Luke xxi. 28. Her deliverance may be begun when the storm is breaking, which may for a time put the church under greater difficulties than before; yea, cause the godly to mistake and tremble at the sight of their mercy, because of the things by which it is ushered in.

3. Another particular which it concerns the godly to understand is, the peculiar snares and hazards of the time, Eccles. ix. 12. There are searching times, when the Christian's way is more difficult and narrow; and then it is the wisdom of the prudent to understand his way, and to known his ground, which the adversary, by subtle and indiscernible approaches, will seek to draw him off; then is a quick, sagacious discerning in the fear of the Lord called for, to be in a watching posture when the net is spread under their feet. It is a sad remark of Ephraim, " Strangers have devoured his strength, and he knoweth it not." Hos. vii. 9. In what a secure and sleeping posture Sampson had his hair cut off! David, through many of the Psalms, is more solicitous for the preventing the snares of wicked men, than for protection from their rage and violence. There is a feeling of the pulse of the times, by which the present distemper and hazard of the church may be known; and this day in a special manner calls us to this grave study. We should closely examine the public snares of the times, and how they approach; for in vain is the net spread in the sight of any bird, Eccl. i. 17.

(1.) Each time has its peculiar distemper and evils, the observing of which concerns the godly,

for their more watchful adverting to the snares of
that time; for the temptation of the time goes as
the present distemper discovers itself, whether in a
hot boiling fever, or in a dead lethargy, and follows those evils which are most contagious, and
where the current of the multitude runs. Sin is
warmed under the favourable aspect and countenance of great men; yea, the present snare lies in
those evils which promise outward advantage and
security from trouble, when the question is stated
between sin and suffering; and it is a special
part of the godly man's work to keep a distance
from the least accession thereto; yea, next to the
salvation of the soul, to be solicitous all along the
way to have his garments kept from the smallest
stain and spot thereof; a touch from a public prevailing evil being found to draw deeper on the
conscience, and recovery and escape thence more
difficult, than from many other personal infirmities.

(2.) There is some part of the truth of God in
each time of the church more questioned and
brought in debate, by which with greater clearness
we may know where a public snare lies; for its
aim is to entangle and assault the godly man,
where in a special way he is called to his post.

(3.) We may discern a prevailing snare by the
tendency there is in a day of trial to question
duties, which were clear and unquestionable when
the judgment was not biassed by any outward in-
citements: for they who thus question a truth because it is unpopular, get an answer according to
the idol of their hearts, as Balaam, who tried that
way, and was successful. A hesitation in the
heart, from want of resolution to suffer for the
truth, will not long be without a scruple in the

head to cause a debate, and then is it easy for a
snare to enter.   With what fear and tenderness
should light be regarded, which, as the apple of
the eye, may by the least thing be hurt, but is not
easily healed!   Thus men insensibly wear out
their former impressions of duty, and before they
are aware have, by a judicial stroke, their judgment determined in that which was before their
desire.   They know little of the depth of a man's
heart, who are not jealous over a change of their
·judgment in an hour of trial, when its tendency is
to spare themselves.

   (4.) We may discern a public snare by the advantage which the adversary gets thereby to divide
the godly amongst themselves; for it is easy to
enter by such a breach, and throw in the bait in so
muddy a water; it being very obvious what advantage a snare has, where jealousy and bitter strife
turn men's eyes from the public hazard, and by
mutual quarrels blunt the edge of contending for the
truth.   There may be a necessity on the godly
sometimes to withstand their friends to the face;
·yea, the most eminent in the church, when the
truth is concerned, Gal. ii. 11 : but this should be
with the greatest caution and tenderness, to obviate
a breach, which is like the breaking in of waters,
whilst the watching adversary waits his advantage
in such a day; and it is too sadly known how small
a wedge, driven with a tendency to that end, makes
way for the entry of a further snare.   We see, 1
Cor. xi. 16, what a sad connexion there is between
a dividing time of the church, and a further departing from the truth; but we must always so pursue
union amongst ourselves, as that Christ and his
cause be not left alone.

   (5.) A preseht snare may be seen by the sudden

change of known adversaries, and by the friendly insinuations of those who were wont to threaten; in such an appearance there lies an ambush, and it is but a change of weapons for advantage. Men should know the voice of the shepherd, lest they follow after a stranger; it being more usual to be stolen off their feet in a calm, than blown down by a storm. It is hard to stand before the blandishments of men, when that more endearing and sweet relish of peace with God is not preserved in the soul; which is a choice means to make the ear deaf to the most charming voice of the enchanter. The adder's poison is under their lips whilst wrath is boiling in their hearts, Psa. cxl. 3; yea, the cruel man can change his countenance when it is fit to lay a snare, and with Joab embrace them in his arms, whom he intends to smite under the fifth rib.

(6.) A snare may be seen in its approach by the prevalence which the fear of man has, and the unusual command it seems to have over the spirits of men, even over those whose zeal and resolution for the truth have in other trials appeared with much advantage; for in the fear of man there is a snare, Prov. xxix. 25, which will pursue when it finds men in a flying posture. The godly man has his breastplate, but he has no armour for his back, when he turns his face from resisting. It is sad when the adversary is taught to follow by our fainting, and the spirit which is in the world seems to be upon the ascendent, with a prevalence even over the spirits of the godly; yea, when they are debased, and made contemptible, in whom the appearance of God and his authority at another time would have made the hearts of their enemies to tremble.

(7.) A public snare is then to be feared, and calls

for a watchful eye, when success waits on a sinful
course; for then new queries will be started, strange
reports spread, with much subtle reflection on the
way of the Lord, to make the godly question the
same.   David found it not easy to stand before this,
Psa. lxxiii. 3.   In such a trial the adversary, by
continued observation, knows how to assault the
followers of the truth, and attack them at the
weakest point; then the scandal of the cross causes
many to be offended, for it is sore for them to suffer
who know not the fellowship of the cross of Christ,
the greatest and nearest fellowship with him upon
the earth.   Yea, in such times the church may
run more hazard from some of her friends, than
from the professed adversary; for it cannot but be
a searching and hazardous time when many are
turning aside, and some of understanding are suffered to fall, who are ready to press their sin as a
duty on others; for seldom do such fall off, but
they are found more active to engage others in
their apostasy, than they were anxious, while holding their former integrity, to pursue the truth's
interest.

(8.) A snare of the time may be discerned by
the tendency thereof to corruption in the church;
when it discovers itself by the hands of Esau,
though it have the voice of Jacob.   We may see
from the Scripture and observation of the church,
at others' cost, what a sad tendency such a thing
has still had to the shipwreck of faith and a good
conscience; and how hard it is to dance about the
fire, and not be burned, or stand in the way and
counsels of ungodly men, and not be ensnared.

(9.) It threatens a snare when inquiry about the
duty of the time is pursued without respect to the
present case and circumstances thereof; for thus a

snare may wait in a thing at other times indifferent, the neglect whereof upon some special circumstances may be a quitting of duty; and the doing or yielding to something, in another case warrantable, may at some times fall under a moral prohibition: as when a thing, in itself indifferent in the worship of God, is pressed by the magistrate as necessary by virtue of his sole command. There should not be an inquiry concerning this in the general, without a particular application to the complex case. A snare is then on the entry when that consideration of the prophet is not much regarded, Is this a time for such a thing? 2 Kings v. 26. For the disciples to refresh themselves with sleep was innocent; but that they could not watch one hour with their Master in his sufferings, must needs vary the case, for it was to desert him.

(10.) There is a sad appearance of some public snare getting advantage, when it is suited to our self-love and private interest; for a snare enters not without a call and finds its greatest strength and advantage within. Yea, conformity to the world, with a wearing out of soul-tenderness, is too often known to have a tendency to an evil course, for the motion is then down the hill. How many in embracing the world have at the next step fallen off from the truth! No weapon has been more made use of against the church, and has ruined more; so that it may be said, where other snares have killed their thousands, this has slain its ten thousands.

4. Another particular, which calls for a serious inquiry, is, What can the righteous do when there is a growing darkness on the church, and the very foundations are shaken, and so many in the matter of duty give over as men astonished, seeing

this evil is from the Lord? It is no small thing
to manage well such a time of the church's trial,
and in so sharp a storm there is need of much
care: but the Scripture of God is near to let us
know how to steer in the darkest night, and from
that blessed record there is one thing clearly held
forth; "The righteous shall hold on his way, and
he that hath clean hands shall be stronger and
stronger," Job xvii. 9.

(1.) All is well, and nothing can happen wrong,
whilst the foundation of God, which is his eternal
counsel, abides sure; though other foundations be
shaken, the godly man lies at a safe anchor, which
will not drag in a stormy day; his great interest
is beyond hazard, though more than an immortal
soul were in that adventure; his heaven is sure,
whereof he cannot be beguiled, whilst things upon
the earth seem most uncertain; and it is well with
the church, were it even sinking into the grave,
since the Mediator will bring it up again. Men's
malice cannot hurt, nor their cursing blast, that interest which God has blessed; for it is sure "there
is no enchantment against Jacob, neither is there
any divination against Israel," Numb. xxiii. 23.

(2.) The truth, and the great interest of godliness, are so known to a Christian, that it needs no
testimony from men, nor incitement from the example of others; it commends itself and witnesses
its reality, though by all the generation amongst
whom we live it should be cried down. To be a
Christian indeed requires that we know the truth,
and be founded on a ground that can support and
quiet the soul in the greatest falling off of others,
though there were none else to walk in that way.
If it were supposed that there were but one serious
Christian in the whole world, there is so great a

discovery and certainty of the truth upon the soul, as would oblige him to declare with Joshua, "But as for me, I will serve the Lord," Josh. xxiv. 15. I shall but add these few grounds of establishment in the way of the Lord.

[1.] That the number seems so small who follow the truth, and are found serious in the study of godliness, can be no ground to question the reality of religion, since men must either quit the Scripture, or admit that the way to life is strait, and that few enter therein. Yea, the small retinue the truth has in the world is an express verification of it. There is not the least warrant to make the suffrage of the multitude a test of the way of the Lord; his followers are a select number chosen out of the world, else the Scripture could not be fulfilled; and the falling of many from the truth is a seal thereto, no less than the coming in of others; and the excellent way of holiness is the more discernibly known by this character, that it is every where spoken against.

[2.] That so great contempt and reproach this day attend the truth and practice of godliness, should prejudice none, but be a further ground to help the Christian to hold on his way, since it is foretold that it should be so. The most excellent of the earth in their time have been accounted the filth and offscouring of the world; but the greatest reproacher has often been forced to give in his retraction, and make a profession of that which before he scoffed at. And, finally, when God comes near by a stroke of his judgment, the proud change their style, and speak in another language upon the awful appearance of death.

[3.] That sentence is not speedily executed against an evil course is also a seal and con-

firmation of the truth, and a ground of establishment in the way of the Lord, Eccles. viii. 11.
Therein men may see, that a short reprieve from
punishment is no pardon, whilst sin runs on to an
after account; that judgment deferred, when therewith a further hardening appears, threatens more
than a quick and present despatch, and shows the
stroke will be the greater when it comes.

[4.] So great an abounding of profaneness and
ungodliness within the church is an undeniable
seal to the verity of the Scripture; it being unanswerably clear, that there could be no darkness, if
there were not such a thing as light; or folly if
there were no wisdom: holiness is thus made
known by its opposite.

[5.] That the truth seems so much entangled
in the confusion of contrary doctrines, and pursued
by error, and the assault of those adversaries who
in every age are seeking to darken it, can be no
ground of prejudice. It is sure the Lord has made
his way plain, nor does the Scripture give any
ground to turn aside unto crooked paths; for these
are clouds of men's own creating, which have such
a tendency to darken the same. We see truth in
all ages is waited on by error, which, with any
brighter discovery thereof, attends it like a thick
fog; though these can never unite any more than
gold and clay can join together. The notion of
error were inconceivable, if the truth had not a
certainty and real being; nor does it conflict with
such an adversary, but for its further triumph.
O! if the solid persuasion of the Scripture were
in earnest pursued, and men's souls were brought
under the power and authority of the truth, as that
which is the word and testimony of the living God,
it would prove a more effectual cure to so dreadful

a distemper of the church, than all the disputes of the time. 1. It is manifest that no error or corrupt doctrine assaults the church, but it is pointed forth by so express an opposition in the Scripture, that we may see a prophetical forewarning thereof, and of men's endeavour to corrupt and darken the truth. The word is written, and in a special way directed, to every time of the church, and to all her trials, by Him who knew and foresaw what opposition his truth in after ages should meet with. In this marvellous record men may clearly see that there is no poison nor corruption in doctrine which infests the church, but which has its proper antidote there provided. 2. Do we not see, even in those mental delusions and heresies which seem most strange, the Scripture most exactly confirmed, and discern that they who are under their influence are like clouds carried about with a tempest, 2 Peter ii. 17, and driven on by a judicial stroke? Though it is amazing to see at what a rate many are turned mad, with a discernible bewitching of their judgment, and a besotting unto most strange and absurd extravagancies; yea, how tenacious and violent they are in their way, when silenced with the clearest discoveries of the truth; yet does not this also witness that there is a righteous God giving them up to strong delusion, and that Satan is let loose with a remarkable power to deceive? 2 Thess. ii. 9—12. O how dreadful is that stroke which is inflicted on the judgment and reason, which in some respect we may say is greater than that which is on the affections! 3. We find the Scripture, by a clear prophetical discovery, pointing at that influence which human authority, and the patronage of those who have a name and repute in the church, should have on the corrupting the doctrine thereof; and therefore the Holy Ghost so particularly guards against the same, and opposes the authority of the written word to the highest pretences of any party: an apostle must not be admitted nor have credit to the truth's prejudice—an angel, yea, a voice from heaven, may not oppose itself to this more sure testimony of God in his word, Gal. i. 8. 4. In this great depth of error we see this truth take place, "Deceiving, and being deceived;" and that, by a marvellous stroke, men's judgments are made captive to their will, and their deliberate acting to deceive others has the same effect on themselves. 5. The Scripture is further made out, when we see how hard it is for men to find land when they are once carried from the truth, and launch out into that horrid gulf of error.

  *Inference* V. The truth of God revealed in the Scripture is not more marvellous and great in its import, than clear and obvious in the evidence of its verification, which has every where such a witness, that there can be no escape from this discovery; and if men will not receive its testimony, they must have it forced on them as their torment: for invention fails, and politics are found too weak, to ward off some impression of the Scripture, which with an awful appearance and authority justifies itself to the conscience without men's consent. This advantage has the truth, that even atheism must bear a witness thereto, and against itself; which fact, if men would but weigh it in the balance of sober reason, would appear a sufficient antidote against its own poison, and a great seal to the Scripture, which would want a special confirmation, if it wanted such an adversary. I must, finally, in behalf of the truth of God, attest the reproachers of this time, who are so much at work to challenge his unspotted way, and call in question his faithfulness, and appeal to that tribunal which the great God has placed in the conscience, if they can, without doing violence thereto, withstand the clear evidences of Divine truth; concerning which I shall here ask,

1. If it be the great prerogative of God to declare things from the beginning to the end, and hold forth the various and most remarkable events which should fall out within time, with their proper circumstances, yea, to discover the great revolutions of the world through all the ages, when second causes in their remotest tendency thereto could not be discerned, is not this then clear and undeniably true of the Scripture? 2. I must make that challenge and attestation which that great servant of the Lord, Joshua, did in such a cause. No one thing has failed of all which the Lord has spoken in the Scripture, Josh. xxiii. 14; nor can men instance any special prediction or promise which has miscarried, or turned abortive. What truth wants its seal and confirmation? yea, what step of Providence can be pointed out which does not square and marvellously accord with the word? I challenge an instance. 3. Does not the written word, as a bright lantern, attend the church from the very porch and entry of time in all her journey, and evidently point at the remarkable times and revolutions of her case, which have now in a great part gone over her head? Yea, is it not clear, that the sun does not more truly shine on this terrestrial globe, than the Scripture shines on and illuminates the whole frame and structure of Providence; and that, in all the strange parts which are acted in the world, there is none who

walks at random; or by his own counsel directs and steers his course; but that the innumerable millions of men who are this day upon earth, in all their various motions are at present fulfilling the determined counsel of God, and their actings are concentric with his great end? 4. Is not this way of godliness, which seems to-day to be every where spoken against, that good old way, in which the footsteps of the saints are to be found since the beginning, no new light having broken up in the world? Through all past ages there has not wanted a continued succession of those who in this reproached way served the God of their fathers, and have sealed the truth, which from one time to another was delivered off their hands to the present generation. I here challenge the greatest atheists; whom can they instance of that blessed company, since there was a church in the earth, who could ever contradict this or bear another witness? 5. Must you not confess, that there is no such depth in the heart of man, or so close and subtle a plot of wickedness there, which is not found out and pointed at in the Scripture? 6. Can this demonstration of the Scripture be denied, that whilst man is a free agent in his actions, and therein acts spontaneously, he has, notwithstanding, in his own breast both a judge and an accuser, which though within him, does without his consent exercise a power over him, and an authority which he would, yet cannot decline? 7. Can men who are themselves strangers to the way of God, deny that serious godliness is a marvellous thing, and that there is something here above nature, which by its effects on others shows a Divine power, that suits and accommodates itself to the various conditions and employments of men;

puts a special honour on the greatest prince, and instructs the wise and prudent, yet will lodge with the poorest artificer in his shop, or with the labouring man in the field; and manifests a native motion from inward principles, when on outward grounds there is not the least incitement; a living thing that has its discernible languishing and wearing out, and its more vigorous actings, as well as any living man? 8. If men have any serious reflection, and do not shut up the Bible, can they forbear to remark how well it answers the various successions of time, and the marvellous variety of things so many ages distant from each other; that there is so great a distance of time between the penmen, yet in its composure it is one entire piece, so connected and closely knit together, that men may see the same spirit in the whole, and each part moving and carrying forward one great design? 9. I shall but further add, if religion has a being and reality, which men cannot deny, without falling far below reason into the condition of the beasts, must there not be a rule also? It is easy to judge in what a strange and monstrous shape religion would appear, were it left to the choice and decision of men. Let the most professed atheists turn their eyes through the whole earth, and in a calm and sober composure of spirit, judge if there be any thing more absurd, than the face and appearance which religion has amongst those by whom this excellent rule of the Scripture is not owned; yea, could men subject themselves to such extravagancies without a Divine stroke on their judgment and reason, which the righteous God, in verification of his word, inflicts on those who shut their ears from the report of the truth, the sound whereof goes forth through the earth?

Here I challenge men, though strangers themselves to serious religion, to account for the great difference between those parts of the world where the gospel shines, and the rest of the nations, excepting on the ground, that the former possess such a revelation of God and of the truths connected with eternity, as is unknown to others.

**THE END.**

BV - #0012 - 210723 - C0 - 229/152/20 - PB - 9781331700555 - Gloss Lamination